The Historical Experience in German Drama

In his still-standard survey of German historical drama, *Das deutsche Geschichtsdrama* (1952), Friedrich Sengle understands "historical drama" as that in which objective history is blended with an *idea* that is the basis of its dramatic coherence and force. This idea inevitably becomes the engine of a dramatic action, inclining the theatergoer to become wholly engaged with dramatic characters in a dramatic present, rather than with "real" figures in a historical past. Such plays (for instance, Schiller's *Maria Stuart*) may remain broadly true to history, but the *experience* they afford is often not historical; that is, it may be emotionally and intellectually compelling, but it will not cause us, in our present, to become engaged with our relationship with past figures and events and their continued relevance for us. Alan Menhennet identifies and analyzes examples of German drama that are historical not only in terms of the provenance of the material, but also in that, while remaining dramatic in nature, they do convey a historical experience. He provides a critical survey of such plays extending from the seventeenth century to the twentieth, in the contexts of literary history, the philosophy of history, and German history from the Thirty Years' War to the Second World War. Major figures treated include Gryphius, Lessing, Schiller, Goethe, Grillparzer, Hebbel, Schnitzler, and Brecht. There is no competing work in English.

Alan Menhennet is Professor Emeritus of German at the University of Newcastle, Newcastle-upon-Tyne, UK. He is author of *Grimmelshausen the Storyteller* (Camden House, 1997).

Studies in German Literature, Linguistics, and Culture

Edited by James Hardin
(*South Carolina*)

ALAN MENHENNET

The Historical Experience
in German Drama

From Gryphius to Brecht

CAMDEN HOUSE

First published 2003
by Camden House

Camden House is an imprint of Boydell & Brewer Inc.
PO Box 41026, Rochester, NY 14604–4126 USA
and of Boydell & Brewer Limited
PO Box 9, Woodbridge, Suffolk IP12 3DF, UK

ISBN: 1–57113–255–4

Library of Congress Cataloging-in-Publication Data

Menhennet, Alan.
      The historical experience in German drama: from Gryphius to
Brecht/Alan Menhennet.
         p. cm. — (Studies in German literature, linguistics, and culture)
Includes bibliographical references and index.
ISBN 1–57113–255–4 (alk. paper)
         1. Historical drama, German — History and criticism.   I. Title.
II. Studies in German literature, linguistics, and culture (Unnumbered)

PT693 .M46 2003
832'.051409—dc21

2002010540

A catalogue record for this title is available from the British Library.

This publication is printed on acid-free paper.
Printed in the United States of America.

For David and Audrey

Contents

Preface

THE "HISTORICAL EXPERIENCE" in drama, as I eventually found myself constrained to call it to avoid confusion with the established term "historical drama," first appealed to me as a technical problem, which I discuss in detail in the introduction. However, while it remains an aesthetic question to be examined in an aesthetic context, it leads us also into areas in which significant intellectual, and above all, political themes arise. We find ourselves confronting issues of crucial importance to the understanding of the past and present, and the building of the future of Germany and Austria. Using the drama, rather than the historical novel, some of the greatest German writers set out to create for their audience a dramatic experience that, as in Shakespeare's *Histories*, is historical and at the same time political. Since historical and critical studies of German drama have tended to focus on the former, somewhat to the detriment of the latter, it seemed to me that I might be justified in attempting to redress the balance a little, not to overturn their judgements, but in the hope of adding an additional nuance to the picture.

Acknowledgments

I WOULD LIKE to record my deep gratitude to Professor Tony Harper for reading the ms. of this book, and for his helpful comments. My thanks for material assistance are also due, and gladly given, to Nicole Böheim and Anke Neibig.

Alan Menhennet
Jesmond, Newcastle upon Tyne, 2001

Introduction

THE THRUST OF THIS STUDY differs from that of Friedrich Sengle's *Das deutsche Geschichtsdrama* (Stuttgart 1952) which is focused on cases in which there is a meeting of "objective" (that is, "real," factual) history and a "tragende Idee."[1] This latter will inevitably be the main engine of a dramatic action, inclining us to become wholly engaged with dramatic characters in a dramatic present, rather than "real" figures in an historical past. The experience to which this is conducive may be emotionally and intellectually compelling, but it will not be historical in the sense that it causes us, in our present, to become engaged with our relationship with past figures and events, and their continued relevance for us. Historical "colour," however profuse, will remain peripheral. Schiller sets his *Maria Stuart* in a recognisable Elizabethan England, but while this provides the circumstances for the action, the spiritual life of the characters belongs overwhelmingly to the eighteenth century. The Maria and Elizabeth who appear are Schiller's creations: we cannot afford to think too much of the "real" ones.

In the kind of play with which we are concerned, history is to some degree internalized: the experience is both dramatic and historical. Isolating this quality requires close argument. We cannot rival Sengle's inclusiveness, while benefiting from the work he has done, in particular in the area of the "national" idea, which appears in the eighteenth century, and blossoms fully in the nineteenth.

"National" and "historical" interests are often intricately intertwined, above all when the need for a nation's consciousness of, and belief in, itself is acute; times of war, for example, of national construction or re-construction. Ibsen turns to history in the period of "National Romanticism," to exorcise the memory of the Danish hegemony[2] and renew, for present purposes, links with an heroic Norwegian past. The Russians drew inspiration from Karamzin, without whose *History of the Russian State* Pushkin's *Boris Godunov* is unthinkable; the Czechs from Palacký's *History of the Czech People*, which was, as Masaryk says, "philosophically conceived,"[3] but also gave a people that was accused by Engels in 1849 of "never having had" one,[4] and designated as "geschichtslos" by the historian Otto Bauer in 1911, a real basis for its sense of nationhood. This is true of the Austrians and the citizens of "Little Germany" as well. Thus we find the "Reichsgründungsschreiber" Treitschke[5] writing to legitimize the new Prussian-based *Reich* — and no doubt, either directly or through his disciples, firing the ardour of many a history-teacher — and the "patriotic" dramatic laureate of the Hohenzollern *Reich,* Ernst von Wildenbruch asserting that "das Schicksal eines Volkes [ist] seine Geschichte. Darum ist und bleibt das historische Drama das eigentliche."[6] This will not be our argument. Wildenbruch has his own Hohenzollern axe to grind. In fact, we accept the association, in strict theory, of the dramatic with an undivided present, and posit a polar opposition between the dramatic and the historical impulses that can create an impulse towards relatively "epic" form. The dramatist cannot, like Scott, suspend his narrative to reflect with his audience, in their shared present, upon the past. But by relaxing the tension of the close-knit dramatic action, he can create space for active reflection by the audience, in its own time, on history *qua* history. The link between nation and history is important for us because the spectator's knowledge of, and sense of community with, the "objective" history with which he is presented, stimulates and enables him to fulfil the reflective function that the historical experience demands. Our main attention, therefore, is concentrated on works treating subjects that originate in, or impinge upon, the Germanic world.

Three aspects demand consideration if we are to describe the *effect* of a dramatic action as "historical." The first two are obvious: temporality and actuality. Events happen "before our eyes," but as soon as, and insofar as we see them as "historical," we experience them in a particular way. The living are also dead, the character who lives in an imagined present, exists also in a factual past. To achieve an historical effect, the dramatist must convey a sense of actual, as well as dramatic, reality: of "then" as well as "now." He can invent, but he must avoid discrepancies with known fact which, however effective, would downgrade history to the status of a mere stage for the "real" action. Grillparzer gives his Rudolf II, and Ibsen his Lady Inger, a fictitious illegitimate son, but both make a contribution to the historical theme. Goethe's transformation of Egmont into a young lover without family encumbrances is a freedom too far.

Or it would be, if the intention were historical. Schiller's objections to *Egmont* are well-known; if we were to judge the play as "historical" —that is, bring to bear on Goethe's hero our knowledge of the actual sixteenth-century Egmont — they would be justified. But when Schiller replaces the historian's with the critic's hat, and argues that the play can be improved *dramatically* by a stricter adherence to historical fact, we shall have to demur. Goethe would have had to work against his clear intention, which was to produce a "drama of character."[7] His self-defence (in a conversation with Eckermann, 31 January 1827) makes it clear that while he is making use of historical material, he is doing so to an essentially non-historical purpose: "Der Dichter muß wissen, welche Wirkungen er hervorbringen will und danach die Natur seiner Charaktere einrichten . . . Hätte ich den Egmont so machen wollen, wie ihn die Geschichte meldet, als Vater von einem Dutzend Kindern, so würde sein leichtsinniges Handeln sehr absurd erschienen sein."[8] Goethe has decided not to write an historical tragedy in this case, but to focus on what Theodor Storm, commenting on his own *Aquis Submersus*, a story set in the seventeenth century, but in which the historical element is really peripheral, called "rein menschliche Konflikte."[9] As in the Age of Goethe, so in that of Poetic Realism, plays could be written with superficially "historical" plots, but no strong impulse toward historical feeling or thought. One such example is the *Elfriede* of Storm's friend Paul Heyse, which the critic Erich Schmidt could judge by purely dramatic criteria. "Ich folgte seelischen Verwicklungen in modernem Stil," he writes, "und kümmerte mich ganz und gar nicht darum, wie das zehnte Jahrhundert und das Gericht der Peers zu reimen sei."[10] Goethe and Heyse are perfectly entitled to use historical material in this (unhistorical) way and we are perfectly entitled to leave the plays in question out of our investigation.

In a fully "historical" drama, the dead exist alongside the living, the imaginary together with the real, in a single space, or at a single point in time. This brings us to our third, more elusive, aspect. Instead of purely dramatic (what Brecht would call "Aristotelian") identification between spectator and character, we need a sense of community, of a continuum. This is an experience of time in that the spectator, aware of himself in his own present, is aware also of a corridor that links him with events he recognizes as past. It is not the almost metaphysical experience of existence "in time," which can be rendered — by Storm for example — in both non-historical and historical settings, and that is brought home to us more strongly by Shallow and Falstaff, who have "heard the chimes at midnight,"[11] than by the death of the "historical" (real) Henry IV. To the latter, we relate in a different way. We are both joined to and separated from him by time, for the purely human relationship by which we may (and to some extent, do) identify is diluted by the political and national issues which make this case important and interesting. Rather than "time rediscovered," this is more akin to what Proust calls the "mémoire volontaire," which involves conscious thought about a past that remains past, and which becomes "history" for us when we see it as separated from us by time, yet linked with us through a temporal continuum. The dramatist needs to articulate the continuum, to show an event as historically, as well as dramatically significant, as Pushkin says in commenting on a "patriotic" play by a contemporary.[12] Shakespeare does this by juxtaposing the old king with the new, and raising the question of the governance of England.

This continuum must be defined by the critic in terms that are broadly ideological. History is more than a chronicle that merely records the facts. It makes meaningful to us what may be remote, both by the way in which it is itself modestly "dramatic" (that is, it visualizes its "characters" as acting within their own present) and, more important for our present purpose, by the (un-, perhaps even antidramatic) process of interpretation. The way in which history does this is inevitably influenced by the ideological basis from which the historian operates. A different concept of history obtained in the age of the Baroque from that of Herder, Kant, Hegel, or Marx. We will not expect the same sense of community from Gryphius as from Goethe, Schiller, Hebbel, or Brecht. And history itself, of course, can breed historical awareness as a factor in the mind of a dramatist and his audience. We caught a glimpse of this in the case of Shakespeare's *Henry IV,* and in the German-speaking lands as well, the rise of national identity and coherence as an issue will make a difference to an author's treatment of his nation's past. The treatment of the Napoleonic era to be expected of an Austrian of the nineteenth (or indeed the twentieth) century, will be different from what we would be likely to find in a citizen of Weimar and the Holy Roman Empire, or in the work of a Christian Dietrich Grabbe, in the days of the German Confederation. Like the French Revolution out of which he sprang, Napoleon became part of the history of many countries. We shall see in due course how Grillparzer and Schnitzler approach that era, but for the present, Pushkin, a man with a keen appreciation of history, illustrates very well the significance of Napoleon for nations other than his own: "He showed the Russian people its high destiny."[13]

Our survey will, then, deal with different situations and attitudes, but there will also be common themes. As far as possible, we will concern ourselves with playwrights dramatising episodes from their own national history. In the case of Andreas Gryphius, where this cannot be done and is in fact least to be expected, we will be considering an event of more than merely local significance, which he will have felt had immediate relevance to his own situation as a German writing in the era of the Thirty Years' War and its aftermath.

In addition, historical drama, of whatever age, has a particular technical problem, which we will see recurring over and over again, and which we will now attempt to outline. Drama arises out of the interactions (usually conflict) between, or within characters who exist in a present time. That what "has happened" or will, or might happen, can play an important role in conditioning what a dramatic character feels, is obvious enough. But as far as the recipient, whether spectator or reader, is concerned, all this is happening *now*. The normal tense of epic narrative, the preterite, does not exist in drama, says Wolfgang Kayser,[14] and since the "present" is in incessant flux, a continuous sequence of individual points which no sooner appear than they disappear, he naturally lays considerable stress on the element of "Spannung," the expectation of what will happen next.[15] We may be in what Grillparzer calls a "supposed present,"[16] but it is the dramatic reality, and the shift to historical reality requires a *relaxation* of tension, what Beyer, commenting on the most important of Ibsen's "saga-dramas," *The Pretenders*, sees as a "breaking of the framework."[17] And this demands the articulation of the continuum that links present with past. It is all very well Meyer arguing after the event that "the spirits of the present" are about in *Huttens letzte Tage*, but as W. A. Coupe points out, he does nothing in the text to conjure them up.[18] In addition, while the context of drama is to a greater or lesser extent individual, the substance of history demands a more general basis of knowledge and thought, with important possible implications for dramatic structure, and perhaps also for things like characterisation. These are factors that propel the drama in the direction of the epic mode. An historical novel has ways of achieving these aims that are not open to the drama. The novelist, and with him the reader to whom he speaks, is a separate presence (whether *announced* or not), independent of the time-scale of the action, and can afford a variety of times and tenses not open to the dramatist. The historical effect depends on the complicity of the reader/spectator; the narrator of a novel, who exists in the same "now" as his reader, can switch perspectives with ease. George Eliot, in *Romola*, can perform a seamless transition from the fifteenth century, in which Savonarola, who *"had*

[a] readily roused resentment towards opposition," actually preached his sermons, into the nineteenth, in which we read them, and find that they ". . . *have* much of that red flame in them . . ." (chapter 54: my emphases).

It is harder, though not impossible, for the dramatist to enlist the complicity of the spectator, that is, to bring into play his knowledge of what happened in, and after the (actual) time of the characters whom he is watching in the (imagined) dramatic present. The Baroque "Trauerspiel," like the oratorio, has ways of stimulating historical reflection, as we shall see in the case of Gryphius, but these are arguably not truly dramatic. They involve treating not the stage as a world, but the world as a stage. The later writer has to make do with devices such as the prologue or epilogue, or elements within the text which will touch off an historical train of thought, symbolic objects, for example, like the helmet and sword of Knud Alfson in Ibsen's *Lady Inger*,[19] or consciously or unconsciously prophetic speeches, as when Wallenstein, at the end of Grillparzer's *Bruderzwist*, refers to the possibility that the coming war might last thirty years. And he must certainly avoid stimulating the spectator's historical sense into contradiction by including too blatant an anachronism or invention. Schiller, who had attacked Goethe for his historical inaccuracies in *Egmont*, invented a confrontation between Maria and Elizabeth that effectively dehistoricizes his two principal characters!

The dominant role of the present in drama emerges forcefully in the exchanges between Goethe and Schiller on the relation of the dramatic to the epic mode in their correspondence in the year 1797 (when Schiller was working on *Wallenstein*, and Goethe on *Hermann und Dorothea*). Goethe's former scepticism as to the value of theory had been modified, largely by contact with his new friend, and Schiller's natural bent for aesthetic speculation had been fully developed. The most important letters for our purposes are Goethe's of 23 December and Schiller's reply dated 26 December. Goethe comments on the modern tendency in all poetic genres to fudge the divisions between the modes, and to move always towards "representation of what is completely *present*," which for him is the mode of drama: ". . . so soll alles sinnlich wahr, vollkommen gegenwärtig, dramatisch sein." Schiller makes a very sharp distinction between the ideas of the epic, where the action "stands still, as it were" and the reader "moves around it," which corresponds well to the concepts of past-ness ("Vergangensein") and of narration, and that of the dramatic, in which the recipient is "streng an die sinnliche Gegenwart gefesselt."

He sums up: "Daß der Epiker seine Begebenheit als vollkommen vergangen, der Tragiker die seinige als vollkommen gegenwärtig zu be-
handeln habe, leuchtet mir sehr ein." With the dialectic characteristic
of the author of the *Ästhetische Briefe*, Schiller then adds that in order
that true poetic art shall ensue, each of the polar pure ideas requires a
"Contrepoids," a corrective movement in the direction of the other,
so that the sensuous in the case of the epic, and moral freedom in that
of drama, shall not be lost. We shall have to take up this point again in
connection with *Wallenstein*, but should note for the present that he
does not seem here to be thinking specifically of the historical drama.

Nevertheless, the idea of a mingling of dramatic and epic is useful
for our present purposes. The historical drama will inevitably be a hybrid genre . . . and not necessarily the worse for that. The dramatist
who wishes to create an historical effect has to enlist the
reader/spectator's aid. He has to make room within drama for a
quasi-epic mood. This makes Kayser's concept of the "Raumdrama"
attractive for us. This Kayser defines as "[das bloße] Dramatisieren des
Lebenslaufes,"[20] a classic case for which would be Goethe's *Götz von
Berlichingen*. A proper discussion of this work must await its proper
place in our (also historical) scheme, but it may not be inappropriate
to recall here that Goethe himself stated that his intention was to
dramatise an actual life-history, in fact the *History* ("Geschichte") of
Gottfried von Berlichingen of the Iron Hand.[21] Kayser's paradigm for
the "Raumdrama" is in fact the historical play, which may well contain
tragedy, but which also "versetzt notwendig in jene Haltung des gegenüberstehenden Beobachtens, die im Grunde episch ist."[22] The
great example, for Kayser, is Shakespeare, and not only in his Histories, and here again, we seem to catch an echo of "Sturm und Drang,"
of Herder and the young Goethe, to which we shall return in a later
chapter.

Not a few important plays which have the potential to be "historical" have been left aside in this study. *Egmont*, which we discussed
briefly a little earlier, is one example; Kleist's *Prinz Friedrich von
Homburg*, which has a more immediately "German" relevance and in
which (since it is a product of the Napoleonic period) the symbiosis
between history and politics might be expected to work more noticea-
bly, springs to mind as another. But here again, we see little evidence
of an intention to achieve what we have called the historical effect.
The potential within the *Homburg* plot for a "national" theme which
links the era of the Great Elector (Battle of Fehrbellin, 1675) with the
Napoleonic present, is obvious enough, and the ending ("In Staub

mit allen Feinden Brandenburgs") seems to suggest that Kleist, who (perhaps with current fashion in mind) himself described the play as "vaterländisch"[23] may have wished to point in this direction. Certainly, his nationalistic sentiments at that time were vehement, and in their way, sincere enough. But they were fuelled by personal concerns and the text as a whole supports the view that here too, Kleist was attempting to solve his own problems, above all the apparent discrepancy between "Gesetz" and "Gefühl" which first made itself felt when the "Prussian" in him came into conflict with the human being. The (potentially, "modern") Kleistian consciousness which predominates here, is "wirklicher als die Wirklichkeit" in Koch's phrase;[24] personal, not historical. These, no doubt, are the "Niederungen psychologischen Kleinkrams" that Lukács praises Scott for having avoided.[25] And the historical substance, the sense of the "old" which is as essential as the link with the present in historical drama, is at best skin-deep, even if the play's "historical" character is less transparent than that of Kleist's *Die Hermannsschlacht* which, as he wrote to H. J. von Collin (20 April 1809) was "einzig und allein auf diesen Augenblick berechnet." It is worthy of note that Hebbel, a man of strong national consciousness, ignores the national-historical angle completely in his very positive review of *Der Prinz von Homburg*.

And indeed the soil of Prussia, for all the importance of the role played by that state in German history — and historiography — was hardly fruitful for German historical literature, as we shall see in due course. There was a "Germany" until 1806, even if, as a political body, it was weak and disjointed. It was the "Vaterland" which Gryphius conjures up in the preface to his *Leo Armenius*, and to which Goethe's Götz swears his loyalty and Schiller's Wallenstein breaks his. After 1806, "Austria" emerged as an historical phenomenon and the search for an "Austrian idea" which, like the quest of the Czechs for a national identity leaned heavily on the historians,[26] was a response to a political reality. So indeed was that of the nineteenth-century "Little Germans" for a *Reichsbewußtsein*. In the rump out of which the "Deutsches Reich" eventually arose, there was a sincere sense of "German" identity, but even after 1871, it was a soul not really at ease in the Prussian body. Not even Treitschke — and certainly not the dramatists of the Wilhelmian *Reich* — can convince us that Prussia, "no slow natural growth, but the artificial construction of Frederick II" as Taylor calls it,[27] was other than mechanistically "state-constructive."[28] It may well be no accident that in the thought of Hegel (for whom, as Nipperdey puts it, human reality was "objektiver Geist")[29] and those who followed him, and in some of the dramas of Hebbel (who was no Austrian, even if he found "asylum"[30] in Vienna) and, in a different way, in the un-dramatic *Stücke* of Brecht, history became an abstraction.

Notes

[1] Friedrich Sengle, *Das deutsche Geschichtsdrama* (Stuttgart: Metzler, 1952), 1.

[2] See in particular *Lady Inger of Ostraat* (1855), which the editors of *The Oxford Ibsen* (vol. 1 [Oxford: Oxford UP, 1970], 17) describe as "assertively Norwegian" and "pointedly anti-Danish."

[3] T. G. Masaryk, *Zur russischen Geschichts- und Religionsphilosophie*, vol. I (1913), (Düsseldorf-Cologne: Diederichs, 1965), 261. Karamzin was, says Masaryk, "auch für die ersten Slawophilen Lehrer der russischen Geschichte" (289).

[4] Engels, "Democratic Panslavism," in *Karl Marx: The Revolutions of 1848 (Political Writings I)*, ed. D. Fernbach (London: Allen Lane, 1973), 231–32, and O. Bauer, *Geschichte Oesterreichs* (Vienna: 1911), quoted by Karl Stadler, *Austria* (London: E. Benn, 1971), 39.

[5] Friedrich Naumann's expression. Naumann names Treitschke, along with Arndt, Raumer, Dahlmann, Gervinus, Baumgarten, Häusser, Droysen and Sybel, among the historians who worked as "predecessors and satellites" of Bismarck to construct the Prussian-German "Reich": cf. F. N., *Mitteleuropa* (Berlin: Georg Reimer, 1915), 38.

[6] Hitler, for example, records how his history-teacher worked on his "national fervour." Cf. Alan Bullock, *Hitler: A Study in Tyranny,* rev. edition (Harmondsworth: Pelican, 1962), 27. For Wildenbruch, cf. Sengle, *Das deutsche Geschichtsdrama,* 182.

[7] A "Figurendrama," in Wolfgang Kayser's terminology: cf. W. Kayser, *Das sprachliche Kunstwerk,* 2nd ed. (Berne: Francke, 1951), 370.

[8] See further A. G. Blunden, "Schiller's Egmont," *Seminar* 14 (1978): 31–44, and Lesley Sharpe, "Schiller and Goethe's Egmont," *Modern Language Review* 77 (1982).

[9] Letter to W. H. Petersen, 12 December 1885.

[10] Reproduced in *Theodor Storm-Paul Heyse, Briefwechsel,* ed. C. A. Bernd, vol. 2, (Berlin: Erich Schmidt, 1970), 140.

[11] Shakespeare, *The Second Part of Henry the Fourth,* III, 2.

[12] "An important historical event": A. S. Pushkin, *Polnoye Sobraniye Sochinenii,* (Moscow: Gosudarstvennoye Izdadelstvo khudozhenstvennoi Literatury, 1949), 1345. The event in question is the absorption of Novgorod into the growing Muscovite state: the consolidation of the state is the central ideological pillar of Karamzin's *History.*

[13] Pushkin 140.

[14] "[zum Drama] in dem es nun kein Präteritum . . . mehr gibt." Wolfgang Kayser, *Das sprachliche Kunstwerk,* 369. Compare Lessing (*Hamburgische Dramaturgie* 77): the action should be presented "nicht als vergangen, das ist, nicht in der erzählenden Form, sondern als gegenwärtig, das ist, in der dramatischen Form." "Die Form des Dramas" says Grillparzer, "ist die Gegenwart" (*Selbstbiographie,* 150).

[15] "da spannt sich alles auf das Kommende"; Kayser 369. A patriotic pageant, says Emil Staiger, could be called theatrical but not "dramatic": "'Bühnenmäßig' und 'dramatisch' bedeutet also nicht dasselbe" (E. Staiger, *Grundbegriffe der Poetik* [1946], 4th ed. [Zurich: Atlantis, 1959], 143). For him, too, "Spannung" is central to "dramatic style." Schiller speaks of a "fortwährende Unruhe" in the spectator, who cannot tear himself away from the "object" (letter to Goethe, 26 December 1797).

[16] "Die Supposition einer Gegenwart": see his essay "Über den gegenwärtigen Zustand der dramatischen Kunst in Deutschland" (1834).

[17] M. Beyer, *Ibsen. The Man and His Work,* trans. Marie Wells (London, 1978), 48: ". . . the topical preaching [when the ghost of Bishop Nikolas speaks] breaks the framework of the play."

[18] Cf. Meyer's "Mein Erstling," and W. A. Coupe, "Hutten, Meyer and the Use of History," in D. Attwood, A. Best, and R. Last, eds., *For Lionel Thomas* (Hull: U of Hull, 1980), 43.

[19] A thread that is skilfully woven into the dramatic fabric.

[20] *Das sprachliche Kunstwerk,* 370.

[21] See Goethe's letter to J. D. Salzmann of 28 November 1771.

[22] Kayser 370–71. Grillparzer, in his *Selbstbiographie,* describes how, in order to bridge the historical gap and justify the (for moderns) "abscheuliche Katastrophe" of *Medea,* he was forced to construct a trilogy, a form which has "etwas Episches" (103–4).

[23] Cf. Letters to Georg Andreas Reimer (21 June 1811) and Fouqué (15 August 1811). For a detailed discussion of the "national" aspects of Kleist's plays during the Napoleonic period, see H. A. Korff, *Geist der Goethezeit,* 2nd ed. (Leipzig: Koehler und Amelung, 1958), Teil IV, 269–311.

[24] F. Koch, *Heinrich von Kleist. Bewußtsein und Wirklichkeit* (Stuttgart, 1958), 43.

[25] Georg Lukács, *Der historische Roman* (Berlin, 1955), 42.

[26] Not only Hormayr and Grillparzer. Hofmannsthal, in his "Austrian essays," still calls on figures from the past like Prince Eugene. Friedrich Naumann, for whom historians are "die Erzieher der Völker," emphasizes the role of a series of writers, from Arndt to Treitschke, in creating an "Imperial consciousness" (*Mitteleuropa,* 33 and 36–38).

[27] A. J. P. Taylor, *The Course of German History* (1945), University Paperbacks edition (London, 1961), 32.

[28] Cf. Treitschke, *History of Germany in the Nineteenth Century,* trans. Eden and Cedar Paul, vol. 1 (London, 1915), 7.

²⁹ Cf. Thomas Nipperdey, *Deutsche Geschichte 1800–1866* (Munich: Beck, 1983), 506–7.

³⁰ Cf. Helmut Kreuzer, "Friedrich Hebbel," in B. von Wiese, ed., *Deutsche Dichter des neunzehnten Jahrhunderts* (Berlin: E. Schmidt, 1969), 390. Hebbel was, says Kreuzer, as "ein relativ isolierter Außenseiter in Wien."

1: Historical Drama of the German Baroque: Andreas Gryphius

W HY BEGIN WITH THE BAROQUE when, if Sengle is to be believed, in spite of a lively interest in historical *fact*, the period produced "keine echte Geschichtsdichtung"?[1] In part, the answer lies in analysis of what Sengle means by the word "echt" — an argument that could also apply to Brecht's *Mutter Courage*. In that play, as well as in Gryphius's *Carolus Stuardus*,[2] to which we devote the bulk of this chapter, the actual events portrayed are seen as being of significance principally, if not entirely, by reference to "historical" criteria which transcend the time in which they occur, and indeed earthly time as a whole. As K.-H. Habersetzer puts it, in commenting on Gryphius's *Papinianus*, "Historie [bleibt] nicht auf ihre Faktizität festgelegt"; it "transcends itself" because of a statement contained within it.[3] But this is itself a "genuine" statement about history, the expression of the Baroque "Geschichtsbegriff," which we shall outline later.

With the exception of *Cardenio und Celinde*, all Gryphius's "Trauerspiele" (as indeed those of Lohenstein)[4] can be seen as historical in this sense. *Carolus Stuardus*, to a lesser extent *Papinianus*, and perhaps also *Leo Armenius*, deserve to be singled out for the framework common to all three heroes. Papinianus and Carolus are unequivocally political martyr-figures with religious overtones. Leo the Armenian has a dual function. He is a martyr in relation to the new usurper Michael Balbus, but at the same time he is an iconoclast and usurper himself, an object of Divine Retribution, as the apparition of the former Patriarch of Constantinople ("Tarasii Geist") makes clear to him in a dream. This, of course, gives these figures a potential relevance to seventeenth-century political debate, but it also confers on them an "eternal," exemplary status which transcends historical time: rather as the biblical David and Saul, in Grimmelshausen's *Ratio Status*, furnish a quasi-emblematic framework for a confrontation of "godly" and Machiavellian models of kingship. We shall certainly have to take account of the (often transparently) transcendental dimension of the earthbound "dramatic" action in a Baroque play. But it is also worth noting that "real time," if we may call it that, plays a part in Gryphius's plays. He shows his characters, at times, as existing within a real historical tradition. As we shall see later, Charles I, as a political figure, is firmly located within his country's history. As a martyr, he belongs in an actual tradition begun by Christ himself. Parallels with Christ abound, and the King places himself in the line which began with St Stephen.[5] Whether Gryphius is exercising poetic licence here is uncertain, but he would have seen it as legitimate. He makes clear that he has enlisted the aid of "Dicht-Kunst" (that is, poetic licence) in the cases of Leo Armenius and Papinianus. Leo is shown falling on the True Cross, and Papinianus refuses to join in the persecution of the Christians.[6] The temporal is — as most commentators agree — simultaneously seen *sub specie aeternitatis;* but it is not, perhaps, often enough registered that this not only makes events "transparent," to a certain extent, to a supra-temporal dimension, it can also provide a link between the terrestrial past and present. The exemplary nature of the event can also invoke the idea of an historical tradition, as when Carolus aligns himself with the first Christian martyr, or Bassianus (Caracalla) identifies himself as an "ander Nero."[7] Gryphius's aim here is to bring into play an historical tradition — as the Notes reveal, Tacitus' *Annals* are a key source in this work — rather than draw a learned parallel, as often occurs in Lohenstein's annotations. The latter, for example, in annotating Subrius Flavius's remark about the cramped nature of the place of execution (*Epicharis* V: 492), first refers to Tacitus, then adds that Charles I complained "auf gleichmässige Arth" about the low level of the execution-block.[8] The two instances in this example are linked, as in a metaphor, by a *tertium comparationis,* but not by an overarching historical tradition; they remain discrete historical "cases."

The predilection for Biblical associations of the radical Puritan Hugo Peter (who sees the King as an Agag and a Barabbas), enables Gryphius to reinforce Carolus's Christ-like associations *ex negativo,* so to speak; most strikingly of all, when he exploits the motif of the axe which, with that of the sea, dominates the play's imagery. Peter gives Hewlet what we must assume is the actual executioner's axe, which he sees as the axe of Divine Justice, with the exhortation ". . . mache dich an Carls unfruchtbar Eichen."[9] The transcendental perspective inherent in the Baroque understanding of reality enables Peter to interpret history awry and the spectator, knowing that Peter's is a "verkehrte Welt," to do so correctly. In a not dissimilar way, that same perspective enables the dramatist, often in conjunction with the principle of retribution ("Rache" or "Straffe"), to enrich the temporal fabric with a prophetic strand.

In *Carolus Stuardus*, which dramatizes the last hours of Charles I of England, we are dealing with a more or less contemporary sensation and political *cause célèbre*. Gryphius began the first version in 1649, and the impact the event made on him is further illustrated by the fact that he introduced, retrospectively, a reference to it in a note to *Catharina von Georgien* (I: 17–18). There is also the added historical dimension that he is able in a revised second version (1663) to exploit the fact that the audience knows that retribution — a prophecy only in the dramatic text — has already taken place. A mass of source-material exists which Gryphius has exploited quite exhaustively. At the same time, he has highlighted the eternal spiritual theme, and, following the lead of the *Eikon Basilike* and other English sources,[10] given the play an added historicality by emphasizing the theme of Charles as a martyr in imitation of Christ, that is, as part of a tradition. And the play, set in a by no means exotic or far-off country,[11] could have acquired an extra piquancy for a German audience by reminding it that there had been upheavals and wars on the continent too. Gryphius himself points this out in the chorus to the second act, and there are a number of references that seem to suggest links to events closer to home.[12] It was not all that long since Germany too had "seen treachery"[13] and we should remind ourselves that when Gryphius began the work, the Thirty Years' War had only just come to an end. Linkage with the present is much more tenuous in the case of *Papinianus*, but it can fairly be pointed out that for the Latinate seventeenth-century reader (and it is clear from the "Anmerckungen" that Gryphius is writing for such readers), Roman history would have been relatively familiar ground, and often had an "exemplary" status almost comparable to that of the Bible, so that cases were easily transferable across the centuries. Thus, in the disquisition on Fortune in the Notes to *Papinianus*, Gryphius quotes a modern epigrammatic epitaph in which the French "Duc d'Ancre" is described as "the Gallic Sejanus."[14]

For the German Baroque, the historical figure was important, as Rolf Tarot has put it in commenting on the great Jesuit dramatist Jakob Bidermann, not as an individual, but as an "über sich hinausweisendes Exemplum,"[15] and could assume a more or less allegorical, or "emblematic" status.[16] The actions in which these figures participate are "real," and documented as if by a modern historian, but the documentation is there, in the first instance, to underpin an interpretation of a much less modern kind, one more reminiscent of the "universal" and "Providential" history, as Collingwood calls it, of the Christian Middle Ages.[17] The heroic dramas ("Trauerspiele") and novels of the Baroque (and these were the genres which dealt with "history," for in Benjamin's words, "the sovereign was (its) prime exponent"[18]) demonstrated, in spite of the "inconstancy" of the world and its apparent dominance by fickle Fortune, the "wunderbare Regierung des Höchsten"[19] in this world. A "higher power" that "determined history,"[20] call it God, "Verhängnis,"[21] or Providence,[22] provided the extratemporal, quasi-eschatological, perspective from which events had to be understood. For the seventeenth century, indeed, events involving disasters in high places, were in themselves "Trauerspiele" — for example the fall of Wallenstein, described in those terms by Johann Rist[23] — and the scene in which they occurred, a "Trauer-Bühne."[24] A "tragedy" could occur within a "Freuden-Spiel" such as Hallmann's *Adelheide:* when Adalbertus sees the heroine about to leap from a high tower into the river below, he exclaims: "O grimmes Trauer-Spiel!"[25] Stories ending in an event which was in itself "lamentable" ("jämmerlich") were, effectively, tragedies and featured as such in popular contemporary collections such as Rosset's *Les histoires tragiques de nostre temps* (1614: in the German version, *Schaw-Platz trauriger Geschichten*), to which Gryphius makes reference in the Notes to *Papinianus.*[26] The impending death of Charles I is for Laud a "Jammer-Spiel."[27] Peter can refer to the scaffold (a place of joy for him!) as the "Traurgerüste" (III, 381), and the English Count can say: "man eilt das Spill zu schlissen" (V, 33). The acting-out of the events which constitute the plot is presented in a form which, as Harald Steinhagen says, is "much less rationally transparent" (that is, psychologically motivated) than is the case in drama as conceived from the eighteenth century onwards,[28] in which the meaning has to arise from *within* the plot. This meant, of course, that contemporary events were just as much "history" as those that had happened a century ago. The real fulcrum of history lay outside time, rather than within it, and Baroque dramatists consistently remind their audiences of this fact. Gryphius, for example, has his "First English Count" in *Carolus Stuardus* cry out to the God who is "outside time (ausser Zeit)."[29] The goddess of Sacred Justice descends from the clouds, the emblematic representation of the borderline between the eternal and temporal realms, declares herself the ruling spirit of the "Traur-Spil" (*Papinianus* II: 525) that is to follow, and ascends to Heaven again.

Our play conforms to the pattern outlined above. It is much concerned with political and juridical principle and practice,[30] but ultimately, the theological ("eternal") perspective takes precedence. The allegorical Choruses between the Acts give the best opportunity for that perspective to become clearly apparent, but it is implicitly or explicitly present throughout. Characters appeal to a referee (God) outside the field of play, refer to the Last Judgement,[31] are described, or present themselves, as "examples" of eternal truths, which are worthy of study by others,[32] and refer frequently to the principle of Retribution ("Rache"). That this principle is very closely related to, if not indeed identifiable with that of "Verhängnis"; perhaps even Providence is instanced by, for example, a line from Paul Fleming's poem "Schreiben vertriebener Frau Germanien an ihre Söhne," in which the poet bewails the miseries of the Thirty Years' War. This is seen, as is commonly the case in seventeenth-century Germany, as an instance of Divine Retribution: "So hat die hohe Rach' es über mich verhangen."[33] In a Note to line 55 of Act V of *Carolus Stuardus*, Gryphius is able to record, retrospectively, that "die Göttliche Rache" has punished the "erschreckliche Leichtfertigkeit" of a soldier who spat in the King's face. The ghosts of Mary Queen of Scots (and of other "murdered English kings" in the first Chorus), and of Strafford and Laud appear, not principally for stage-effect,[34] but as presently living visitants from another dimension, to emphasize the *eternal* history to which the action at present going forward on earth, in truth belongs. They are indeed emissaries of that spiritual dimension and can participate in the process of retribution, as their role in the "Poleh" scene (V: 157–260) shows.[35]

They also draw attention to the overarching *national* history in which the action is embedded. The shades of Strafford and Laud provide commentary and prophecy, but are not detached from their own former actuality, their roles and fates in the period leading up to the Civil War. The actual Queen of Scots is, of course, also "past history" (for example for Cromwell, III, 236), as are other monarchs whose sticky ends are listed by her ghost in its catalogue of England's sins against the monarchical principle, and chronicled in the Notes. The latter are not part of the dramatic action, though they contribute significantly to the historical stratum of the play as a whole. Even discounting them for the moment, it can be said that there is a significant deposit of pre-seventeenth-century British history in the text itself[36] and that this helps, as do the frequent "Neronian" and

Tacitean echoes in *Papinianus*,[37] to create an awareness of a life lived in past "actual" time, though *within* eternal time.

There is an awareness of a concrete future as well, an awareness particularly connected with the theme of retribution. There are many more or less general references to dire consequences for Britain in the future, but the most interesting are the two cases in which the Restoration is foretold and the punishment of the regicides described. Here, the eternal and the temporal overlap in an interesting way. The prophetic vision derives from a spiritual source which is naturally accessible to the ghosts of Strafford and Laud, and does not need to be shown (II, 143–59). When it is inflicted on the semi-demented Poleh (V: 193–237), Gryphius, with a nice sense of the difference between him and spirits like Laud and Strafford, reveals it by means of lifting the inner curtain of the Baroque "Verwandlungsbühne" and presenting "vertoningen" (exhibitions, dumb shows), in the manner of one of his models, Vondel. In both cases, the process is directed by the principle of retribution,[38] which appears in bodily form in the final chorus.

These moments call into play the potential historical knowledge of a spectator or reader of 1663 by superimposing the future on the present, but they do so in a way that breaks the dramatic web. We are presented here with a *suspension* of dramatic time and reality, such as happens also in the Choruses. One is reminded of the technique of the Baroque Passion-oratorio where the "dramatic" element, represented by the passion-story in the text, is punctuated by meditative episodes (chorales, eventually arias and choruses).[39] The oratorio-text is, of course, a text for music (where "dramatic" has a different meaning), but it affords us a useful comparison in that it involves the audience in shifts of temporal perspective. Smallman does not discuss, nor does he need to discuss this issue, but for literary drama, it is important, and for historical drama, crucial. Under the surface of the recitative, formally a narrative in the past tense, there is always a latent dramatic present, which crystallizes in the statements of soloists, or *turbae*. But it is also history, established for the believer as fact, and located in a specific past. The meditative sections belong to a relatively, or even absolutely time-free zone and they therefore inevitably expose, whatever the artist's intention, the relative temporal locations of both story and audience. Even allowing for the power of music, we have to register a break in the continuous flow of the action. Also, by making the story an object of periodic contemplation from an "eternal" standpoint, this technique introduces into the structural equation of the whole a static factor, perhaps more "epic" (in the sense of the observer's stance referred to by Kayser[40]) than dramatic.

That *Carolus Stuardus* is an "historical" work in this sense is clear. The question that needs to be addressed now is whether, in this case, history is contained within a framework which, even if it is tempered by "epic" tendencies, can still be called at least in some sense dramatic. There is certainly a static quality in the human "action" proper, most obviously in the two rock-like figures, Carolus and Cromwell, who could be seen as men of inaction. Yet this is a dynamic inaction; their (respectively positive and negative) *constantia* is thrown into relief by the tension and movement around them. In contrast to the (perhaps totally "epic") technique of the "Histories" of a pre-Baroque writer such as Jakob Ayrer, who produces what could be called chronicle (rather than true history) in dialogue-form, Gryphius does have an eye to the creation of dramatic time in this play. By "dramatic time," we mean that "present" without which there can be no dramatic action, the coherent and urgent sequence of "present" moments which forms the medium in which the characters interact, and generates tension, and the sense of forward impulsion. Even in "epic drama," insofar as it is drama at all, this cannot be dispensed with. In his *Erbauung der Stadt Rom*, for example, Ayrer extracts a series of occurrences from Livy, and presents them in sequence, but is if anything less "dramatic" than his source. The sense of linkage and causation between events is minimal. Numitorius's remark when, having killed the usurper Amulius with the help of Romulus and Remus, he picks up the crown and sceptre and begins *his* reign, is characteristic: "Du hast nun lang genug Regirt."[41] Gryphius's awareness of the need for a sense of dramatic, as well as transcendental time, is particularly well instanced by his exploitation of the new material which he has incorporated into the second version. He wishes certainly to improve the accuracy of the historical record as he sees it, but also to enhance the sense of urgency which arises out of the fact that time is in fact hastening forward toward the moment of execution which, is the centre round which the whole revolves. Fairfax is given a new and more sympathetic role, bolstered by the determination of his wife to save Carolus if she can. His "dark" counterpart as a driving-force, namely the Independent leader Hugo Peter, also has his role significantly developed, not least in driving forward plans *for* the execution. These characters, significantly, dominate the whole of the new first Act. This sense of urgency in the "active" characters also enhances our awareness of the *constantia* of the outwardly static figures.

From the point of view of what must seem the inevitable outcome, in particular for one whose mind is set on eternity, what little
earthly time is left seems itself an eternity. But however relative its importance in the eschatological scheme of things, it is within that
earthly time that the drama occurs, and Gryphius makes sure we are
aware of it. Carolus, for whom there is nothing left to do but wait and
remain steadfast, is from the beginning anticipating the end of his
suffering: "Die Zeit fällt zimlich eng," he says in Act II when it is, as
Juxton replies, "noch früh."[42] We feel how slowly time is passing.
When Fairfax uses practically the same words,[43] the effect is very different: there is "no time to lose." The coming day is a "threat" (I, 3)
for Fairfax's wife; it sets a clock running of which we are still being
reminded in the fourth and fifth Acts.[44] There is a counterpoint of
times, a swirling of hopes and fears around the immobile central play-
ers. The latter do not lack energy and strength, but they must use it to
stand still; Cromwell must not give in, Carolus must not break down.
For them, time is long and what they have to do in it is precisely
nothing. The plotters and planners, on the other hand, are, or can be
conceived as being, in motion. There can be little doubt that Gryphius, with the introduction of the "Gemahlin," and development of
Peter, strengthened the play's movement, and hence its dramatic
"Gegenwart" (in Grillparzer's terms), but equally little doubt that he
wished it to be a subordinate moment, a foil at best. The impulse is
given by the "Gemahlin" who, with her dreams of fame for herself
and her husband, echoed, ironically, in the same Act by that other
arch-planner, Peter,[45] belongs to the world of *vanitas*, that phenomenon in which time shows its inconstant face and which is conjured up
by Strafford's ghost ("Das Rasende verkehren Der ungewissen Zeit"
(II, 42–43) and another "spectator"-figure, Juxton in what is almost a
"keynote" speech (II, 291–307). That dimension, in which man is
truly at the mercy of Fortune because he lacks the insight to see
through it, is one that Carolus, in spirit, has already left behind him. A
similar contrast is observable between the immovable Papinianus, a
martyr for the truth who "pocht aller Zeiten Noth" (III, 472) and
those who swirl around this rock in the eddies of court intrigue, such
as Julia's Chamberlain, who speaks (V, 1) under the pressure of "die
enge Zeit." It may be the case that, as Herbert Heckmann has said,
the hero's great opening monologue has "unmasked" the reality that
follows,[46] and shown its *relative* insignificance, but it is still a reality
and an important, and strongly dramatic constituent element in the

whole. Even in the Biblical narrative of the Passion, we can discern "dramatic time."

There is, then, a basic dramatic plot-structure, but its time-sequence is interrupted by prophetic episodes and by choruses, and generally subverted by a tendency, in the choruses and elsewhere, to reflect on it from a vantage-point outside time. The audience is not confined to the auditorium; there are spectators on stage (among the cast!) as well. At first glance, it would seem that reality is also being subverted — and to the extent that this is necessary to achieve the reflective stance, that is clearly the case, since dramatic reality and dramatic present go together. But we know that Gryphius was very anxious to keep as close as he could to the historical actuality, often to the extent of using the actual words of historical figures, the most striking case in point being the King's final speech, of which he remarks in the Notes that he could have constructed something briefer, but thought it important to have Carolus speak ". . . wie er sich selbst mit seinen eigenen Farben außgestrichen."[47] And by making us aware of this fact — for Gryphius does not assume that the audience has (as yet, at least) itself studied the sources he cites — the Note, superfluous in terms of "pure" drama, has made a useful contribution to the end-effect of the play as *historical* drama. The reader, who is also a "spectator," of course, if he reads a drama properly,[48] will experience an inevitable dilution of the dramatic effect in the process of consulting the Note. But as Flemming says, it is the "content" (Gehalt) rather than the dramatic experience that is Gryphius's chief concern.[49] This involves a constant willingness on the part of the ideal recipient to suspend the dramatic experience in the interests of "correct understanding": "zu richtigem Verstande," as Gryphius puts it in his prefatory remarks to the annotations of *Carolus Stuardus.*[50] "Content," as far as historical drama is concerned, means not only the action's exemplary, extra-temporal meaning, but also the awareness that what we are seeing not only is happening, but also *has* happened.

This brings us to the question of the "Kurtze Anmerckungen," their nature and their function within the work as a whole. Notes, by definition, lie outside the drama in its quintessential form, that is as performed before our eyes in the dramatic present, and even in drama as read, that is as a purely literary genre, they constitute a disruption of that present. The Notes to *Carolus Stuardus* are often quite long and detailed — unusually so for this author, who is much less lavish in his provision for the "curious reader" than is Lohenstein.[51] They fall short of being scholarly history: a commodity that Gryphius, with his "unvergleichliche Wissenschaft,"[52] was quite learned enough to have supplied had he wished to do so. One is tempted to repeat the question Gryphius asks at the end of the Notes to *Papinianus:* "Und so vil vor dises mal. Warumb aber so vil? Gelehrten wird dises umbsonst geschriben / Ungelehrten ist es noch zu wenig."[53] His prefatory remarks to the Notes are also somewhat Delphic: he adds them, he says, to "please others," not because he himself thinks they are "hoch-nöthig."[54] Perhaps this reflects his awareness, expressed in the same place, that this practice is often frowned on. But it is clear that he annotates to please himself, not others, and, as he puts it in the second version of *Carolus Stuardus,* to expand and enrich his reader's experience. In some cases at least, his motivation could be called "historical."

Gryphius certainly wishes to make a political point, and may well have a particular political "intention," as Habersetzer puts it,[55] in this work. But he is not just writing propaganda, and certainly not just chronicling the events as fact. He is showing their significance as history, which extends far beyond the fate of the characters on the stage, though the very historicity of the events is important as evidence for his argument. He uses the choruses ("Reyen"), as indeed does Lohenstein, to bring out the implications of an individual action within the wider sweep of history,[56] but he uses the technique of annotation, in the particular case of the trial and execution of Charles I, to involve the reader, whom he conceives as educated, and certainly capable of reading Latin, but not primarily a "Gelehrter," in examining, with him, the actuality, as well as the eternal significance, of an episode in English history.

These Notes are not merely source-references, there to prove that Gryphius is a conscientious scholar. In many cases, they help to develop and support the presentation of the King as a martyr, an "ermordete Majestät." And they can be affective as well as informative: the long section on the Prayer Book, documenting its history and Charles's strong self-identification with it, culminating in the emotive assertion that his execution was in fact a judicial murder and he a political and religious martyr, is a valuable contribution to his historical characterisation, and as moving as anything in the text itself. The Note is in fact an important supplement to, indeed extension of the text. A not dissimilar case is that in *Leo Armenius,* in which the martyr-status of the central figure, a kind of pre-figuration of Carolus,[57] which is not always as clear as it might be, is supported by a Note to the line (IV, 138) in which the apparition prophesies the fate of a conspirator: "Dir wird / was Leo trägt." True, the sorcerer points out in the text that the oracle might mean death (lines 155–58), but by making clear that that this refers to retribution subsequently meted out to a regicide, the Note adds historical weight (a vision of the future otherwise unavailable to the reader, who is hardly likely to have Zonaras at his fingertips) to the dramatic irony of the ambiguous phrase. At the same time, it enhances Leo's martyr-status (as a monarch, rather than an individual) by introducing the words of the avenging Theophilus: "Warumb habt ihr Hand an den Gesalbten deß HERRN geleget? Und seid nicht nur zu Todschlägern sondern auch zu Vatermördern an ewrem Keyser worden?"[58]

The Notes are naturally sometimes written for the satisfaction of the scholar,[59] and dispensable for dramatic purposes, but sometimes, at least, they can be seen as integral, and a positive contribution to the work as a whole, in its task of showing and interpreting history. The full effect can only be achieved when the two sides are taken together. This is obviously so in the case from *Leo Armenius* quoted above, as in that of Carolus's exhortation to the Bishop in V, 461 ("Bleib . . . stets indenck meiner Worte"); only when we read the relevant Note do we appreciate the point Gryphius wishes to make, namely that this most Christian king does not wish his son to revenge his death on any individual.[60] In *Papinianus*, Julia alludes to the last words of Severus (II, 177–78), but does not quote them, which she could easily have done. Instead, Gryphius, who clearly regards them as integral to the proper effect of his drama, which is about kingship as well as martyrdom, provides them in a Note.[61]

The king's exclusion from Hull is registered in the text (III, 481) with a brief, dry statement. The relevant Note evokes the scene graphically and emphasizes the political seriousness of the episode with what purport to be the words of the very person who endured this "insolens facinus et aperta obsequii detrectatio." The *Eikon Basilike* is then recommended by Gryphius as "mehr denn würdig / daß es wol gelesen / und recht erwogen werde."[62] That Gryphius himself had taken this advice and that he sees the validity of the work as universal, is clear from the Note on *Papinianus* (Act I, line 35), in which he refers his reader/spectator to some "sehr nachdenkliche Wort" in this work. The "Hull" Note in *Carolus Stuardus*, like many of the others, is more than mere documentation. It is part of the case for Divine Right that the play quite openly sets out to make (an attitude it shares with *Papinianus*)[63] and — if we posit the play as read, albeit by one who, like Gryphius,[64] would be capable of envisaging it in stage terms — it could even be seen to strengthen the emotive as well as the ideological exposition of that case. Reading this Note can be seen as a dramatic extension of the viewing of the scene (a "static" conversation), whether on the physical stage, or the stage of the imagination. It adds both a visual element, with the image of the King and his followers "left dangling outside the city gates in foul rainy weather," and an emotional one, by allowing the King to express directly his deep sense of the affront offered to him, both as an individual, and as a representative figure. We cannot but recall Flemming's statement that while performance was "wohl gewünscht," it was "nicht gesichert," and that the normal form of communication for these plays was the book rather than the stage.[65]

It is time now to draw threads together and attempt an objective assessment of *Carolus Stuardus* as an historical drama. One thing is clear from the outset: its Baroque perspective, in which historical "truth" is not identical with, and cannot be expressed within, the boundaries of the world of fact, distinguishes it immediately from the forms and practices of historical drama as we are accustomed to them from eighteenth- and nineteenth-century examples. And yet (apart from its demonstrative function), actuality holds a genuine interest for the author and his putative reader, so much so that, although he is well aware of objections to this practice,[66] he uses the technique of annotation, both as scholarship and sometimes even as narrative, to strengthen and develop this aspect of his work. The non-naturalistic techniques which Gryphius uses (Choruses, apparitions, prophetic visions), not only introduce the "eternal" dimension into his text, but serve to enrich our knowledge of the earthly history of which the characters are a part.

In their different ways, both these techniques and many of the Notes[67] also help to foster the temporal aspect of the historical experience. In the case of *Carolus Stuardus*, of course, the time gap between Gryphius's events and his audience is quite small. But quite apart from the fact that within the framework of the Baroque concept of history, *all* history is "contemporary" in the sense that it is on an equal extratemporal footing, Gryphius shows his characters in the context of British national history as well by tracing the thread of events which leads directly to Charles back, certainly as far as Jacobean and Elizabethan, perhaps even medieval times. Mary Queen of Scots is the principal vehicle in the text, but the Notes also make a significant contribution. The long discourse on Anglo-Scottish relations (Note to II, 112) is the outstanding example. Another occurs in the Note to V, 104, in which Gryphius indulges in an excursus on the Prayer Book which is not strictly necessary in the context, "denen welchen die Engelländische Kirchen Gebräuche unbekant . . . zur Nachricht." The "Nachricht" helps to create an historical context: this book has existed "von Königin Elisabeths Zeiten an," Gryphius tells us, and after describing it, he launches into an account of Charles's disputes with the Presbyterians, in which he in a sense "dramatises" him as a politico-religious martyr: "beständig"(constant) in his support of the liturgy, subject to "grosse Verfolgungen und Widerwertigkeiten," and eventually, in spite of the fact that he is "König dreyer Königreiche," ". . . von seinen Unterthanen ermordet."[68] This last remark, of course, underscores the point already made in the play's subtitle.

As was clear in the introduction, the desire to achieve an historical effect must impose a certain strain, an "epic" tendency, on the close-knit structure towards which the dramatic impulse naturally seems to drive the playwright. He feels the need to provide his audience with information (an "historical exposition," perhaps) which the author in whom the dramatic motivation dominates would reject as disruptive of his desire to create and maintain a "dramatic present." He must also locate his "dramatic" action within a wider context and facilitate an historical perspective on events for his audience. The hybrid called "historical drama" must find some sort of compromise if it is to deserve the second element in its title. We would submit that within the parameters of Baroque theory and practice, Gryphius has done this; not, certainly, by adopting an overtly "epic" technique such as the trilogy, but by bringing the transcendental into the action, and by making use of the footnotes. It could be argued that this "devalues" the (individual and factual) dramatic action which is contained within that framework, but the counter-argument would be that this is to ask a man of the seventeenth century to think and write as if he had been born a century later. Gryphius certainly seems to us to deserve the title of "dramatist," in the same way as that title is often bestowed upon J. S. Bach. Certainly, to remain within the literary context, it is only necessary to place his works alongside the naively "epic" plays of Ayrer, essentially stories narrated "spielweiß," as the author puts it in the "Vorredt" to his *Tragedie und gantze Historie von Erbauung . . . der Stadt und Stiffts Bamberg*,[69] to see that Gryphius represents at the very least a giant step in that direction.

Notes

[1] *Geschichtsdrama,* 9.

[2] There were two versions, the first written soon after the execution of Charles I but not published till 1657, the second, revised and expanded version (which will be the basis for our discussion) appeared in 1663, after the Restoration.

[3] K.-H. Habersetzer, *Politische Typologie und dramatisches Exemplum* (Stuttgart: Metzler, 1985), 60. For Habersetzer, Papinianus is the *exemplum;* Charles I is a case of "political typology."

[4] We do not have space for a detailed examination of the plays of Daniel Casper von Lohenstein — which could certainly be justified on academic grounds — but can refer the reader to Gerhard Spellerberg's study: *Verhängnis und Geschichte* (Bad Homburg, 1970). With due allowance for individual differences, much of the general comment in this book is relevant to our case also. It is, in essence, history as the interpretation by the "emblematischer Verstand" (36) of the working-out of an eternal and transcendent "plan" (of "Verhängnis") that concerns Lohenstein, in both the action and the allegorical Choruses ("Reyen"). He indicates the role of Habsburg Austria in this scheme and pursues this approach to history further in his novel, the *Arminius.*

[5] ". . . als jener riff . . . etc.," p. 78, V, lines 339–40.

[6] For *Leo Armenius,* cf. Gryphius's comments in the preface: "Daß der sterbende Keyser / bey vor Augen schwebender todes gefahr ein Creutz ergriffen ist unlaugbar: daß es aber dasselbe gewesen / an welchem unser Erlöser sich geopffert / sagt der Geschichtschreiber nicht / ja vielmehr wenn man seine Wort ansiehet / das widerspiel; gleichwol aber /weil damals die übrigen stücker des grossen Söhn-Altares . . . zu Constantinopel verwahret worden: haben wir der Dichtkunst / an selbige sich zu machen / nach gegeben / die sonsten auff diesem Schawplatz jhr wenig freyheit nehmen dürffen." Andreas Gryphius, *Gesamtausgabe der deutschsprachigen Werke* (GA), vol. 5, ed. H. Powell (Tübingen: Niemeyer, 1965), 4. In the case of *Papinianus,* see the note to line 86 of act I: "*Baronius* zwar wil *Papiniano* zumessen / als wenn er mit dem blutt der Christen sich . . . beflecket / es mangelt aber an einem Beweis" (GA 4, 257). Werner Eggers points out that in the case of Leo Armenius, Gryphius has suppressed the accusations of unorthodoxy contained in his source, Cedrenus: cf. Eggers (Note 15), 159.

[7] Bassianus himself, act III, line 2. Lest we miss the point, Gryphius emphasizes in a note (260) that he is thinking of the murder of Britannicus. Cf. also the conversations between Bassianus and Laetus (II, 40–46) and Papinianus and Cleander (III, 431–67). Nero died in A.D. 68; Bassianus (Caracalla) reigned from A.D. 211–17.

[8] D. C. von Lohenstein, *Römische Trauerspiele,* ed. K. G. Just (Stuttgart: Hiersemann [BLVS], 1955), 291. Gryphius has his hero remark on this fact on two occasions, but without a footnote. The point is reasonably clear, and has in any case been made by Peter and his confederates in the first act (lines 300–302).

[9] 40, III, 78. Cf. Matt. 3, 10: "And now the axe is laid to the root . . . etc." Gryphius is careful to link Peter with the real axe in question (cf. "Anmerckungen," III, 77). The blasphemy is compounded at the end of the same speech by the reference to Malachi 4, 2 ("Noch ungeborner Sonn . . .").

[10] For a list and discussion of Gryphius's sources, see the edition with Commentary of the play by Hugh Powell (Leicester: Leicester UP, 1955), cxxxv–cxxxviii. Unless otherwise stated, references will be to this edition.

[11] Carolus (or his realm?) is identified to Europe's rulers as "der große Nachbar" (line 532 of act III).

[12] *Carolus Stuardus,* 36–37. This Chorus is in both versions, though differently positioned. The Lord Chamberlain of the Palatinate reminds us of the Germany of the Thirty Years' War in his description of Carolus as the man "Nach welchem Deutschland sah" (51) and Laud's vision of Civil War and a devastated land ("Flüsse Leichen voll . . . ein verwüstet Land Und umbgekehrte Städt" (26), and the reference of the First English Count to the Civil War as a consuming fire (53) seem to echo Gryphius's to the Thirty Years' War in the Preface to *Leo Armenius* ("Indem unser gantzes Vaterland sich nunmehr in seine eigene Aschen verscharret," GA vol. 5, 3) and in various sonnets, most notably "Threnen des Vaterlandes."

[13] In the figure of Wallenstein: cf. II, 556: "Auch der Adler siht Verrähter" (which can also be interpreted, as Powell points out [note 210], as a reference to the "Fronde.").

[14] GA 4, 264 (note to line 205 of act IV). The man in question was an Italian adventurer named Concini, who was the favourite of the Queen Mother at the time of the *Fronde.*

[15] "Nachwort des Herausgebers" to J. Bidermann, *Ludi Theatrales,* vol. 1 (Tübingen: Niemeyer, 1967), 18.

[16] For allegory, cf. in particular Walter Benjamin, *Ursprung des deutschen Trauerspiels* (1928), rev. ed. by R. Tiedemann (Frankfurt, 1963). Pure allegory, of course, occurs only in the Choruses; as Werner Eggers says in the case of Gryphius, the members of the historical *dramatis personae* are identified as "berechtigte Träger der angegeben historischen Namen," but the dramatist then makes them "unmask" themselves as "examples" W. Eggers *Wirklichkeit und Wahrheit im Trauerspiel von Andreas Gryphius* (Heidelberg, 1967), 46. For the "emblematic" aspect of German Baroque drama, see Albrecht Schöne, *Emblematik und Drama im Zeitalter des Barock* (Munich, 1964).

[17] R. G. Collingwood, *The Idea of History* (1946) (Oxford, 1961), 50. On this theme and its relevance to Gryphius's "Trauerspiele," cf. the remarks on "divina . . . providentia, qua res humanae administrantur," in the commentary on Job (1646) of Balthasar Corderius, cited in H-J. Schings, *Die patristische und stoische Tradition bei Andreas Gryphius* (Cologne-Graz, 1966), 155–56.

[18] Benjamin 51–52.

[19] The words of Anton Ulrich von Braunschweig in his *Syrische Aramena,* quoted by Günther Müller in *Deutsche Dichtung von der Renaissance bis zum Ausgang des Barock* (1927), (Darmstadt, 1957), 249.

[20] E. M. Szarota, *Lohensteins Arminius als Zeitroman. Sichtweisen des Spätbarock* (Berne-Munich, 1970), 231; M. Wehrli, *Das barocke Geschichtsbild in Lohensteins Arminius* (Frauenfeld-Leipzig, 1938), 19 ("geschichtsbestimmende Macht").

[21] A transcendental principle, "vor aller Zeit gewesen" (Spellerberg 43). It opens up the wider temporal perspective and allows, for example, of prophetic moments, as when Felicitas speaks, in the final "Reyen" of *Ibrahim Sultan*, of "Was das Verhängnüß Guttes hat gesponnen" Lohenstein, *Türkische Trauerspiele,* ed. K. G. Just (Stuttgart: Hiersemann, 1953), 219. Lohenstein may have felt a greater measure of "Vernunft-optimismus" than did Gryphius: see B. Asmuth, *Daniel Casper von Lohenstein* (Stuttgart, 1971), 39). However, Lohenstein still sees human judgement as fallible, and the maintenance of "Macht" and the pursuit of "Tugend" as essentially incompatible.

[22] E.g. Bidermann, *Belisarius:* "Qui stetit in summo felix . . . Agitur deorsum ad nutum Providentiae"; *Ludi Theatrales,* ed. cit., vol. 1, 77.

[23] See Johann Rist, "Was ist dieß Leben doch? Ein Trawrspiel ists zu nennen," in H. Cysarz, ed., *Deutsche Barocklyrik* (DLER) I (Leipzig: Reclam, 1933), 216.

[24] In Hallmann's *Die sterbende Unschuld oder Catharina Königin in England* (1673?), when the Queen, just before her death, collapses in a faint, one of her ladies-in-waiting exclaims: "Ach Sie ermuntre sich auf dieser Trauer-Bühne": J. C. Hallmann, *Sämtliche Werke,* ed. G. Spellerberg, vol. II (Berlin: de Gruyter, 1980), 221.

[25] J. C. Hallmann, *Sämtliche Werke* III(2), (Berlin: de Gruyter, 1987), 472.

[26] See GA 4, 268.

[27] Act II, line 115. Gryphius himself refers to it as such (note to V: 285).

[28] See Harald Steinhagen, *Wirklichkeit und Handeln im barocken Trauerspiel* (Tübingen, 1977), 25.

[29] Page 52 (act III, lines 549–50). Strafford's ghost is able to interpret the future as prophesied by the spirit of Archbishop Laud as God's holy Judgement (II, 159–60: "Herr, wer erkennet nicht . . . etc.").

[30] The relation between the action of *Papinianus* and current political debate about the legitimacy of rebellion is well described by Habersetzer 87–94. Here too, though, the main emphasis is on the historically transcendental virtue of "Großmut."

[31] E.g. p. 71 (V, 63): "Der Bischoff stellt ihm [i.e. Carolus] vor den übergrossen Tag . . . etc."

[32] E.g. Carolus: ". . . schaut wie die Macht verschwinde Auff die ein König pocht," 60 (IV, 9–10) and 13: Gemahlin: "Bebt, die ihr herrscht und schafft! Bebt ob dem Trauerspiel" (I, 11), 25: Laud: "Mehr denn zu wahrer Spruch / durch unsern Fall bewehret" (II, 85), 70: Graff: "Laß diß den Fürsten nur ein Schau- nicht Vor-Spill seyn" (V, 16) and 81: Juxton: (the world is) ". . . ein Schau-Platz . . . auff dem ein ider findt / Daß alle Majestät sey Schatten / Rauch und Wind" (V, 431–32).

[33] See Paul Fleming, *Teütsche Poemata* (1642; reprint: Hildesheim: Olms, 1969), 117.

[34] One feels that Hallmann, in a scene that seems to echo this one, *does* have the ghosts of the Bishop of Rochester and of Sir Thomas More appear to the sleeping Catharina for the stage-effect, though he has them disappear, on this occasion, without the statutory explosion ("ohne Knallen")! (vol. II, 217).

[35] Cf. the role of the ghost of Severus (Bassianus's father and predecessor) in the fourth Chorus of *Papinianus*, where he appears together with the "Rasereyen" (Furies), who are fulfilling the will of "die Rache" (GA IV, 235).

[36] Not only past kings are mentioned. The "First Count," for example, recalls the Gunpowder Plot from the days of his youth (III, 561–67, 53) and the memory of the Spanish Armada crops up in Fairfax's exchanges with his wife (I, 173–74, 17) and with Cromwell (III, 236–37, 44).

[37] Among the parallels and contrasts, the comparison between Papinianus and Seneca is perhaps the most interesting. The latter had, of course, "exerted the powers of his skill and eloquence," as Gibbon puts it, to condone Nero's action, whereas Papinianus had refused, and taken the consequences (see the *Decline and Fall of the Roman Empire*, I: 5–6).

[38] II, 149, 26 ("Indem erscheint die Rach") and V, 193, 75 ("Weh mir! Die Rach erscheinet!") Carolus also looks forward to a Restoration, but in less specific terms (II, 419–23). The link between "Rache" and the opening of a perspective into the historical future is also illustrated by the final scene of Hallmann's *Catharina* (ed. cit., 232–33), in which Catharina's ghost appears to Henry and draws his attention to a series of twelve "shows" on the inner stage, the last of which, interestingly, is the execution of Charles I: a leap, in fact, from the Tudor to the Stuart line!

[39] Evidence for Gryphius's own time is sketchy, but Basil Smallman believes it is likely that chorales, at least were part of the structure of the German Passion-oratorio in the first half of the seventeenth century: cf. Basil Smallman, *The Background of Passion Music. J. S. Bach and his Predecessors* (London, 1957), 79–80.

[40] Cf. Kayser's "Haltung des gegenüberstehenden Beobachtens," quoted above, chapter 1, note 12 and text. There might be a parallel with the at least theoretical presence of Marxist analysis in Brecht's *Mutter Courage*.

[41] J. Ayrer, *Tragedi, Erster Theil von Erbauung der Stadt Rom; Dramen*, vol. I, ed. Adalbert von Keller (reprint: Hildesheim: Olms, 1973), 66. Ayrer, who followed in the footsteps of Hans Sachs, wrote his plays at the turn of the sixteenth and seventeenth centuries. There is no room to pursue the comparison between Ayrer and Gryphius further here, but it may perhaps be noted in passing that much of the apparatus for a historical contemplation of events through what we have called "suspension" of dramatic time, can be detected in embryo in Ayrer (the demise of Amulius, for example, is described by Numitorius as a "Rach" sent by the divine powers [66]), but this element remains theatrically undeveloped and there is little sense of the interpenetration of the temporal and eternal.

[42] Act II, line 271; 29. And it is still "early" when Hacker meets Peter at the beginning of act III (38, line 15).

[43] I, 217; 18: "Doch fält die Zeit sehr eng."

[44] 67 and 68: Gemahlin: "Wie das so ruchloß dann verschertzt die schönste Zeit?" (line 276); I Obriste: "Ich eil." Gem: "ohn Zeit verliren" (line 297). In the fifth act, the haste has transferred itself to the other side: 70 (line 33): "Man eilt das Spill zu schlissen"; 73: "Ihr Wütten lässset sie nicht lange Zeit verliren."

[45] Cf. Gemahlin, act I, 14 (line 34: "mein eigen Ruhm"; line 37: "meinen Ruhm"), 18 (line 196: "Sein eigen Ruhm") and 19, lines 234–41. Peter refers to Hewlet's forthcoming "Ruhm" in line 260 of the same act (19).

[46] Herbert Heckmann, *Elemente des barocken Trauerspiels. Am Beispiel des "Papinian" von Andreas Gryphius* (Darmstadt: 1959), 30.

[47] *Carolus Stuardus*, 104.

[48] In this very note (to V, 285), Gryphius speaks to the "Zuseher und Leser," *Carolus Stuardus*, 104.

[49] "Auf den Gehalt kam Gryphius . . . alles an": Willi Flemming, *Andreas Gryphius. Eine Monographie* (Stuttgart: Kohlhammer, 1965), 210.

[50] GA 4, 140.

[51] The Notes to *Carolus Stuardus* require nineteen and a half pages in the *Gesamtausgabe*. None of the other plays requires more than three, with the exception — significantly — of *Papinianus* (fourteen and a half.) While not all annotations make a contribution to the reader's "historical experience," this suggests that there is a correlation between "correct understanding" and historical "content." The un-historical *Cardenio und Celinde* has no Notes at all! This is also true, of course, of the first version of *Carolus Stuardus* for which some sources at least (for example, the *Eikon Basilike*) would surely have been available. The reason for this may perhaps lie in the fact that this text was not written, in the first instance, with the general public in mind.

[52] The expression of Gryphius's son-in-law and biographer, Balthasar von Stosch, as quoted by Powell xxix.

[53] GA 4, 269.

[54] GA 4, 255.

[55] See the discussion of "political typology" in K.-H. Habersetzer, *Politische Typologie und dramatisches Exemplum* (Stuttgart: Metzler, 1985), 35–42. Habersetzer argues persuasively that Gryphius even hoped to spur the Great Elector to take up arms against England (46–59).

[56] On several occasions, most notably in the final "Reyen" of *Sophonisbe*, where he makes use of the doctrine of the "Four Monarchies" derived from Daniel 7, Lohenstein places the actions taken from both ancient and (in the case of the "Türkische Trauerspiele") modern history in a historical-cum geo-political context that sees the Habsburg Empire as in a sense the fulfilment of the design of "Verhangnis." See in particular Lohenstein, *Afrikanische Trauerspiele*, ed. K. G. Just (Stuttgart: Hiersemann, 1957), 350–53.

[57] See the preface, in which Gryphius refers to the frequency with which, in history, thrones have been acquired through "Auffruhr und Krieg," and adds that "bey uns newe" it is not unheard of "unter dem schein deß Gottes dienstes (wie Michael und seine Bundsgenossen) ungehewre Mord und Bubenstück ins werck zu rich-

ten." GA 5, 4. The subtitle of this play, "Fürsten-Mord," points forward to that of *Carolus Stuardus.*

[58] GA 5, 95.

[59] E.g. the note (to *Papinianus* V, line 356) on methods of execution, in particular Gryphius's stern reproof to a commentator who has accused another of a mistake in relation to the execution of Ann Boleyn! (GA 4, 267–68). Though even here, we can discern some kind of "historical" relevance.

[60] Cf. GA 4, 137 (line 461) and 159.

[61] Cf. GA 4, 259. The long note to IV, line 293 is particularly interesting. In a sense, it "historicizes" the whole scene, in which Papinianus is stripped of his dignities — clear enough from the action as such — by identifying him specifically as "Praetorii Praefectus" (cf. 265–66). Gryphius prefaces this annotation with the remark that whoever wishes to understand this scene properly ("recht verstehen") must go to the original source, Hadrianos's *Notitia Imperii Orientis et Occidentis.* This is surely another indication that the author thought of his play as stage drama, certainly, but as a drama "performed" by a reader.

[62] See 98. The relevant lines are not in the first version. A similar example of historical expansion by annotation is contained in the Note to page two of *Catharina von Georgien,* in which Seneca's *De Tranquilitate* is given as a source, and the reader is urged: "Besihe das gantze Capitel durch und durch," and Gryphius remarks pointedly that this play was completed "well before" the execution of Charles I (GA 6, 222). This is therefore a case of the retrospective addition of an historical perspective! The play, probably written about 1647, was first published in 1657. This is more than a grace-note, of course: the linkage with Charles is meant as an enhancement of the dramatic and ideological impact of the lines spoken by "Die Ewigkeit" in the prologue to *Catharina.* See also the reference to the *Eikon Basilike* in the note to line 35 of Papinianus's opening monologue (GA 4, 256), which draws a parallel with Strafford.

[63] See GA 4, 233–35, especially p. 234: ". . . Der Fürst ists der uns schafft . . . etc."

[64] Gryphius was, of course, acquainted with contemporary stage-production, from Holland and elsewhere. That he wrote in terms of a *seen* performance is clear, for example, from the notes on performance which he appends to the "Anmerckungen" of *Papinianus.*

[65] Cf. W. Flemming 149–50. Flemming, in summing up, asserts that Gryphius's drama is "kein bloßes 'Buchdrama.'" But the rest of Flemming's summing-up is worth quoting: ". . . aber auch kein bühnenwirksames Theaterstück, vielmehr ein Literaturdrama, das zu nachdenklichem Aufnehmen aufforderte, sowohl beim Lesen wie beim Spielen" (171).

[66] Cf. the Introduction to the "Kurtze Anmerckungen" of *Papinianus,* GA 4, 255.

[67] Through extended excerpts from sources, these "Anmerkungen" often involve the reader heavily in the actuality of events preceding the action, when the action itself hardly seems to demand it. That to Act II, line 433, for example, extends over nearly two and a half pages and takes us back to the minority of James I.

[68] Note to V, 103.

⁶⁹ Cf. Jakob Ayrer, *Dramen,* vol. I, 576. The pronouncedly "epic" method by which the author proceeds is well illustrated by the prologue to the *Comedia vom König Edwarto dem Dritten* where "Jahn Clam" first summarises the plot, then announces: "Wie sich das aber als zutragen Wern euch jetzt die Personen sagen Die nach mir wollen kommen ein" (*Dramen* III, 1927–28), or by that to the *Erbauung der Stadt Rom:* "So wöll wir euch jtzt recetirn / Die schön Histori . . . etc." (*Dramen* I, 17).

2: The Age of Enlightenment: *Aufklärung*

ALTHOUGH THE ENLIGHTENMENT, in Germany, had to share the eighteenth century with an opposing tendency which can be called in broad terms "Romantic," we can reasonably say it enjoyed the ascendancy until the early 1770s. From that point on, it continued, into the first decade of the nineteenth century, to make a significant contribution to German literature and thought, through the work of writers of the older generation like Lessing and Wieland, and of others (most notably, for our purposes, Schiller) who certainly underwent a "pre-Romantic" phase (the so-called "Sturm und Drang") but returned in part at least to the values of the Enlightenment during the period usually designated as "Classicism," or "Weimarer Klassik."[1] We have, accordingly, subdivided this phase of our enquiry into two chapters. In what we defined as the era of "Aufklärung" (*circa* 1720–1770), the rationalism which is always rightly associated with the idea of the Enlightenment shows itself from its more timidly restrictive side. Like the later "Classicist," the *Aufklärer* believes in the primacy of man. However, he is acutely aware that the "philosophical" truth of what he thinks or writes can be undermined by that of the emotions and the imagination, yet he puts his faith in the head rather than the heart. Truth, in history, is on the one hand the factual record, and on the other, an interpretation in the light of his own enlightened criteria, which he wishes to impose on past ages as well as his own. With growing confidence, and the insight into individuality gained during the outburst of pre-Romantic revolt which was the "Sturm und Drang," the generation to which Schiller belongs is ready to venture further, though with the onset of maturity, respect for reason has reasserted itself. In Schiller, indeed, deeply emotional though he always was, it can be said that the authority of the reason, and its inherent respect for order, had never been overthrown. Even his most rebellious hero, Karl Moor in *Die Räuber*, having begun by asserting the freedom of the Self from the constraints of "das Gesetz," eventually finds true sublimity by subordinating the principle of individuality to that of Law.

In the chapter he devotes to the historical drama of the *Aufklä-rung*, Sengle can find no more than "Ansätze." In theory, "poetry has nothing to do with history."[2] The view the Enlightenment took of history was probably not quite as "a-historical" as has been argued in the past, but it was also arguably not conducive to a state of mind that would allow past times a validity of their own. Its form of rationalism, working through abstraction, brought the past before the tribunal of its own essentially time-less present, and formed a barrier to any sense of *historical* community. The German Enlightenment's "pragmatic" school of historians, whose first outstanding representative is Johann Lorenz von Mosheim (1694–1755), lays a solid foundation in matters of accuracy and objectivity, and of careful consideration of the factors conditioning historical events, "der weiteste und unbefangenste Blick in die maßgebenden allgemeinen Zusammenhänge," as Hettner has put it.[3] However, there is a difference between seeing that the past has to be understood in terms of its own *circumstances*, as Lessing's friend C. F. Nicolai, for example, can be said to have done,[4] and allowing it validity and relevance to the present day, in its own right and its own ethos. It is the criteria of the civilized age of reason that condition the climate in which history is understood and judged. Circumstances can be individual; the nature of things and of Man, is universal, and as Gottsched insists, "unveränderlich." This is the attitude that prevails from Voltaire's *Essai sur les moeurs* onward, and as a practising historian, in Cassirer's judgement, Voltaire, probably the chief model for the historiography of the Enlightenment, "rediscovers his own ideals in the past."[5]

The distant past of the Germanic nations did attract some interest, but it was still thought of as in itself broadly "barbaric." Even Scott is enough of an *Aufklärer* to see the belief in ghosts prevalent among his border heroes as "acceptable [only] to *barbarous* tribes (my emphasis)."[6] When Lessing, in *Laookon*, describes "the old Nordic heroic spirit," he is not tempted to anticipate the nineteenth-century's enthusiasm for "Germanic" heroism. He resurrects the tenth-century Danish hero "Palnatoko," only to erase all sense of historical community with the comment: "Unsere Urältern waren Barbaren."[7] He finds his heroic models among the Greeks, who were for him, as for Winckelmann, proto-*Aufklärer*, "denkende Wesen"[8] who, under the beneficent influence of true "Nature," acted "nach Grundsätzen." J. E. Schlegel's *Canut* (1746) is set in eleventh-century Denmark, but the Nordic heroic spirit has been relentlessly refined out of it, except in the case of the villain Ulfo, who is sometimes interpreted as prefiguring the individualism of the "Sturm und Drang," but is in fact there to set off, by his "Raserei," the true humanity of an enlightened eighteenth-century "Menschenfreund" in old-Danish clothing.[9] In the 1770s, when bards were in fashion, Wieland recognized the "nervichte Stärke" of his ancient forbears, but denied any idea of historical community with them: "[wir sind] so sehr von dem unterschieden, was unsere Vorfahren zu den Zeiten der Barden waren, daß kaum ein gewisseres Mittel wäre, unsere Poesie unbrauchbar und lächerlich zu machen, als wenn wir sie in eine Velleda verkleiden wollten."[10] History was, in essence, progress towards enlightenment, and the thought of revivifying the dead selves over which the *Aufklärer* had risen, had no appeal for Wieland. He felt the charm of medieval stories, but turned them, in his verse-tales, into "polished jewels"[11] of essentially Rococo style. Lady Jane Grey remains a martyr in his version (1758), but while historical fact is respected, sixteenth-century Protestantism is transposed into the "tender" key of Enlightenment Sentimentalism.

Even quasi-sanctified Roman heroes like Cato or Brutus, immensely popular tragic subjects in this period,[12] had to have their Stoic virtue softened, or "corrected." There may be tinges of "historicism" in Nicolai, but as in the case of Lessing's historical standpoint in the *Erziehung des Menschengeschlechts*, the universalistic, and historically indifferent, "correct" criteria of Enlightened rationalism, are the criteria by which all events are judged. Like Wieland, Nicolai is aware that "die gesunde Vernunft entwickelt sich nur nach und nach," but he feels — also like Wieland — that "man ist auf dem besten Wege dazu" — and that he himself has already arrived.[13] There is no ground here for empathy with "oldness." The nominally ancient can come over to us as modern, or rather, as existing, by virtue of abstraction, in a timeless "universal" context. The name "Sparta" occurs in Gottsched's *Agis* (1745) with monotonous regularity, but as far as its content is concerned, it might as well have been set in Leipzig. Agis is not a Spartan, but simply "der Fürsten Muster." Schönaich, in his *Montezum* (1763), refines the Aztecs in accordance with the Enlightenment stereotype of the Noble Savage.[14] The concept of history as "fact" is what underlies the concern of many authors of the time for historical fidelity and their reluctance to use the "poetic freedom" given already by Aristotle. Lessing, in his *Hamburgische Dramaturgie*, delights in exposing this timidity and pedantry, but in placing the licence that the "much more philosophical" aim of poetry confers[15] in the framework of "inner probability," he is at one with Gottsched, who had evoked the principle ("es ist alles sehr wahrscheinlich eingerichtet") to justify the invented material introduced by Deschamps into the sparse account of Cato given by the sources: "Niemand [wird] was Widersprechendes darin antreffen."[16] "Nature," rather than history, decides what is probable (that is, consonant with truth). Drama, says Lessing, may take its plots from history, but it aims at a non-historical outcome: to turn "die unnützen Schätze des Gedächtnisses" into "Nahrungen des Geistes." History, he says in discussing Weisse's (lurid, but totally un-Shakespearean) *Richard der Dritte*, may show us examples of apparently undeserved suffering, for we cannot see the "good reason" that must lie in the "unendliche[r] Zusammenhang der Dinge." The dramatist must make out of the isolated "members" of history a "whole" that mirrors the rational (and therefore moral) order of God's creation.[17]

The mere fact that something is historically documented does not make it aesthetically acceptable. *Lessing* considers the argument that the "superstition" of Cronegk's *Olinth und Sophronia* may have been compatible with "many good qualities" in the period in which it is set (in more "simple" parts of the world, even to the present day). He leaves little space for historical understanding in drama: "Er schrieb sein Trauerspiel eben so wenig für jene Zeiten, als er es bestimmte, in Böhmen oder Spanien gespielt zu werden."[18] There is little room for historical understanding when "truth" and "nature" are at stake. This emerges yet more clearly in his comment on the use of apparitions. It would be unfair to judge the introduction of a spectral visitant in an ancient Greek play "nach unsren bessern Einsichten." A modern, who holds such enlightened views, or in any case is writing for an audience that does, cannot be allowed this licence, not even if he sets his action back in those "more credulous" times. For not only is the dramatist "no historian," he is also, as Lessing remarks in his criticism of Wieland's *Lady Johanna Gray*, "the master of history."[19] However familiar the nominal historical setting, the dramatic present still takes precedence. Defending Thomas Corneille's *Comte d'Essex* (Voltaire had attacked its historical inaccuracies), Lessing argues that he could have claimed that the spectator may have read his history-books, but that it is not the "historical," but his (i.e. Corneille's) Elizabeth to whom he responds.[20] The dramatic present wipes out the historical past.

The general tendency of the eighteenth century to bourgeoisification (later continued at a philosophically higher level by the Weimar Classicists), also lessens the historicality of dramatic subjects taken from the past. Indeed, the most striking dramatic creation of this period, the *bürgerliches Trauerspiel*, sets up a significant barrier to the

THE AGE OF ENLIGHTENMENT: *AUFKLÄRUNG* ◆ 37

use of historical subjects at all, by virtue of its preference of family affairs to affairs of state. In historical studies too, there was a tendency to look for the "Mensch" rather than the individual. As Nicolai (whose point of view is that of the "aufgeklärter bürgerlicher Stand")[21] says is the case with Voltaire's history,[22] historical figures, when they appear in plays, tend to be seen in terms of a generalised moral "humanity." Formally too, the taste of the Enlightenment — and this includes Lessing — for integrated, regular, classicistic structure, militated against the "epic" form which is naturally favoured, as will appear in the case of Goethe's *Götz von Berlichingen*,[23] by an approach that is "historical" in our sense of the word. Gottsched, the founding father of the "Klassizismus" of the *Aufklärung*, did write one play on an historical topic (the Massacre of the Huguenots) which seems to demand an "epic" treatment, but attempts in his *Parisische Bluthochzeit* (1744), as Robert R. Heitner puts it, to "constrain the material within the classicistic form," with predictably catastrophic results.[24] Although they were "patriots" in their way, the German dramatists of this era generally found the German past uncongenial as subject-matter, preferring to go either to Classical antiquity or (in the *Bürgerliches Trauerspiel*) to a modern domestic milieu to find the virtues they could admire. Admittedly, even in such stony ground, there are fruitful patches, and Sengle singles out J. E. Schlegel and Klopstock as precursors of the "vaterländisch" (patriotic) tendency. We shall return briefly to this "national" aspect at the end of this section. For the moment, the concept of history, and general sensitivity to the historical, which predominated in the "Aufklärung" will occupy the foreground.

Lessing, like Nicolai, does not depart in any essential aspect from the "pragmatic" method which was standard for the German Enlightenment.[25] I have said that in his most important tragedy, *Emilia Galotti* (1772), Lessing "drags" an ancient theme into modern times.[26] I do not want to depart from that formulation, but this seems an appropriate moment to develop the point implicit in that indication of a forcible quality in the process of transfer. There *is* an historical dimension in the theme Lessing has chosen, which even his systematic attempt to create "eine bürgerliche Virginia" (his phrase), has not been able totally to eliminate. This, in turn, has to do with the contemporary relevance for the eighteenth-century *Aufklärer* of the history of Ancient Rome, in particular as a school of heroism and virtue. We find this reflected in the "Moral Weeklies,"[27] and in the fondness of dramatists for themes from Classical history. Figures like Cato (treated by the founding father, Gottsched, in his *Sterbender Cato* of 1731) and Brutus were almost honorary contemporaries. Echoes of Horace's "dulce et decorum est pro patria mori" occur, for example in Cronegk's unfinished Crusader-drama *Olinth und Sophronia* (1760),[28] and in Lessing's *Samuel Henzi.*[29] Even this more or less contemporary action can be conceived in quasi-Roman terms; the play is shot through with the rhetoric of "Tugend" (i.e. "virtus"), "Freiheit" and "Vaterland,"[30] and the parallel with Brutus is drawn by Wernier in the opening scene: "O wer gleich Bruto denkt, sich auch gleich Bruto wagte." It feels as ancient as it is modern, as Roman as it is Swiss, and much more so than it is potentially German. But while this is evidence, perhaps, of a desire for a tradition, and of respect for the concept of nationhood, the ideas remain abstractions and there is no real sense of historical continuity or community. For a play that could link the past with the Holy Roman Empire, we must wait for Schiller and, in a different way, Goethe. We shall come upon this theme again when we turn to Schlegel's *Hermann.* For the moment, our concern is with *Emilia Galotti*, where the crucial figure is not so much the daughter as the father, with that of the projected son-in-law, Appiani, as a kind of pendant.

Before we turn to Lessing, it is helpful to note that the Virginia-story, originally in Livy, seems to have been quite popular in the eighteenth century, and had already been given a dramatic treatment in Germany, namely that of Johann Samuel Patzke, which has been helpfully analysed by F. J. Lamport.[31] Patzke's *Virginia*, published in 1755, is a close contemporary of Lessing's "bürgerliches Trauerspiel" *Miß Sara Sampson*, and seems to share (or at least, to wish to share) the sentimental middle-class attitudes which inform that work. Patzke tells us in his "Vorbericht" that he intends to concentrate on the "rührende Begebenheit der Virginia" rather than the political motif of the overthrow of Appius.[32] As Lessing makes clear in his *Hamburgische Dramaturgie*, an emphasis on "Rührung" (a pity based on the self-conscious and essentially rational sympathy of a "virtuous" heart) makes figures of prominence and affairs of state less, rather than more suitable for tragedy, because sympathy is based on a perceived similarity between character and spectator.[33] With that emphasis, much of the historical content of the story disappears. A state, says Lessing, "ist ein viel zu abstrakter Begriff für unsere Empfindungen," a statement which (since a state is an historical phenomenon) seems to remove a principal potential source of the sense of community of which we have spoken as a vital element of historical drama proper. Especially since we are talking of the Roman state, the republic and its heroic virtue, a subject with which educated Germans of the Age of Enlightenment were intimately acquainted as a result of their classically based education, and which, in the absence among *Aufklärer* of any strong sense of a German identity in the political (as opposed to moral and cultural) sense, or of a real interest in the Middle Ages, was perhaps the nearest thing they had to a sense of continuity with the past.

The ending, the father killing his own daughter, is a problem for Patzke as later for Lessing, and Lamport remarks shrewdly that it can be seen as a mark of the author's political "naivety" that he thinks it possible to depoliticize the story.[34] The theme of "Roman-ness" bulks large in the tragic motivation: Virginia has to prove herself a "Römerinn," as her father has trained her to be.[35] The result is a sense of contradiction: an action which strives to be psychologically "modern," relies on the heroic ethos of Ancient Rome, which, paradoxical as it may seem, still commands respect in the more "menschlich" eighteenth century,[36] to make its catastrophe convincing. Lessing is at least consistent in setting the action in a more modern Italy, but even a "bürgerlich," or a "modernised" Virginia, is still a Virginia. At the critical point, Emilia refers directly to the father who "in days gone by" killed his daughter to save her honour: "Aber alle solche Thaten sind von ehedem! Solcher Väter gibt es keine mehr!"[37]

The crux of this play is the principle of "virtue," and the crucial character is that modern (but not fully modern*ised*) "Vater," Odoardo, who, having instilled respect for ancient tradition in his daughter, is now being called upon to act in accordance with it. Lessing makes no direct association with ancient Rome, but there is perhaps an echo of the Stoic ideal of freedom in Odoardo's assertion (V: 4) that "Wer kein Gesetz achtet, ist ebenso mächtig, als wer kein Gesetz hat," and he lives by a stern ideal of virtue which, like that ideal, is seen as both admirable ("the pattern of all manly virtue" [Appiani, Act II, scene 7]) and extreme. The Prince and Claudia criticize it as "rude" ("rauh")[38] and they have some right on their side. Lessing's *Philotas* (1759), written in the period of the Seven Years' War, in which his friend (Ewald von) Kleist went to an "heroic" death, also wavers between admiration and criticism of ancient virtue, rather as the Stoic hero is both lauded and criticised in Brawe's *Brutus.*[39] A similar ambivalence appears in the attitude of the Enlightenment to the tradition of "old German" heroism embodied above all in the figure of Arminius. "Rough virtue" is to be applauded as the antonym of "courtly vice" (e.g. in Wieland's *Hermann* [Canto I, lines 66–68]),

but not as the boorishness of Raufbold and his pards in Zachariae's
Der Renommist.[40]

No one would suggest, of course, that *Emilia Galotti* is an historical play, but together with Patzke's work and others that evoke the
world of ancient Stoic and republican virtue, it presents the reader or
spectator, voluntarily or involuntarily, with an historical dimension.
The social and political world of the eighteenth-century absolutist
court, whose image was often one of luxury and vice, did raise moral
questions for the essentially *bürgerlich* writers of the *Aufklärung*, even
if most of them genuinely wished to avoid a concentration on socio-
political issues and confined their political hopes to at best a reforming
Enlightened Despotism. They did not wish to return to antiquity, and
they did reject the (as they saw it) unfeeling Stoic *apathia* in its pure
form. Nevertheless, their view of "virtue" and "vice" was coloured by
their reading of ancient authors and although they accepted official
Christian doctrine, ancient heroes and heroines were more congenial
to the writers of the *Aufklärung* than Christian martyrs — or indeed,
apart from Klopstock and his disciples in the '60s and '70s, than ancient Germans — as models of virtue. Their choice of dramatic topics
confirms this, and against the fact that Emilia, whose "piety" is part of
her motivation, does allude to early martyrs as precedents, we can
point to Lessing's scathing dismissal of Cronegk's depiction of martyrdom in *Olinth und Sophronia.*[41] Emilia, in any case, also has some
"Roman" steel in her, and she certainly knows which key to press
when she wishes to goad her father to action. Von Wiese, while he is
aware of the Roman origin of the theme, discusses Odoardo's character exclusively in terms of a "christlich-moralisch" mind-set,[42] but
while we would agree that Odoardo is a "modern" man, as is Lessing,
there is an "ancient" strand in the thinking of both that should not be
entirely ignored. In rejecting the idea that Goethe's *Werther* might be
a true portrait of Karl Wilhelm Jerusalem, the heroic moral standard
to which Lessing refers is that of Greece and Rome: "Glauben Sie, daß
je ein römischer oder griechischer Jüngling sich so und darum das Leben genommen? Gewiß nicht."[43] Ancient history offered a good opportunity to focus on the issue of virtue. There was no easy direct link
with the historical tradition of "Germany" itself. The Middle Ages
were not yet respectable to a defensively aggressive rationalism, and
we have to wait for the "Sturm und Drang" to see an exploitation of
the heritage of the sixteenth century.

There was, however, an attempt to make use of another Germanic
tradition which, perhaps by virtue of its very remoteness (and its

THE AGE OF ENLIGHTENMENT: *AUFKLÄRUNG* ◆ 41

closeness in time to ancient Rome), did not present such problems. The figure of "Hermann" (the Arminius of Tacitus) had a measure of relevance for the middle-class eighteenth-century thinkers and writers who were the main driving force of the *Aufklärung*, in that it had strong associations of a plain virtue untainted by the luxury and laxity they saw as endemic at court. From Gottsched onward, the theme of "old" German virtue, which turns out to be very like the natural simplicity beloved of the *Aufklärer*, features quite prominently in their writing. It is not unworthy of notice that a Prince who was seen as free of such "modern" taint, like Joseph II, could be linked (somewhat incongruously it has to be said) with Hermann by J. M. Miller.[44] That the figure was an acceptable vehicle for the degree of German national feeling that did exist at that time, can be seen from references in the writings of Gottsched, Uz, and others.

Johann Elias Schlegel and Friedrich Gottlieb Klopstock were the two most prominent writers who — in different ways — attempted to bring the theme to the stage and who could perhaps be said to have thereby created the beginnings of a national German, "vaterländisch" drama. It has to be added, though, that these beginnings were modest. Schlegel works, in his *Hermann* (1740–41), within the strict limits of the regular classicistic drama on the French model — which he also follows in including an (unhistorical) love-plot — and generates little sense of the world of the ancient Germans. Schlegel's brother Johann Heinrich tells us that he felt "aus seinem Gefühle und aus der Erfahrung" that a theme taken from national history ("in der Geschichte des Volkes") would have a particularly strong effect on an audience,[45] which suggests the theoretical potential of a "vaterländisch" play within him, but his mentality is too much that of the *Aufklärer* to allow this to approach fruition and introduce, for example, an "epic" tendency into the strict classicistic form. Peter Wolf sees the play as having a "strongly national" character "von der gedanklichen Seite her."[46] However, the play's "German" patriotism remains an abstraction and its colouring is as much Roman as it is Teutonic. It is not *mere* "Kolorit"; it is central to the play's heroic ethos, but this gives it no more historical substance. Goethe found a performance he saw in 1766 very dry, "ungeachtet aller Tierhäute."[47] While the theme of freedom bulks large, this freedom is an heroic abstraction, easier to relate to the Roman republic than to eighteenth-century Germany, as is Brutus's tirade against the Kings in Schlegel's *Lucretia*. Revolutionary doings are afoot at the end of this play, as Schulz says,[48] but they are *too* "rauh," too remote in time and in manners, to provide a sense of community for an eighteenth-century audience. When Gottsched attempted to relate the German-Roman contrast in *Hermann* to the present contrast (as he saw it) between Germany and France, Schlegel was quick to dissociate himself from such an interpretation.[49]

Klopstock's trilogy of half-dramatic, half-lyrical sketches, "Bardiete" as he called them,[50] depart from the classicistic form, and were written in a mood and during a period of genuine patriotic enthusiasm, in particular the 1760s, which also saw a prolonged outburst of patriotic lyricism (that is, "Thuiskon," "Der Hügel und der Hain," and the re-casting, in "Wingolf," of "Auf meine Freunde" [1748] from classicistic into an almost indigestibly Germanic mode).[51] Although there is no reason to doubt the sincerity of this "Deutschtümelei," there is no substance of historical tradition behind the strange names and concepts these poems contain. In the same way, Hermann's world in the "Bardiete" is too hazy and remote, and the possible links with the modern Holy Roman Empire too tenuous, to generate a sense of community, and with it, a drama that we can see as more than merely formally, or at best, embryonically "historical."[52] In fact, a promising beginning in the latter direction was made by Goethe at about the same time, but that is another story and belongs to another chapter in *our* story.

Notes

[1] Goethe's principal contribution, as far as historical drama is concerned, belongs under the broad "Romantic" heading, and he is accordingly treated in our fourth chapter.

[2] Sengle 13. The basis of this tendency is Aristotle's distinction (accepted by both Gottsched and Breitinger) between the truth of history and that of poetry. Lessing returns to this topic again and again in the *Hamburgische Dramaturgie* (for example, Stücke 17, 19, 29–32.) The truth of "character" (that is, universally and eternally valid "human nature") sufficed for him and the "Genie" (the man of talent) could afford to laugh at the pedantry of mere "historical knowledge" (Stück 34).

[3] Hermann Hettner, *Geschichte der deutschen Literatur im achtzehnten Jahrhundert,* rev. ed. by G. Erler (Leipzig, 1961) vol. 1, 227. Mosheim had a deservedly high reputation as an ecclesiastical historian: cf. Hettner 227–28.

[4] E.g. Frederick II must be seen in his own "Verhältnisse[n]": H. Möller, "Nicolai als Historiker," in B. Fabian, ed., *Friedrich Nicolai* (Berlin, 1983), 143. Nicolai's criteria are: "all historical work to be founded on contemporary sources, interpretation in the specific historical context, what can be proved from sources to be

separated from the merely probable, the formation of hypotheses and — strictly separate — chronology and causality" (150).

[5] Gottsched, *Ausführliche Redekunst* (reprint: Hildesheim: Olms, 1973) I: 43. For Voltaire, see Cassirer, *The Philosophy of the Enlightenment*, trans. F. C. A. Koelln and J. Pettegrove (Boston: Beacon P, 1960), 221.

[6] Walter Scott, *Minstrelsy of the Scottish Border*, ed. T. Henderson (London: Harrap, 1931), 55.

[7] G. E. Lessing, *Sämtliche Schriften*, ed. K. Lachmann and F. Muncker, vol. 9 (1893; reprint: Berlin: de Gruyter, 1968), 8–9. References to this edition will be cited as LM.

[8] J. J. Winckelmann, *Geschichte der Kunst des Altertums*, in *Werke in einem Band* (Berlin-Weimar: Aufbau, 1969), 183.

[9] Canut, his patience finally exhausted, sends Ulfo away to die (act III, scene 3) with the words: "Er müsse durch sein Blut der Welt die Lehre geben: Wer nicht will menschlich sein, sei auch nicht wert zu leben." Formally, the play is strictly classicistic: the unities are rigidly observed, there is a cast of only seven, and references to Scandinavian history and geography are minimal.

[10] Comment in the *Teutsche Merkur* of 1773, quoted in James W. Marchand, "Wieland and the Middle Ages," in H. Schelle, ed., *Christoph Martin Wieland* (Tübingen, 1984), 36.

[11] Goethe's comment, quoted in Marchand 43.

[12] See the entries in the subject-index of Reinhart Meyer, *Das deutsche Trauerspiel des achtzehnten Jahrhunderts. Eine Bibliographie* (Munich: Fink, 1977).

[13] Nicolai, quoted in Möller 160.

[14] See *Deutsche Literatur in Entwicklungsreihen*, Reihe Aufklärung, vol. 3, 135. Schönaich's play is described by Heitner (see Note 22), 404–5.

[15] *Hamburgische Dramaturgie*, Stück 19; *Lessings Werke*, ed. F. Bornmüller (Leipzig-Vienna: Bibliographisches Institut, n.d.) vol. 4, 86.

[16] J. C. Gottsched, *Sterbender Cato*, ed. H. Steinmetz (Stuttgart: Reclam, 1964), 16.

[17] Stücke 30 and 79: *Lessings Werke*, vol. 4, 133 and 351 respectively.

[18] Stück 1: *Lessings Werke*, vol. 4, 10–11.

[19] See *Lessings Werke*, 51, and the 63rd "Literaturbrief": "Der Dichter ist Herr über die Geschichte . . . etc" (LM viii, 168).

[20] *Hamburgische Dramaturgie*, Stück 24, 107–8. Cf. Stück 31, 140: "Voltaire ist mit seiner historischen Kontrolle [on Corneille's Rodogune] ganz unleidlich."

[21] Möller 144.

[22] Möller 144–45: Voltaire turns the "Lebensgeschichte der Regenten" into the "Geschichte der Menschen." Compare Lessing's remarks on Kings and Princes in *Hamburgische Dramaturgie*, Stück 14.

[23] Cf. Sengle 13–14 on the natural antipathy for the historical approach among proponents of "strict form." J. E. Schlegel is, like Gottsched, a stout defender of the Unities. Lessing claims for the dramatist the right to contract (zusammen rücken)

historical time and events as he likes (*Literaturbriefe* 63, LM viii, 168). He seems almost to pre-figure Herder in his comment on Shakespeare's "Freskogemälde" in his discussion of Weisse (*Dramaturgie,* Stück 73), but dodges the issue by isolating *Richard the Third* in the category of "historisches Schauspiel."

[24] *German Tragedy in the Age of Enlightenment* (Berkeley-Los Angeles, 1963), 72. Lessing ("Literaturbrief" 63) is scathing about Gottsched's adherence to historical fact in this play.

[25] For Nicolai and pragmatism, see Möller 152. Further to Lessing's thought and practice in historical matters, see my essay "Historical and Dramatic Truth in Lessing," *Lessing Yearbook* 19 (1987): 67–83. It is the critic in Lessing that is most provoked and inspired by historical enquiry. He is resolutely a "modern," and wants from the past "fact, not life" (69).

[26] "Historical and Dramatic Truth," 78.

[27] Cf. W. Martens, *Die Botschaft der Tugend,* 340–41: "Ein rechter Patriot . . . zeichnet sich durch die Tugend aus, und insofern darf er nach der Meinung mancher Sittenschrift an den Patriotismus der Römer anknüpfen."

[28] "Wie süß," says Sophronia, "ist selbst der Tod, das Vaterland zu retten": J. F. von Cronegk, *Schriften* (Karlsruhe 1776), vol. I, 316.

[29] "Wie selig ist's fürs Vaterland sich grämen!" *Lessings Werke,* vol. 2, 455.

[30] In the opening scene, for example, "Freiheit," and cognate words, occur fifteen times, and "Vaterland" on five occasions. In Henzi's opening speech in Act II, scene 2, the word "Tugend" occurs four times, "Freiheit" twice and "Vaterland" once.

[31] F. J. Lamport, "Patzke's *Virginia,*" *New German Studies* 8 (1980), 19–27.

[32] Quoted in Lamport 20.

[33] See particularly Stück 14, paras 1–2.

[34] Lamport 26. Whether there is anything more than a theoretical modern relevance, is another matter!

[35] Cf. Lamport 24.

[36] See for example Gottsched's *Sterbender Cato* and Brawe's *Brutus.* The heroism of Schlegel's Hermann is, as Schulz points out, entirely "Roman." G.-M. Schulz, *Die Überwindung der Barbarei. Johann Elias Schlegels Trauerspiele* (Tübingen, 1980), 77.

[37] Act V, scene 7; Cf. Lessing's letters to Nicolai (21 January 1758) and his brother Karl (1 March 1772).

[38] Cf. I: 2 (Der Prinz: "Ein alter Degen, stolz und rauh . . . etc."), II: 5 (Claudia: "O, der rauhen Tugend!").

[39] Cf. Marcius: "Der Tugend Majestät Die sich in ihm [Brutus] in vollem Pomp enthüllt Gebot Bewunderung," and 243: Publius: "Ein Menschenfreund zu sein, bist du zu sehr ein Held." (J. Minor, *Lessings Jugendfreunde* [Berlin-Stuttgart: Bibliographisches Institut, n.d.], 220 and 243). Antony includes Brutus among "deluded Stoics" who prefer a "shimmering misfortune" to a "modest happiness." "Straffbares Glück," replies Brutus, "ist der Antone Wahl, des Weisen Haß" (269).

[40] For this theme, cf. my essay "Vom 'Friedewünschenden Teutschland' zum 'Bedrängten Deutschland'" in W. Barner, ed., *Tradition Norm Innovation* (Munich: Oldenbourg, 1989), 154–58.

[41] *Hamburgische Dramaturgie,* 1–2. For Emilia, cf. Act V scene 5: "Nichts Schlimmers . . . etc."

[42] See von Wiese, *Die deutsche Tragödie von Lessing bis Hebbel,* 6–38. Lessing, says Hebbel, has "emasculated" a deeply tragic subject into a court intrigue: H., *Sämtliche Werke,* ed. H. Geiger, vol. 2 (Berlin: Tempel-Verlag, 1961), 731.

[43] Letter to J. J. Eschenburg of 26 October 1774.

[44] See "Vom 'Friedewünschenden Teutschland' zum 'Bedrängten Deutschland,'" 150. For others, see 153–56 and 158–60.

[45] Quoted by Schulz, 72–73. Schlegel also considered writing an *Otto von Wittelsbach.*

[46] P. Wolf, *Die Dramen Johann Elias Schlegels* (Zurich, 1964), 105.

[47] Quoted by Ernst Beutler in Goethe, *Sämtliche Werke* (Artemis-Gedenkausgabe), 4: 1071.

[48] Schulz 64.

[49] Schulz 84–85.

[50] *Hermanns Schlacht* (1769), *Hermann und die Fürsten* (1784), *Hermanns Tod* (1787).

[51] Klopstock's dramatic form betrays a strong lyric impulse, and the principal expression of Germanic patriotism which he inspired occurs in the lyrical work of the "Göttinger Hainbund."

[52] As Korff says, "bei Klopstock ist alles Idee" (*Geist der Goethezeit,* IV: 317). Justus Möser's *Arminius* (1748) is, says Heitner, simply a vehicle for a debate about the ideal form of government.

3: Weimar Classicism: Friedrich Schiller

IN SPITE OF the fact that Schiller was a professional historian, and a dramatist of the first rank, the omens for the achievement of an historical drama that conveys an historical experience are not particularly favourable. As a realist, he does not truly progress, in his presentation of history, beyond the attitudes and methods of the *Aufklärung;* as a poetic and dramatic idealist, he has a tendency to go beyond historical reality altogether and to make the "actual" events "symbolic."[1] In one case only, that of *Wallenstein,* we shall argue that a special combination of circumstances nudged him in the direction of a drama that articulates an historical community between past and present. However, for all their very considerable dramatic merits and conscientious concern for what Korff calls the "stoffliche Oberfläche"[2] of history, *Don Carlos, Maria Stuart, Die Jungfrau von Orleans,* and *Wilhelm Tell* show that this was not a true conversion. It is true that Schiller's fervent idealism and love of freedom provided openings that the nationalism of the nineteenth century was able to exploit. However, no matter how severe the battering that the "alte Form," the Holy Roman Empire, was taking during the Wars of the French Revolution,[3] and no matter how uncertain the future, neither *Wallenstein* nor the *Ästhetische Briefe* give convincing evidence of a desire on Schiller's part to revolutionize *it.* He was a German, but not of the kind celebrated by the historian and publicist Heinrich Class ("Einhart," "Daniel Frymann"), paladin of "Deutschtum," pupil of Treitschke and admirer of Gobineau and Lagarde, and President of the Pan-German League. Class suggests an affinity between Schiller and the Prussian-oriented *völkisch* nationalism of the later nineteenth century when he links the Schiller-centenary with "überströmende Begeisterung" for all-German unity, and asserts that *Die Jungfrau von Orleans* and *Tell* raise the banner of "völkische[n] Opferwilligkeit."[4]

Schiller's historical thinking is more deeply and narrowly rooted in the Enlightenment than is that of Herder, who had already begun to pave the way for the principle of individuality in general and for a stronger appreciation of the individual character of periods and peoples in particular, in his *Auch eine Philosophie der Geschichte* (1774) and who had retained this sensitivity to the individual element in his homage to "Humanität" in the more "Classical" *Ideen zur Philosophie der Geschichte der Menschheit* (1784–91). Schiller's turn, after his *Geschichte des Abfalls der vereinigten Niederlande,* toward a teleological "universal history" linked with a belief in the humanistic "Bestimmung" of man, does not mark a decisive break with the universalistic historiographical methods and values of the Enlightenment. Kant, after all, leaves the practical application of his ideas to others. His own "history" is at best speculation, "durch Philosophie versucht."[5] His influence can certainly be seen in Schiller's inaugural lecture of 1789, and in *Etwas über die erste Menschengesellschaft,*[6] but the criteria by which Schiller judges historical characters and events are still those of "unser menschliches Jahrhundert."[7] *Die Sendung Moses,* which appeared in the same year and contains very strong echoes of Lessing's *Die Erziehung des Menschengeschlechts,* still approaches history from a rationalistic standpoint, seeing a process of "Ausbildung des Verstandes"[8] which leads to a present in which the "richtige Begriffe"[9] of God, available in ancient Egypt only to an enlightened elite, can be enjoyed by all. In his second major historical work, the *Geschichte des dreißigjährigen Krieges,* what we might call the "tragic" view of history, the view of Schiller the dramatist, in which a great transcendental "Schicksal" seems to irrupt into mundane human affairs and "Weltgeschichte" can become "Weltgericht," begins to make itself felt, especially in connection with the fate of Gustavus Adolphus.[10]

The "philosophische Köpfe"[11] to whom and for whom Schiller speaks in his inaugural lecture "Was heißt, und zu welchem Ende studiert man Universalgeschichte?" see the history of the world as uniform, "consistent with itself, like the laws of nature." This "Nature" is in essence that of the *Aufklärung:* the concept of nature which allows Lessing to argue that wherever and whenever he may have lived in history, a *dramatic* character must conform to certain universal laws,[12] or Wieland to say in 1793: "Ursachen und Umstände haben zu allen Zeiten und unter allen Himmelsstrichen ähnliche Wirkungen."[13] Universal history is universal, not in the Herderian sense of infinite and varied riches in a vast single room (and Schiller would certainly have known the *Ideen*), but because it is "einfach (i.e. one and uniform) wie die Seele des Menschen."[14] The methodological implications are closer to those of the pragmatic school of the Enlightenment at which, as we shall see, Herder had already directed a somewhat premature Romantic salvo which, through Goethe, had not been without influence on German drama. A rather different concept of the "historical" from that of Schiller seems to have remained with Goethe, as can be seen from his comment in the *Wanderjahre* that even historians do not think truly historically: "denn der jedesmalige Schreiber schreibt immer nur so, als wenn er damals selbst dabei gewesen wäre, nicht aber, was vormals war und damals bewegte."[15] He writes, that is, without conveying a clear consciousness of the relativities of time which condition the relationship between the life and thought of his day, and those of the life he is describing. Goethe wants, not so much the facts, as the living individual *being* of history, history "von innen hinaus," as he phrases it in describing the experience of reading the Roman historians in Italy.[16]

Schiller goes "back to the past," but he carries the eighteenth century with him. His judgement of Viglius von Zuichem, president of the Netherlandish Privy Council and friend of Erasmus, is revealing. An upright and able man, as Schiller concedes, Viglius was not free of the prejudices, as Schiller sees them, of his own age. Unlike Erasmus, who indeed could be abstracted from his own time and made into a hero of the Enlightenment,[17] Viglius does not measure up to the standards of the eighteenth century. He is no "philosophischer Kopf":

> Ein *Gelehrter*, aber kein *Denker;* ein erfahrner Geschäftsmann, aber kein erleuchter Kopf, nicht starke Seele genug, die Fesseln des Wahnes, wie sein Freund Erasmus zu brechen. Zu schwach und zu verzagt, der kühneren Leitung seines eigenen Verstandes zu folgen, vertraute er sich lieber dem bequemeren Pfad des Gewissens an; eine Sache war gerecht, so bald sie ihm Pflicht war.[18]

If only Viglius had learned the lesson of Kant's *Was ist Aufklärung?* ("sapere aude": "Erkühne dich, weise zu sein," as Schiller translates it in the eighth of the *Ästhetische Briefe*), he could have escaped from the prison of his own time! The amalgam that is required for the true historical dramatist can be deduced from this case. What is "Wahn" for Schiller was for Viglius a matter of conscience and the heart which, one has to assume, could thoroughly engage the emotions in a conflict between duty and humanity. Schiller would have been eminently suited, without giving up his own convictions, to bring that conflict to "dramatic" life, in theatrical or in narrative form. Yet here, he talks of this situation as "more comfortable." In the very phraseology ("schwach," "verzagt," "der kühneren Leitung seines eigenen Verstandes"), one seems to hear Kant: "Faulheit und Feigheit sind die Ursachen, warum ein so großer Teil der Menschen, nachdem sie die Natur

längst von fremder Leitung frei gesprochen, dennoch zeitlebens un-
mündig bleiben."[19] This is Kant, moreover, transposed entire into the
sixteenth century. Schiller wishes to be as true as he can to the facts,
and as effective as he can be in the "Darstellung" for which his major
historical works are renowned, but he either does not seek, or cannot
find the historical ground which would enable him to present another
age and its convictions with a sense of its validity as part of a living reality: a (potentially dramatic) present which is also a past. He does
not, as Herder might put it, "ask history" for the criteria by which
Viglius should be judged. The "allgemeiner Maasstab" of the "Zweck
der Menschheit"[20] remains too firmly in the forefront of his mind, to
the detriment, not, perhaps, of a philosophically "just," but certainly
of a vital appreciation of the circumstances of a past age. These "human" values are universal and, in the words of the introductory announcement of *Die Horen* (1795), "über allen Einfluß der Zeit
erhoben."

This ideological background is less easily observable in the second
of Schiller's major historical studies, the *Geschichte des dreißigjährigen
Krieges*, partly, no doubt, because he finds little to kindle his idealism
in a conflict which threw Germany back into "barbarische(n) Wildheit," partly because he is now impatient to move on to the *Wallenstein* project. In the introduction, however, in which he dilates on the
historical role of the Reformation (which the German Enlightenment
saw as a spiritual source), Schiller is writing as a child of the Enlightenment. Like Wieland, who believes that Germany "owes its constitution" to the Thirty Years' War, he is reconciled to its "horrors" by the
"wohlthätige(n) Folgen" which he, like the rest of Europe, still en-
joys, even in the 1790s.[21] The "inviolable and sacred" Peace of Westphalia, as Schiller describes it in his concluding paragraph, and the
"Westphalia system" (Taylor)[22] for which it laid the foundation, is the
precondition of those introductory comments and belongs as much to
the present as it does to the past. The audience's awareness of these
developments as its own (extra-dramatic) present, which constitutes
the "future" of the characters, promotes both its political, and its historical understanding of *Wallenstein*. It is that fact, perhaps, more
than any other, which makes this a work which is at least partially
"historical" drama in our sense of the term.

There is no evidence that Schiller ever conceived of *Wallenstein* in
anything other than dramatic terms, but there were elements in the
material that made the achievement of true dramatic form extremely
difficult. The original five-act concept swelled into a tripartite

"Suite"[23] of plays; a climactic tragedy preceded by a very long and dramatically irregular exposition. Schiller never felt himself able to free the tragedy from the historical-political "Staatsaction" in which it was embedded, and of which he complained on several occasions[24] during the long period of composition (1796–98). His *aim* remained to the end "theatralisch-tragisch," as he put it in a letter to Goethe,[25] and he seems still to have hankered, in 1799, after the single-play format.[26] No doubt these statements were sincere, but in addition to the army, another antagonist needed to be brought into play, namely the Empire. It is the role of the two Piccolominis, in a kind of dialectic, to bring this about and one doubts whether Schiller, in the end, regretted the decision to write *Die Piccolomini*, with which he could certainly have dispensed, had he so wished. The dramatic-aesthetic theoretician in him may have grumbled, but the historian would have felt some satisfaction, and it is noteworthy that the latter shares the prologue with the dramatist on equal terms. These voices correspond roughly on the one hand, to the Schiller who aimed, as he had proclaimed in the programmatic introduction to *Die Horen*, to eschew local and temporal preoccupations in favour of universal and eternal ones, and on the other, to the man who had a genuine interest in history and politics, had just attempted to come to terms with the French Revolution in his *Ästhetische Briefe*, and was soon to do so again in *Das Lied von der Glocke* (1799).

The dramatic-epic duality is not the only one in *Wallenstein*. The parameters of the dramatic action proper are described by war, yet even in conventional dramatic terms, peace is an important factor in the equation. Wallenstein presents himself as a "Friedensfürst," Octavio also sees himself as working toward it, and Max's vision of peace[27] is intended, at least, as one of the poetic highlights of the whole work, one of those moments where the demand of the "heart" for beauty and humanity is satisfied. The "historical" implications of this ideal will be dealt with later; we are concerned here with questions of practical contemporary relevance. Schiller is writing, and his audience reading or hearing, the play under the aegis of what was still the Germany which had risen, on the foundation laid by the Peace of Westphalia, the source of its "gesegnete(s) Gleichgewicht,"[28] to a state of an at least potential "humanity." This "willkommner Friede," as it is described in the prologue to *Wallenstein*, acts as an axis in time, between peace and war, "then" and "now." What revolves around it is the Holy Roman Empire, the "Deutschland" of which both Wallenstein in the play, and Schiller the historian of the Thirty Years' War, speak.

The name of this peace also contains the memory of the war which it ended, and the threat to the "Reich" which it was seen as having averted. The Nineties of the eighteenth century were also times in which the threat of war and political upheaval hung over Germany. Schiller himself, in *Die Horen*, talks of "the approaching sounds of war" and "the conflict of political opinions." No doubt he was sincerely trying, in Hans Kohn's words, to turn his readers' minds away from politics to universal human interests,[29] but it is hard to see how the awareness of such harsh realities can be entirely shut out. That awareness hangs also in the refined atmosphere of the *Ästhetische Briefe* and it resurfaces in the reference in the Prologue to *Wallenstein* to events on "des Lebens Bühne." However much of a "metapolitical," aesthetic tour-de-force Weimar Classicism may have succeeded in being,[30] it did not exist, and could not have existed in a vacuum and its ideas were certainly not conceived with no reference at all to reality. Goethe was no doubt not the only German in whose mind present events raised an echo of "die schrecklichen Tage des Dreißigjährigen Krieges," as Schubart called them,[31] the traumatic war in which the Empire had been ripped almost to shreds. He notes "with sadness," in a letter of 1792, that the Privy Council has declared the war against the French to be a "Reichskrieg," and draws a parallel with the previous example of an all-embracing "national" war: "Europa braucht einen dreißigjährigen Krieg um einzusehen, was 1792 vernünftig gewesen wäre."[32] Schiller, still a "Zeitbürger," as he says in the second of the *Ästhetische Briefe*, would have been aware of parallels between the disorder of the Thirty Years' War and that of the contemporary revolutionary times; indeed, he saw "barbarism" both in seventeenth-century Germany and in contemporary France.[33] In an interesting letter to Kotzebue (9 November 1798), in connection with a possible performance in Vienna, Schiller shows his awareness that the Austrian censor might find this a ticklish topic, and that can hardly have been solely because the Emperor Ferdinand and his advisers do not appear in a totally favourable light.

We are confronted here by the potentially unifying, but also centralizing force of German "patriotism," the call for which, linked to the idea of a crusade against the French Revolution, was much in evidence in the 1790s. Wieland, in particular, responded to this in various essays in the *Teutscher Merkur,* in which he showed himself as thoroughly "German," but still an adherent of the decidedly uncentralized system of the old "Reich," though he felt, as did many, the need for reform, and even allowed himself to hope that the dangers of this "critical" time might also provide an opportunity, a chance for a "new compact" between the German people and its many rulers.[34] Goethe, no doubt, also thought as a "German" of the type whose patriotism was distributed in a delicate balance between the idea of a unifying cultural German-ness and the political entity whose constitution (Wieland refers to its "Verfassung") made each individual German a citizen first and foremost of the constituent state in which he happened to live, and militated against the emergence of a politically unified nation-state. Under the heading "Das deutsche Reich," Goethe queries the very existence of "Germany":

> Deutschland? Aber wo liegt es? Ich weiß das Land nicht zu finden,
> Wo das gelehrte beginnt, hört das politische auf. (A2, 455)

Wieland could see local patriotisms, even a common German "Nationalgefühl," but no pan-German patriotism.[35] The difficulties, and sometimes absurdities of the fragmentation of Germany through "Kleinstaaterei" were recognised and bemoaned by many, such as F. C. von Moser (*Von dem deutschen Nationalgeist*, 1765), who can find no source of German unity more specific than "das deutsche Herz,"[36] and Justus Möser, who notes in his *Patriotische Phantasien* that the Empire is "kein recht vereinigtes Ganze."[37] Wieland himself had complained in 1780 that the German "Staatsverfassung" was an impediment (to) "jeder Bestrebung, die auf allgemeines Nationalbestes, allgemeinen Nationalruhm, allgemeine Nationalreformen abzweckt."[38] However, it was the only political vehicle for the sense of German unity which came to the fore again in the period of the Revolutionary Wars, both in more populist organs such as Schubart's *Vaterlandschronik* (1791)[39] and in Goethe's "Classical" *Hermann und Dorothea*.[40] Wieland, by no means a reactionary but always a practical thinker, makes the point: only "Patriotismus, Eintracht, Gehorsam gegen die Gesetze und Anhänglichkeit an unsere Konstitution [können] das gemeinschaftliche Vaterland retten."[41] Whatever his idealistic and aesthetic preoccupations, it is unlikely that Schiller, as he worked on a subject at whose centre lay the question of the hero's "Anhänglichkeit an unsere Konstitution," could have been unaware of what was going on around him.

In the prologue which he wrote originally for the performance of *Wallensteins Lager* with which the Weimar theatre was re-opened in 1798, but which turned into a programmatic statement which became an integral part of the whole, Schiller writes, in what seem to be deliberately discrete sections, first as an historian, then as a dramatist. He speaks first of the humanistic promise of the late eighteenth century, the "sublime" moment in history "in dem wir strebend uns bewegen," then of the "Kampf gewaltiger Naturen" which is going on on the world-stage, and then relates it directly to the war and peace of the seventeenth century, with a precise indication of the time-relationships:

> Zerfallen sehen wir in diesen Tagen
> Die alte feste Form, die einst vor hundert
> Und fünfzig Jahren ein willkommner Friede
> Europens Reichen gab, die teure Frucht
> Von dreißig jammervollen Kriegesjahren. (Prologue, section 7)

He then refers to the poetic process, which he presumes will enable his audience to look (perhaps with an aesthetically heightened "Empfindungsvermögen," such as the *Ästhetische Briefe* sets up as a goal) "more cheerfully into the present and into a future distance rich with hope." The "Dichter" is now the dominant voice, though in his evocation of the perhaps tiresome, but indispensable "Zeitgrund" (section 8), the possible parallel between present and past confusions, in the same "Reich," emerges once more:

> Ein Tummelplatz von Waffen ist das Reich . . .
> Der Bürger gilt nichts mehr, der Krieger alles.

Schiller then turns decisively to the dramatic mode and focuses on Wallenstein as a character, not in the historical past, where (for lack of precise knowledge) the image of the actual man "wavers" ("schwankt") in a haze of uncertainty, but as a living human figure in the dramatic present that can be known more precisely ("menschlich näher") and is accessible to the spectator's eyes and heart ("euren Augen . . . eurem Herzen": section 9). The wavering of *this* Wallenstein is not uncertainty as to character, but the result of character itself and more than anything else, perhaps, it makes him the object of tragic Necessity ("the pure form of the terrible," "high Nemesis"[42]), driven by events when he had thought to drive them.[43] That in the vast majority of cases, there is no divergence between these two (conceptual) Wallensteins, is a measure of the success of Schiller's Herculean effort to poeticize his "truly unpoetic material,"[44] to transform "eine so dürre Staatsaction in eine menschliche Handlung."[45] For good or ill, though, a residuum of this "unpoetic," essentially political material must remain, centering on the problem of Wallenstein's relation to the institution of the Empire, and the status of the Emperor. The contradiction of the diametrically opposed views of the two factions during the war itself, which made the Emperor either "hostis publicus imperii," or "der wichtigste Garant der rechtlichen Einheit und des politischen Fortbestandes des Heiligen Römischen Reichs deutscher Nation," according to whether one read the Swedish or the Catholic propaganda,[46] could not be resolved in the eighteenth century. And so we have Wrangel at one point (*Wallensteins Tod* I: 5),[47] and Octavio elsewhere, presenting themselves as saviours of the Empire.

Wallenstein's ambitions, and the means by which he sets out to achieve them, involve us in an analysis of these issues. He presents himself, both in the debate with Questenberg (DP II: 7) and in his attempt to win over the cuirassiers (WT III: 16), as the champion of the German people as a whole, and of "das Ganze,"[48] the Empire as opposed to the interests of the Habsburg dynasty. We know, from his self-revelatory monologue (WT I: 4) before the interview with Wrangel, that he has royal ambitions and that he realizes that he will have to act in a revolutionary manner, to overthrow the legitimate, established authority ("die Macht, Die ruhig, sicher thronende") in order to achieve them. His great enemy will be the conservative mentality, what he refers to dismissively as "das ewig Gestrige," but if that "Macht" is co-terminous with the Emperor, how does that square with his professed loyalty to, and desire to bring peace to, the "Reich"? And where is "Germany," if not there? The lance corporal who leads the deputation of cuirassiers puts the "Gretchenfrage":

> Du willst den Kaiser nicht verraten, willst uns
> Nicht schwedisch machen? (WT III: 15)

To which he can reply only with vagueness reminiscent of the historical Wallenstein,[49] a reference to a "Knäul" which "(muß) zerhauen werden." Is he simply lying? Is his concern for Germany mere self-seeking prevarication? Schiller would not have wanted to "disqualify" him as a tragic hero: indeed, as he wrote to Böttiger, he had taken away "das Rohe und Ungeheure," and attempted to compensate by endowing his hero with a certain "Ideenschwung" (letter of 1 March 1799). Is it not more likely that, however much of a Man of Destiny Wallenstein feels himself to be,[50] he is himself intellectually entangled in a "Knäuel," from which there is no clean exit? The dramatic Wallenstein must know, and be able to express, how he proposes to achieve his aims. Schiller can find a broad aim for him: according to Octavio, who has had it "from the Prince's own mouth," he wishes to "compel" the Emperor to agree to a peace which he does not want (DP V: 1), but it is hard to see how this could have worked. Even allowing for the possibility that Octavio is putting the thing in its worst light in his attempt to draw his son away from Wallenstein, one is inclined to accept his prediction: "Der bürgerliche Krieg Entbrennt" Schiller surely does not want us to see his hero as either sordid or stupid, but in this respect, the historical character cannot be brought "menschlich näher"; the dramatic figure is subject to the same constraints as is the historical one as we know it. It raises for debate political issues (the survival of the political status quo, the legitimacy or otherwise of revolution) which events in both the seventeenth, and the late eighteenth centuries, conspired to make crucial, and which are thus highly likely to spark off historically tinged reflection in the audience. In the past, they are in the present, and vice-versa.

The balancing-act which was the Holy Roman Empire made it particularly difficult to achieve reform and preserve unity at the same time. In the seventeenth century, the principal internal problem was the threat of domination by the Catholic House of Habsburg; in the 1790s, as we have seen, there was a keen awareness of the need for German unity, and of the difficulty of achieving it. In addition, serious thinkers knew that reform of German society was a pressing need. The French Revolution itself had thrown this into relief, and there was a genuine search in progress for the means of achieving a more "bürgerlich" and "menschlich" society. We shall turn to this theme in due course. What is striking for our present purpose is the fact that this (in its way) radical thinking was predominantly anti-revolutionary. The love of order, or at least fear of disorder was a characteristic of the eighteenth century as a whole — and it was the order of the Empire, indeed, that the Peace of Westphalia had, for Schiller, put on a new and firm foundation. The course of the French Revolution seemed, to Schiller and many others, to be one of increasing disorder, and its rejection was the inevitable consequence.[51] This lays the foundation for a political debate (explicit and implicit) which has inevitable historical implications, while it may perhaps be said to have, in turn, a dramatic function, in that it helps to create a sense of tragic Necessity. It shows the strength of the force (the conservative thinking) which Wallenstein would have had to overcome, in order to make Questenberg's nightmare ("der Fürst ist Kaiser!": DP I: 3) become reality.

It is certainly true, and *Wallensteins Lager* has already made the point,[52] that the civil order is under severe threat and the courtier Questenberg speaks in terms which suggest a revolutionary Armageddon:

> Im innern Land des Aufruhrs Feuerglocke
> Der Bauer in Waffen — alle Stände schwürig —
> Und die Armee . . .
> Verführt, verwildert, aller Zucht entwöhnt
> Vom Staat, von ihrem Kaiser losgerissen,
> Vom Schwindelnden die schwindelnde geführt (DP I: 3)

Questenberg uses here an image (Schwindeln) that could easily have linked Wallenstein, in the audience's mind, with the French revolutionaries and their German sympathisers,[53] but as Octavio points out in reply, these firebrands have not yet heard "des Frevels wahren Namen." Wallenstein's charisma, as Buttler notes as late as WT V: 1, can call forth the "Schwindelgeist" in others and as Octavio is soon to discover, threatens to do so in his son Max. However, there is a powerful potential counterforce, which Octavio still hopes he will be able to activate. It is true that it can be labelled "conservative," but that need not mean simply the force of inertia ("das ewig Gestrige"). It can also be seen as respect for law,[54] the instinct for order which was so much a part of the thinking of eighteenth-century German humanism and is seen as the foundation for the peace which is essential if a truly "human" society (Schiller's alternative "revolution") is to grow. These ideas, relevant both to Schiller's age and the age of which he is writing, are developed in the interchange between Octavio and Max in the succeeding scene.

Max too has fallen under Wallenstein's spell; he too, like the "dizzy" people of Eger as Buttler describes them, believes in Wallenstein as a "Friedensfürst." He has the passionate nobility of the idealist, but also a susceptibility to the charisma of the "Great Leader" figure and an impatience with slow-moving, mundane regularity, which seem to contain an echo of Marquis Posa and could, one feels, easily lead him too into somewhat dubious, if "straight" (that is, direct) paths, were it not for the inherent purity of soul, the "Unschuld" in which Octavio has put his trust, and which turns out to be more powerful even than love. But his sweeping dismissal of "tote Bücher" and "alte Ordungen" (DP I: 4), values which were being threatened in the seventeenth century[55] and questioned more radically still in the age of revolution, sounds a warning note. Once it is apparent that his heavenly kingdom will not come about on earth, Max is prepared, not just to ride alone, but to lead a whole regiment to destruction.

Octavio's reply is not a reactionary, but an evolutionary model which traces the path to a goal ("zum Ziel") which sets peace above war, humanity above the iron will of the revolutionary leader, and is more commensurate, on its mundane practical level, with the idealistic vision of a "menschlich" millennium in which the *Ästhetische Briefe* culminate:

> Mein Sohn! Laß uns die alten, engen Ordnungen
> Gering nicht achten! Köstlich unschätzbare
> Gewichte sinds, die der bedrängte Mensch
> An seiner Dränger raschen Willen band;
> Denn immer war die Willkür fürchterlich —
> Der Weg der Ordnung, ging' er auch durch Krümmen,
> Er ist kein Umweg. Gradaus geht des Blitzes,
> Geht des Kanonballs fürchterlicher Pfad —
> Schnell, auf dem nächsten Wege, langt er an,
> Macht sich zermalmend Platz, um zu zermalmen.
> Mein Sohn! Die Straße, die der Mensch befährt,
> Worauf der Segen wandelt, diese folgt
> Der Flüsse Lauf, der Täler freien Krümmen,
> Umgeht das Weizenfeld, den Rebenhügel,
> Des Eigentums gemeßne Grenzen ehrend —
> So führt sie später, sicher doch zum Ziel.[56]

It could well be significant that no reply is made to this argument, formulated, not uncharacteristically for Schiller, through a lengthy metaphorical analogy. Schiller makes good use here of his poetic imagery to associate "das ruhig, mächtig Daurende," as Octavio calls it in his next speech, with the natural way, and with the precondition of all culture, the "Friedensgrundsatz."[57] Max himself has just seen, through eyes enlightened by love (the protective haven where, in a world of war, idealism can flourish), an area in which peace still reigns undisturbed. Here, the soldier reverts to the role of "Bürger," which is the basis of "Menschlichkeit."[58] Max still associates Wallenstein with peace and the Emperor with war, so that the principal *dramatic* tension of *Die Piccolomini* — the clash between father and son which comes to a head in Act V — remains unresolved. But we feel sure that when his eyes are opened, as they eventually are in WT II: 2, where his "prince of peace" invites him to take sides in the "Krieg Der zwischen deinem Freund und deinem Kaiser Sich jetzt entzündet," his *political* choice will be the same as Octavio's ("Ist das ein guter Krieg, den du dem Kaiser Bereitest mit des Kaisers eignem Heer?"). Max's moral choice, that which governs behaviour, is of course different (the "straight," as opposed to the "crooked" path which sets a taint on the actions both of Octavio and of Wallenstein),[59] but this is because, as we shall see, he belongs to the future: for the historically reflective, as well as the dramatically involved spectator. In the present, and this applies both to the seventeenth and the eighteenth centuries, he represents, morally, "das Schöne" in Thekla's words (WT IV: 12), whose lot can all too easily be tragic; as a practical man of business or politics, he could easily have been a disaster, a variant on the Posa-figure in *Don Carlos.*

Max, and his historical meaning, is a theme whose consideration we must postpone for a while. It is well to remind ourselves at this juncture of the point from which we began, namely that in all probability, Schiller did not want to write an historical play in our sense of the word. There is a tension between tragedy and history, as there is between morality and politics. Schiller's criteria remain moral; he demands "Würde," as Max does, and clearly dislikes and distrusts "Staatskunst," yet having chosen a hero from the world of "realism," he cannot avoid it. Out of this tension emerges the fascinating and disturbing character of Octavio Piccolomini, a man whom Schiller the poet and dramatist cannot love, but of whom, as a historico-political observer, he must approve. His defence of Octavio in a letter to Böttiger (1 March 1799) is revealing: the man uses (morally) bad means to a (politically) good end. Lesley Sharpe is justified in remarking that Octavio "loses stature" in his confrontation with Max, but whether this is because he uses "the conservative argument"[60] depends, to a large extent, on whether we are judging morally (and dramatically) or politically (and historically). Octavio makes much the same point to Max in DP V: 1 that Schiller makes to Böttiger ("Wohl wär es besser, überall dem Herzen Zu folgen . . . etc."); he is morally repelled by the thought of deceit, but the sense of duty, also morally based, compels him to use it. The fact that Max, who sees this as casuistry, has the last word, inevitably gives him the emotional (and dramatic) advantage, but at the same time, we cannot but feel that Schiller is making us detach ourselves from the drama momentarily, look at the historical and political situation, and see the possibility of a different conclusion.

The historical factor in which we are interested is based on factuality rather than the "mythic," on temporally rather than transcendentally based thinking. Schiller as the conscientious historian (within the lights of the "Aufklärung"), certainly did what he could to put his seventeenth-century action on a firm basis through a thorough use of sources (mainly eighteenth-century books, but including some older works, such as the *Theatrum Europaeum*, and a piece by Abraham a Sancta Clara, to which we shall return).[61] He altered (or played down)[62] the facts only occasionally, and for good dramatic reasons which do not subvert the historical reality, but the historical dramatist needs to do more than that. No one expects that he should transform himself into an inhabitant of another age (that would in fact militate *against* an historical effect), but he must give that age, not just in the bare factuality of a chronicle, but as a living milieu, a sufficient degree of real existence to make us, who look back at it, aware of the historical continuum in which we co-exist with it. The old must *be* old, and real. Here, we run into the obstacle, not only of Schiller's dramatic intent, but also of his inability to empathize with the period which he is trying to recreate. Jutta Linder has spoken of his striving for "eine überaus exakte Rekonstruktion spezifischer Zeitumstände und allgemeiner historischer Voraussetzungen,"[63] and there is no reason to doubt the genuineness of that striving, but the *spirit* of the Baroque Age is very largely missing. The accomplished pastiche of seventeenth-century language in the "Kapuziner"-scene (*Lager*, sc. 8) serves to throw the eighteenth-century spirit of the rest into even sharper relief. Schiller's letter to Goethe of 19 October 1798 shows that this scene is a tour-de-force which he had enjoyed writing, but also that it is meant to stand out as a "Fratze," even in ostensibly seventeenth-century surroundings. Since Gottsched, the Baroque taste had been stigmatised as "barbaric."[64] Schiller seems neither to have known, nor cared much about seventeenth-century German literature: the fact that he thinks that the "Knittelvers" is characteristic of that period is itself characteristic!

One cannot help but feel that the Capuchin is, in part at least, an indulgence in anti-Catholic satire on the part of an "enlightened" writer, for whom Reformation and reason go together. Certainly, the greatest barrier to sympathy between Schiller and his seventeenth-century characters lay, not in their belief in God, but in that chief bugbear of the Enlightenment, "Aberglaube": the readiness to believe on an irrational basis, in particular in powers, both within Nature and beyond it, that can influence and direct human affairs. Wallenstein's dabbling in astrology was a known fact and Schiller would never have seriously considered suppressing it, but as we shall see, he found it extremely difficult to handle. The theme is also part of the general background, and we do find some attempt to introduce it into the *Lager*. Grimmelshausen, certainly, presents the soldier of the period as superstitious and a firm believer in Fortune, and there are moments in the *Lager* in which we catch a (fortuitous) echo of the world of Simplicissimus and Springinsfeld, notably the reference to the belief that Wallenstein was "fest," that is, his skin had been made impervious to bullets by magical means.[65] The goddess of Fortune is mentioned,[66] but one wonders, again, whether this is a truly Baroque "Fortuna." The recruit signs on for a voyage in her "ship"; it is a venture, certainly, but more Crusoe-esque than Baroque. It lacks the passive fatalism contained in Springinsfeld's statement that he has been "des Glückes Ball," the plaything of a capricious goddess.

That the majority of details and references that give a sense of seventeenth-century "atmosphere" should occur in the *Lager* is significant, for there, of course, they can be attributed to superstition among the soldiery[67] and the dignity of the tragedy is not infringed. Schiller's passionate attachment to what Korff calls "the pure realm of the ideal"[68] which drives him, in *Die Jungfrau von Orleans*, into the "romantic" world of the Wondrous, was capable of inspiring romantically inclined youths like Novalis, or Hölderlin. However, for him, the pure ideal remains pure idea, and the Wondrous has at most symbolic validity. When he designated the *Jungfrau* as "a romantic tragedy," he was demanding the same licence to enter "the old romantic land"[69] in a spirit of aesthetic play that Wieland had claimed in his fairy-tale poems. The historical Wallenstein's belief in astrology is a reality that cannot be as easily neutralised. Schiller wrestled long and hard with this material, eventually finding a formula that made it acceptable to him, but removed it from the historical arena into that of the symbolic idea. What could have been a potent historical factor turns out not to be so, as a result of the reluctance of the unbelieving eighteenth-century dramatist to undermine the tragic status of the seventeenth-century character, by granting his belief any validity in its own historical right. It is not just Schiller's lack of belief — Grillparzer, no less a rationalist, gives a much more convincing picture in the case of Rudolf II. The historian in him cannot summon up enough faith in historical reality to overcome the resistance of the poet and tragedian. Recalling that Ferdinand II's Catholicism (which we might accept as "fanatical") is described in the *Geschichte des dreißigjährigen Krieges* as "superstition,"[70] we are not surprised to find Schiller referring (to Goethe, 7 April 1797) to the belief in astrology as "barokk," a synonym, in the eighteenth century, for bad taste and absurdity. In the same letter, Schiller talks of the need "diesem astrologischen Stoff eine poetische Dignität zu geben." That he felt that the astrological detail might undermine the dignity proper to tragedy, is clear from his letter to Goethe (4 December 1798) apropos of the opening scene of *Wallensteins Tod*, in which, for the only time, and as he makes clear, out of strictly dramatic necessity, he brings the astrological tower into the stage action. The original attempt, involving the construction and interpretation of a pentagram with five F's,[71] he and Goethe both felt to be a "Fratze," something having the undignified quality of a caricature. Although this was suitable for a mere Capuchin (who in any case appears only in the epic, rather than dramatic, *Lager*), it was out of place in a tragic hero. In the final version, the representation of the *speculum astrologicum* (to Goethe, 4 December 1798) gives way to a much more tragically "dignified" use of the astrological symbolism, and in the process, much of the potentially "historicizing" effect of the episode is sacrificed.

It could well have been effective as historical drama; that is, as an episode which presents the past as full-blooded action, as in the "Vehm" scene in Goethe's *Götz von Berlichingen*, or the alchemy scene in Grillparzer's *Bruderzwist;* but while Schiller shows himself a conscientious pragmatic historian by not suppressing the astrological element, he is not *that* kind of historian. Elsewhere, he endows the motif with "poetic dignity" by making it symbolic. In the scene in which Wallenstein defends astrology (and his trust in Octavio) to Illo and Terzky (WT II: 3), he introduces ideas, such as that of the "Weltgeist" and the "Mikrokosmus" which — though they seem more *Faust* than *Wallenstein*! — suggest that this (in itself mistaken) belief is the product of a sensitivity to higher realities and truths that sets this "realist" apart from the mere materialists like Illo. When he maintains that there is "no such thing as chance," he is expressing (within his limitations) that instinct to look for a higher meaning and purpose beyond "die gemeine Natur"[72] which exists in a purer form in this play in the character of Max. This is what enables the latter to excuse Wallenstein his apparent superstition (DP III: 4). In defusing the motif, though, Schiller, while preserving the historical fact, has removed it from the historical context. Max, who, as we shall see later, has his own historical function as a character who is both tragic and prophetic, acts here simply as the vehicle for an historically alien spirit.

The task of giving the past a solid physical presence is, as we noted at the very outset, more difficult for a dramatist than for a novelist for, while the detail of the past can be brought before us on a stage in concrete form, it is also a present form, and the audience's awareness of the past-ness of what it sees is threatened by its immediacy and by the force of the ongoing dramatic action. The Fourth Act of *Die Piccolomini*, while as brilliant a piece of stage-writing as Schiller ever achieved, is an episode in which the tension of the dramatic action is lessened. In this Act, the work as a whole comes nearest to the ideal of historical drama, and the "epic" mood is at its strongest.

The subject is one of the few truly solid historical details introduced by Schiller, namely the Declaration ("Revers") of Pilsen which, it could be argued, need not have been actually *portrayed* at all, or which, at the very least, is given far more space than is dramatically necessary. Without denying that it makes a contribution to important dramatic themes, we are still surprised that Schiller, in the full knowledge that his exposition was in danger of swelling out of control, still chose to devote a whole act to it (and, incidentally, to extend still further the period in which his hero would have to be offstage). Schiller brings the actual document physically before us. The Latin tag ("Ingratis servire nefas") and the text, which is read by Max (DP IV: 1) follow a seventeenth-century source to a large extent, and do genuinely help to alienate the action from the audience's present — not totally, but sufficiently to give the sense of history. It is characteristic, though, that Schiller feels the need to bring the language up to date to some extent. "Vielfältig empfangener Disgusti," with its genuinely "Baroque" integration of a Latin plural into German, becomes "vielfältig empfangener Kränkungen."[73] In the fourth scene of this act, Buttler, not yet the incarnation of Nemesis, appears as the soldier of Fortune and links Wallenstein, "der Fortuna Kind," with Bernhard von Weimar and Mansfeld. It is not the fickleness of fortune that is in the forefront of his (or the spectator's) mind here, but the fluidity, the instability of age-old social patterns and distinctions that characterizes the Thirty Years' War period. The idea of history as a time-continuum, is itself adumbrated: it is "ein großer Augenblick der Zeit," which is favourable to the resolute and strong spirit: "Nichts ist so hoch, wonach der Starke nicht Befugnis hat, die Leiter anzusetzen." That echoes of the 1790s might reverberate at this point can easily be imagined.

In scene 5, Schiller makes even more striking use of a historically symbolic object, and introduces a character who is particularly aware of the history of his nation, and of its continuity. Ironically, that figure is the "Kellermeister," not a German, but a Czech, and even more ironically, the whole episode, chalice and all, is in all probability an invention of Schiller's.[74] The banqueters, flushed with insolence and wine, have called for the "Great Chalice" (Kelch), part of the booty taken at Prague after the Battle of the White Mountain, for use as a drinking cup. The butler explains the first (emblematic) figure with which it is adorned to the German adjutant Neumann, who compliments him with being "wohl bewandert In Eures Landes Chronik," which is traced in outline from the Hussite Wars of the fifteenth century down to the acquisition of the Letter of Majesty from Rudolf II. The importance of the chalice itself, which is part of the goblet's symbolism, to the Czech Utraquists, is made clear and emphasized by the fact that the butler is a descendant of the Hussite rebels. The second picture can be read by Neumann without difficulty: it shows the Defenestration of Prague. Two images of rebellion, then, encapsulating the history of a nation. However, it is not Czech national feeling that interests Schiller, who no doubt thought of Bohemia as a part of "Germany" and would surely have been unaware that the first stirrings of the Czech national "rebirth" were appearing as he wrote. What is important to him is the tradition of Protestantism and the theme of rebellion, and what he is trying to show, as with the "Parricida" episode in *Wilhelm Tell*, is that some rebellions are more justifiable than others. The Hussites fought "für eine gute Sache doch"; the events of 1618, on the other hand, are seen as the beginning of a revolt against the Empire, and a period of (so far) "sixteen years" in which peace has vanished from the earth. It is interesting that Schiller should give the time span so precisely: we know where we are, historically, in this act more than anywhere else in the trilogy. Had Ferdinand called a halt to punitive action after the Czech surrender, all could have been well for Germany and German Protestantism, though at the expense of Czech nationhood.[75] Immediately after this, the health of Bernhard of Weimar is drunk, the most striking, perhaps, of a string of names which help to place this act more securely in its historical period.

The theme of peace features also in the scene we have just discussed, through the butler's lament over its absence. It is time to focus more directly on this theme, and on the figure that gives it the highest profile in an environment dominated by military men, namely Max Piccolomini. At first glance, it might be thought that this should read: "Octavio," but it is Max, by his idealism, and indeed by the very impracticality of that idealism, who best represents the concept as we intend to use it. By "peace," we mean to imply not just the absence of war, but the development of that culture of true humanity for which, as we have seen, Schiller believes that the Peace of Westphalia acted (and, through the "Westphalian System," continues to act), as the necessary material basis. It is this culture, this revolution of the mind and heart, which Schiller proposed in the *Ästhetische Briefe* as the only sure way to a solution of the political and social problems which the French Revolution had failed to resolve. It is, as Schiller's own lucubrations show all too clearly, much easier to formulate "in der Idee," as a philosophical abstraction, than as a course of practical sociopolitical action, but it was certainly not meant as an evasion of the need for real change. As we have seen, Schiller held the rights which the French revolutionaries had attempted prematurely to seize by illegitimate means, to be "sacred." The Kingdom of God (or perhaps one should say, Humanity)[76] *was* meant to come about on earth and a considerable amount of thought was being devoted to the means by which it might be brought about (such as in the later books of Goethe's *Wilhelm Meisters Lehrjahre*, to be continued in the *Wanderjahre*). The most likely vehicle seemed to be a highly refined and idealized, perhaps one might say, "ennobled" concept of the *Bürger*, foreshadowed, perhaps, in Lessing's *Nathan der Weise*, but brought truly to the fore, as Wilhelm Flitner says, by the need to rethink practical socio-political priorities that had been precipitated by the French Revolution.[77]

The first prerequisite for practical *Bürgerlichkeit* is of course a peaceful and orderly environment. The direct relation between the Thirty Years' War and the breakdown of civil order, a constant thread throughout the work, is established from the outset, in the prologue, and formulated in terms of a diametrical opposition of soldier and *Bürger* ("Der Bürger gilt nichts mehr, der Krieger alles"). This theme is developed at length in *Wallensteins Lager* (particularly in the "Recruit" scene [7]). Max then articulates the ideal of peace, and the "beautiful" humanity for which it is a symbol, in *Die Piccolomini* (I: 4), in a speech which is poetic rather than practical or even philosophical; one dominated by the demands of the "heart." This is appropriate, because it is a dream-cum-vision of the future which, in the present environment, can exist only in the heart, "in unsers Herzens Innerstem," as Thekla, wiser in her generation than the impractical Max, tells her lover when they are left briefly alone together (DP III: 5).

The heart, for Schiller, is the place where the reason makes its absolute demand for humanity[78] and in finding the freedom of the heart, Thekla, awakened by her love for Max, has taken a decisive step towards *Bürgerlichkeit* by freeing herself from the conditioning of her class. But inner beauty of soul is in her case not the passive "Tugend" of the *Äufklärung*. Thekla is not a heroine in the mould of the *bür-gerliches Trauerspiel*, which, after Lessing, had degenerated into a sentimentalised representation of "was populär, häuslich und bürgerlich ist." The words are Schiller's;[79] a likely target of his criticism would have been the domestic dramas of A. W. Iffland. Thekla suffers, it is true, but one cannot imagine her saying — no doubt for the audience's benefit — with Iffland's Ruhberg: "Mit Standhaftigkeit will ich mein Herz verbluten sehen."[80] Thekla's scope for independent action is limited, but she is more of a rebel than that. She and Max cannot change the "old order," as Gert Sautermeister puts it, but their love contains the seeds of a "new life," even if, at present, it can blossom only in a self-conscious "Idylle."[81] No doubt some of Schiller's scorn for the Ifflandian "happy end"[82] resounds in Wallenstein's comment that he is expected to play the "weichherz'ger Vater," and "was sich gern hat Und liebt, fein bürgerlich zusammengeben" (WT III: 4). This is the sterner, "real" world, the "ganz gemeine Welt," as Countess Terzky has called it in ironic parody of Max's "Wie schal ist alles nun und wie gemein" (DP III: 3). However, even in realistic mode, Schiller cannot be championing "das Gemeine," and when Wallenstein rejects an alliance with Max as "gemeine Verwandtschaft," it is the self-imagined King of Bohemia, political revolutionary though he is,[83] who is doing the reactionary, common and mean thing, and the young lovers who, with no chance of fulfilment in their own reality, point us toward the future. In the work as planned, there is no scope for a full development of the love-action, what might have been a kind of reprise of *Kabale und Liebe* on a higher level. The plan for *Die Prinzessin von Zelle* (1803–1804) could, had it been executed, have become something of the kind and the figure of Princess Adelaide of Bretagne, in the *Warbeck*-fragment, shows similar proclivities.[84]

Because Schiller was working to the guidelines of what he called "die engen Grenzen einer Tragödienoeconomie" (to Goethe, 28 November 1796), it is not surprising that he should complain, from time to time, of the sheer mass of material with which he had to cope.[85] While he was still thinking in terms of a single five-act drama, he sees the first two-and-a-half Acts (!) as "fast ganz nur Exposition" (to Christian Gottfried Körner, 25 December 1797). Although we can grant that a great deal of preparatory exposition was required, so that the action proper, when it at last begins to move forward, should have the quality of tragic Necessity at which he was aiming, one feels also that at least some of this pain was self-inflicted. Indeed, we would question whether the experience was one of undiluted pain. The historical drama proper is a hybrid of dramatic and epic, and its motivation is similarly mixed. There is a genuine historical interest as well, a desire to present and understand things "as they (actually) were," which can impel what might to begin with be conceived in dramatic terms as exposition, toward the epic, the formal literary mode of the historian proper. A certain tension between the dramatic and historical impulses, the kind of thing which drove Schiller, in his famous review, to make criticisms of Goethe's *Egmont* that the dramatist pure and simple would never have made, is easily conceivable in the case of *Wallenstein* also, and it need not always have been a negative influence. These considerations can lead to a more just appreciation of *Die Piccolomini* in particular.

We know that the relation between the dramatic and epic was a subject of discussion for Goethe and Schiller in December 1797. This discussion overlaps into that of *Wallenstein* in Schiller's letter of 1 December. He speaks first as a dramatist and complains about the way in which the text is "swelling." He is still thinking in terms of "*Exposition*," of which most dramatists would surely say that it were well if it were done quickly. This exposition, however, "verlangt Extensität." The dramatic-epic dualism is reflected in that of action (which requires "Intensität"), and exposition. Schiller continues: "Es kommt mir vor, als ob mich ein gewisser epischer Geist angewandelt habe." He does not believe that this will damage the work, however, since this is "vielleicht das einzige Mittel, diesem prosaischen Stoff eine poetische Natur zu geben." It is here, of course, in what was to develop into *Die Piccolomini*, that Schiller the historian can come into his own. He has, as he himself agrees, also taken advantage of the "Gemütlichkeit" which flows from the relaxation of dramatic discipline to indulge his penchant for expansiveness as a writer of verse, but the diction cannot, surely (as Storz seems to imply),[86] be the only cause of the "Breite" to which Schiller refers, or indeed of the poetic quality of the text. The portrayal of the historical material which is so prominent in this part of the work is itself anything but "dry" and "joyless," because the mere facts are shaped and reflected upon and the issues arising from the facts, such as the political points we have already discussed, clearly have an intrinsic (if undramatic) interest for the author. At the same time, it incorporates much of the thinking, and of the anxieties, of the period of the revolutionary wars. It even seems to anticipate the arrival centre-stage of the figure of Napoleon, though on balance, the suggestion of Fricke and Göpfert that any contemporary allusion must be to Dumouriez (who *did* defect),[87] seems more plausible, in the absence from Schiller's letters of the time of any reference to the Corsican. At the same time, the *idea* of a Napoleon-figure, a "Herrscherseele" in Max's expression,[88] who might be able to offer a "straight path," and cut through the Gordian knot into which the threads of German political life had tangled themselves, could well have had an attraction for the more impatient political idealist. As we see, though, it is an attraction which Schiller, who has created a Marquis Posa in the past, finds dangerous in the extreme. And in *Don Carlos* too, of course, Schiller was addressing ideas and issues of his own day, though in this case, he can be accused of having simply abstracted a plot from the past for unhistorical purposes.[89]

This reminds one strongly of Schiller's remark, in the theoretical discussion with Goethe, that by allowing the author to "move around" the action, and thus to reflect on it, the epic spirit provides him with a "poetic freedom in relation to his material" which in fact the modern dramatist needs. He writes this in a letter to Goethe (26 December 1797) which could well have been influenced by his experience with *Wallenstein*. And the "poetic" aspect provides the opening for the development of the historical potential of the material. Certainly, Schiller is intent on strict dramatic form, and aesthetic considerations take precedence in his mind over political ones. He is following the philosophy announced in *Die Horen* and giving the aesthetic priority over the pragmatic. That does not mean that he is indifferent to the issues of the day, or to the political and social issues raised by his seventeenth-century material, as indeed emerges in the prologue and, in indirect, sometimes symbolic form, in those parts of the work in which we can see the influence of the historical, reflective impulse. Formally, this is also an "epic" impulse. It is not the epic spirit which informs the Shakespearean Histories, or which we sense in the historical thinking of Herder and in Goethe's *Götz*, or in later examples such as the "saga-dramas" of Ibsen. That will concern us in our next chapter. The decision to accommodate the exposition in a full five-act play gave scope for the development of ideas and ideals, and for a fuller treatment of the character of Max, who, though he is invented, is arguably the most historically interesting character in the whole work. Whereas one can see a dramatic integration in the case of the Max-Octavio action, the love-action has at best the dramatic function of a foil, indeed, it can hardly be justified on grounds of dramatic necessity. Schiller is quite right to say, in a letter written very soon after the one in which he spoke of an "epic spirit," that it is in this respect "nicht theatralisch" (to Goethe, 12 December 1797).

The love-action is developed in scenes four and five of the third act of *Die Piccolomini*, after Max has already shown his devotion to Wallenstein on the one hand and to peace and "Menschlichkeit," which provide true nourishment for "the heart," on the other. The heart is the seat of "das Schöne," that inner capacity for beauty in which the aesthetic and the moral are in harmony, and which is the essence of true humanity, as it is of love. Thekla is the more pragmatically clear-sighted, and at the same time the more idealistically oriented of the two; Max is the activist, who wants the Kingdom now. She talks of "preserving" the treasure within, he of going direct to Wallenstein and putting into practice his first impulse: "Wie drängte michs in diesem Augenblick, Ihm um den Hals zu fallen, Vater ihn zu nennen" (DP III: 4). Our concern here is to see whether this has an historical application; whether we think, that is, not only of the contrast between "real" and "ideal," but of the relation between past, present, and future. Are the lovers, as lovers, removed into a sphere that is "zeitlos,"[90] as seems to be the view of Storz, or are they meant as a symbolic reference to what not only ought to, but also will be? Schiller is clear, as in the *Ästhetische Briefe*, about the distinction between ideal and reality, hence the play he makes (in DP III: 4) with the images of "dream," of a magic "island," of a "secure treasure in the heart" to which one can return, as an escape from reality, but he hints at least that *that* "reality" may not be permanent. Max's happiness, dimmed for the moment by the un-poetic reality of the camp, *was* "wirklich," and after the "astrological" episode, over which the lovers' spirituality casts a serene and playful light, Schiller uses the "Mars" motif to motivate a second vision of future peace on Max's part ("Bald wird sein düstres Reich zu Ende sein!"). He sees Wallenstein making peace and retiring to his estate to live "to (and for) himself" and presiding over the growth of "jede Kunst" and "alles würdig Herrliche."

While Schiller's powers of poetic description fall short of the loftiness of his philosophical concepts, so that, as in his portrayal of "heilige Ordung" in *Das Lied von der Glocke*, "die bürgerliche Welt [wird] ungewollt Selbstzweck,"[91] this is clearly another attempt at a representation of "freie Menschlichkeit" (cf. DP I: 4) as a potential practical reality. Max's hero will not make (indeed, does not desire) this peace, but we, the audience, know that in fourteen years, peace will come (and *did* come), the peace which, as we saw, Schiller the philosophical historian regarded as the basis of the eighteenth-century culture of humanity. And while the outcome of the French Revolution dented the optimism that had suffused a poem such as "Die Künstler," Schiller certainly did not feel the black despair that drives Max to what is to all intents and purposes suicide. He is too much the child of the Enlightenment, with its rationalistic universalism and cosmopolitanism, to be able to forge a real continuity with the seventeenth century, or to think in truly national terms, but at the same time too much a disciple of the Enlightenment and of Kant to lose faith in human progress, and the benevolent "purpose" of Nature in history. He is certainly no naïve optimist, and often feels the need for consolation. A flight into the idyllic world of the "heart" may be all that is available to Thekla in the tragic reality that surrounds her, just as the poet in *Der Spaziergang*, in the face of the recurrent "cycles" of history, "flees," as Meinecke sees it,[92] into the elegiac-idyllic haven of an eternal "fromme Natur" in which the sun that shone on Homer shines also on us. But the final stages of the great philosophical statements of the *Ästhetische Briefe* and of *Über naïve und sentimentalische Dichtung* are evidence that the Schiller of the 1790s had not given up on the hope for culture and humanity in the "real world" of history.

Notes

[1] See, for example, H. A. Korff, *Geist der Goethezeit* 2nd ed. (Leipzig: Koehler und Amelung, 1958), vol. 2, 251. Schiller is oriented not toward the past, but toward a dimension which equates to the mythical, "(der) Ewigkeit, dem ewigen Gedächtnis der Menschheit."

[2] *Geist der Goethezeit,* p. 249.

[3] Cf. the Prologue to Wallenstein, lines 61–78. Whether or not Schiller had the young Napoleon in mind here, as Ludwig Bellermann suggests (*Schillers Werke* [Leipzig-Vienna: Bibliographisches Institut, n.d. (Meyers Klassiker-Ausgaben) vol. IV] 23n.), remains a moot point.

[4] *Deutsche Geschichte. Von Einhart* (1909) (Leipzig: Theodor Weicher, 1926), 255 and 388. For Lagarde, see 287, after a description of the "Judengefahr" which perhaps stays just this side of crude anti-semitism. Treitschke is eulogised on 403, Gobineau on 405. The publisher of *Einhart* quotes reviews in which *Daniel Frymanns Kaiserbuch* (1925) is described as "ein glühendes Bekenntnis zum völkischen Deutschtum" ("Pommersche Tagespost") and "allen völkisch-vaterländischen Kreisen dringend zu empfehlen" ("Schwarz-weiß-rot") For the Pan-German League, see Fritz Stern (note 95) 215–16, and Bracher (note 4), 35–36.

[5] See his *Idee zu einer allgemeinen Geschichte in weltbürgerlicher Absicht* and *Muthmaßiger Anfang der Menschengeschichte,* in I. K., *Was ist Aufklärung? Aufsätze zur Geschichte und Philosophie,* ed. J. Zehbe (Göttingen: Vandenhoeck und Ruprecht 1967), 41 and 76.

[6] The influence of Kant's essay on a philosophy of history "in weltbürgerlicher Absicht" is manifest in the inaugural lecture: cf. *Schillers Werke* (Nationalausgabe), vol. 17, ed. Karl-Heinz Hahn (Weimar: Hermann Böhlaus Nachfolger, 1970), 373–74 ("Nicht lange kann der philosophische Geist . . . ein teleologisches Prinzip in der Weltgeschichte."). In the case of the second lecture mentioned (published in *Thalia* in 1790), the influence of Kant is specifically acknowledged (398n.). Unless otherwise stated, all references to Schiller's works will be to this edition, referred to as NA.

[7] NA 17, 375.

[8] NA 17, 383.

[9] NA 17, 396. Cf. Lessing's "bessere Einsichten!" (Chapter 3, Note 15).

[10] Cf. Book III, NA 18, 279: "Die Geschichte, so oft auf das freudenlose Geschäft eingeschränkt . . . etc." There are events which point the mind towards "eine höhere Ordnung der Dinge."

[11] NA 17, 362–63. An expression redolent of the mood of Enlightenment!

[12] *Hamburgische Dramaturgie*, 57: "Banks hat ihn [Essex] zu sehr nach dem Leben geschildert. Ein Charakter, der sich so leicht vergißt, ist kein Charakter . . ." Lessing is chastising Joseph Banks for having stuck too rigidly to the historical reports in his portrayal of the Earl of Essex. Contradictions, he says, can be accepted in history as possible dissembling ("Verstellung"), since we can rarely know the inmost thoughts of an historical figure. But Nature, which must be the poet's model, allows of no self-contradiction. See also Stück 19: The guide for proper characterisation is a probability derived, not from "fact," but from reason: "Was ein jeder Mensch von einem gewissen Charakter unter gewissen gegebenen Umständen thun würde."

[13] C. M. Wieland, *Über teutschen Patriotismus;* in *Werke* vol. 3, ed. R. Döhl (Munich: Hanser, 1967), 747.

[14] NA 17, p. 21.

[15] See the *Maximen und Reflexionen;* Goethe, *Sämtliche Werke* vol. 9 (Artemis edition; reprint: Munich: Deutscher Taschenbuch Verlag, 1977), 585. Cf. also 629: "Keine Nation hat ein Urteil als über das, was bei ihr getan und geschrieben ist. Man könnte dies auch von jeder Zeit sagen." All references to Goethe in this book will, unless otherwise stated, be to this edition.

[16] Artemis-edition, vol. 11, 167 (*Italienische Reise*). Compare 132: ". . . die Geschichte [schließt sich] lebendig an."

[17] See, for example, Wieland's portrait in the essay *Erasmus*. Lessing does something similar with the figure of Luther in his controversy with Goeze.

[18] NA 17, 117–18.

[19] Kant, *Was ist Aufklärung?* 55.

[20] See *Die Gesetzgebung des Lykurgus und Solon*, NA 17, 423–24. In *Auch eine Philosophie der Geschichte*, Herder remarks that a Leonidas might have been "ein witziger Mann unsres Jahrhunderts," but was not: "darüber frage die Geschichte" (J. G. Herder, *Werke* [Weimar: Volksverlag], 304).

[21] See NA 18, 10. For Wieland, cf. his "Zusatz zum Schreiben der Revolutions-Gesellschaft in London," *Wielands Werke* vol. 15, ed. W. Kurrelmeyer (1930; reprint: Hildesheim: Olms, 1989), 396.

[22] NA 18, 384. Cf. Taylor, *The Course of German History,* 13–24. Taylor, who writes with a knowledge of what came later, is understandably less enthusiastic than Schiller, but he does say that the Peace "gave Germany long years of modest quiet" (13).

[23] See Schiller's letter to A. W. Iffland, 15 October 1798.

[24] E.g. in his letter to Körner of 28 November 1796: "Es ist im Grund eine Staatsaction und hat, in Rücksicht auf den poetischen Gebrauch, alle Unarten an sich, die eine politische Handlung nur haben kann."

[25] 17 March 1799 ("Wenn Sie davon urtheilen . . . etc.").

[26] He wrote to Georg Heinrich Nöhden, who had translated his *Fiesco* and *Don Carlos* into English, on 5 June 1799: "Auch die Wallensteinischen Schauspiele bin ich gesonnen in ein einziges Theaterstück zusammenzuziehen, weil die Trennung derselben tragischen Handlung in zwei verschiedene Repräsentationen auf dem Theater etwas Ungewöhnliches hat und die erste Hälfte immer etwas Unbefriedigendes enthält."

[27] *Die Piccolomini* act I, scene 4. References (given in future in brackets in the text) will be in this form, the constituent parts of the "trilogy" being quoted as WL (Wallensteins Lager), DP (Die Piccolomini) and WT (Wallensteins Tod) respectively. The text used will be that of the "Nationalausgabe," vol. 8.

[28] See NA 17, 369, lines 10–11 and 25–26.

[29] Hans Kohn, *The Mind of Germany. The Education of a Nation* (1960; London: Macmillan, 1965), 28.

[30] Cf. Dieter Borchmeyer in V. Žmegač, ed., *Geschichte der deutschen Literatur vom 18. Jahrhundert bis zur Gegenwart,* vol. I/2 (Königstein/Ts: Athenäum, 1979), 5: "ein metapolitisches Jenseits von ancien régime und Revolution."

[31] C. D. Schubart, *Deutsche Chronik* (1774), 460.

[32] Letter to Voigt, 10 October 1792.

[33] Cf. NA 18, 10: "ein dreißigjähriger, verheerender Krieg, der die kaum auflebenden besseren Sitten der älteren barbarischen Wildheit zurück gab," and the letter to Friedrich Christian von Augustenburg of 13 July 1793.

[34] For the combination of danger and opportunity, see "Etwas zur Beruhigung der patriotischen Bürger von . . ." (1794). The idea of a "neuer Bund" is adumbrated in "Schreiben an den Herausgeber der Teutschen Merkur, nebst der Antwort" (1793): cf. *Wielands Werke* vol. 15, ed. W. Kurrelmeyer (1930; reprint: Hildesheim, 1987), 639–42 and 777 respectively. See further Alfred E. Ratz, "Ausgangspunkte und Dialektik von C. M. Wielands gesellschaftlichen Ansichten" and G.-L. Fink, "Wieland und die französische Revolution," 379–98 and 407–43 respectively.

[35] *Über deutschen Patriotismus, Wielands Werke,* vol. 15, 590–91. He speaks of a "Nationalgefühl" in the "Schreiben an den Herausgeber . . .," 776. See further

Irmtraut Sahmland, *Christoph Martin Wieland und die deutsche Nation* (Tübingen: Niemeyer, 1990), 148–216.

[36] Cf. J. Murat, "Klopstock, citoyen français et patriote allemand" in G.-L. Fink, ed., *Cosmopolitisme, Patriotisme et Xénophobie en Europe au Siècle des Lumières,* (Strasbourg, 1985), 202. For an account of Moser's ideas and their reception, see J. Gagliardo, *Reich and Nation. The Holy Roman Empire as Idea and Reality* (Bloomington, 1988), 55–65, and Sahmland 108–23.

[37] Justus Möser, *Patriotische Phantasien,* ed. S. Sudhof (Stuttgart: Reclam, 1970), 78. At the same time, this empire is the author's "Vaterland" (206).

[38] Quoted by Ratz in "Ausgangspunkte und Dialektik von C. M. Wielands gesellschaftlichen Ansichten," 386.

[39] Cf. J. Clédière, "Idéal Cosmopolite, Vertus Allemandes et l'Image de la France dans la *Deutsche Chronik* de Schubart" in Fink, *Cosmopolitisme et Xénophobie,* 261: "Wer kann uns antasten, wenn wir alle eins sind?"

[40] ". . . wäre die Kraft der deutschen Jugend beisammen . . . etc." (3, 192; Vierter Gesang, lines 98–100). The fact that this turns out not to be the right path for Hermann does not necessarily devalue the patriotic sentiment.

[41] Quoted by Fink in "Wieland und die französische Revolution," 438.

[42] Cf. Schiller's remarks to Goethe on Shakespeare, letter of 28 November 1797. If any one of Schiller's tragic heroes resembles Macbeth, it is surely Wallenstein.

[43] Cf. Schiller's letter to Goethe of 2[?] October 1797: "Da der Hauptcharakter eigentlich retardierend ist, so thun die Umstände alles zur Crise und dies wird, wie ich denke, den tragischen Eindruck sehr erhöhen."

[44] Letter to Goethe, 28 November 1796.

[45] Letter to Körner, 10 July 1797.

[46] See Christoph Kampmann, *Reichsrebellion und kaiserliche Acht* (Münster, 1992), 207.

[47] "Gerettet haben wir vom Untergang Das Reich."

[48] "(Ich führ) ihn [diesen Stab] . . . zu des Ganzen Heil"; "Mir ists allein ums Ganze."

[49] As C. V. Wedgwood has put it, "noble conceptions float hazily" in Wallenstein's letters: C. V. Wedgwood, *The Thirty Years' War* 1938 (Harmondsworth: Pelican Books, 1958), 306.

[50] "Ich fühls, daß ich der Mann des Schicksals bin" (WT III: 16).

[51] See Schiller's letter to Friedrich Christian von Augustenburg of 13 July 1793: "Der Versuch des Französischen Volks, sich in seine heiligen Menschenrechte einzusetzen . . . (hat) nicht nur dieses unglückliche Volk, sondern mit ihm auch einen beträchtlichen Theil Europens, und ein ganzes Jahrhundert, in Barbarey und Knechtschaft zurückgeschleudert" (NA 26, 262). Cf. *Ästhetische Briefe* 2 and 7. The world "needs a total revolution," but a revolution "in seiner ganzen Empfindungsweise" (Brief 27).

[52] See especially WL 6 (Zweiter Jäger): "Keine Ordnung gilt mehr und keine Zucht."

[53] Compare Weislingen in Goethe's *Götz* (A4, 695): "Ich sehe kein ander Mittel, den Schwindelgeist zu bannen," Wieland in *Über teutschen Patriotismus, Werke* (Hanser) III, 753: "die schwindlichten Franzosen," and the poet and publicist C. D. Schubart: "Und doch schwindelt den Bauren in Böhmen der Kopf vom Geist der Unruhe" (*Deutsche Chronik* [1775; reprint: Heidelberg, 1975], 585). Schubart calls Wallenstein "ein schwindlichter Ebentheurer" (218).

[54] The Emperor is still, as he has been described in the *Geschichte des dreißigjährigen Krieges*, the "rechtmäßiger Herr" (NA 18, 323), the embodiment of "rechtmäßige Gewalt" (314).

[55] Cf. Ranke, *Geschichte Wallensteins*, 289: "Die alten Ordnungen und Institute . . . wurden nicht beobachtet."

[56] The reference to Order recalls the section on "Heilge Ordnung" in *Das Lied von der Glocke*. Further to the positive side of this character, see W. Wittkowski, "Octavio Piccolomini. Zur Schaffensweise des 'Wallenstein'-Dichters," in K. L. Berghahn/R. Grimm, eds., Schiller. *Zur Theorie und Praxis der Dramen* (Darmstadt, 1972), 428–44.

[57] See the inaugural lecture, NA 17, 370: ". . . welcher allein den Staaten wie den Bürgern vergönnt, ihre Aufmerksamkeit auf sich selbst zu richten, und ihre Kräfte zu einem verständigen Zwecke zu versammeln."

[58] DP I: 4: "O schöner Tag . . . etc."

[59] Cf. DP V: 3 ("Mein Weg muß gerad sein") and WT II: 7 ("Dein Weg ist krumm, er ist der meine nicht.").

[60] See Lesley Sharpe, *Friedrich Schiller. Drama, Thought and Politics*, 2nd ed. (Cambridge, 1994), 236.

[61] For a list, see NA 8, 408–9.

[62] The historical Wallenstein, for example, was "a lame, bent, nerve-ridden wreck of a man" (Wedgwood, *The Thirty Years' War*, 313). Wallenstein's monologue (WT III: 13) gives a different impression.

[63] Jutta Linder, *Schillers Dramen. Bauprinzip und Wirkungsstrategie* (Bonn, 1989), 36.

[64] Gottsched, *Ausführliche Redekunst*, I: 77. The "Capuchin" scene is based on Abraham a Sancta Clara's "Auf, ihr Christen," to which Goethe had drawn Schiller's attention.

[65] This, of course, is black magic. The motif occurs on numerous occasions in Grimmelshausen; for example, the Provost-sergeant in *Simplicissimus* is "fest."

[66] Cf. WL sc. 7 (Wachtmeister: "Auf der Fortuna ihrem Schiff Ist Er zu segeln im Begriff"); and "Auch Wallenstein ist der Fortuna Kind" (Buttler, DP IV: 4).

[67] Though Schiller does add a corrective, even here, in the voice of the "Erster Jäger" ("Was wollt Ihr da für Wunder bringen . . .").

[68] *Geist der Goethezeit*, vol. II, 261.

[69] Cf. line 2 of canto I of Wieland's *Oberon*.

[70] See NA 18, 76: "Die Jesuiten . . . hatten ihren Aberglauben in die Brust eines Helden gesät."

[71] See NA 8, 466–69.

[72] Cf. Wallenstein, in his speech of mourning for Max (WT V: 3): "Um die gemeine Deutlichkeit der Dinge Den goldnen Duft der Morgenröte webend."

[73] See NA 8, 489. Nor is the word "Revers" used.

[74] See NA 8, 490. In the original version (reproduced on 464–65), the cup is merely a "Pokal," and the motif is undeveloped. Clearly, Schiller made use of the space afforded by the expansion into a five-act play to introduce an historical dimension!

[75] Cf. the *Geschichte des dreißigjährigen Krieges,* NA 18, 89: "Aus einer Rebellion in Böhmen und einem Exekutionszug gegen Rebellen (such as the one against Mainz in Schiller's own time!) wurde ein Deutscher und bald ein Europäischer Krieg." "Deutsch" here presumably means one in which basic principles of the Imperial constitution come into play.

[76] E.g. in *Ästhetische Briefe* no. 4, Schiller talks of a "reine und objektive Menschheit in der Brust seiner Bürger . . . der Mensch in der Zeit veredelt sich zum Menschen in der Idee" (see also Brief 27); Prince Friedrich Christian von Augustenburg, Schiller's patron, and his minister Count Ernst von Schimmelmann, inspired by *Don Carlos,* sweep class distinction aside in their letter to the poet of 27 November 1791: "Wir kennen keinen Stolz, als nur den, Menschen zu seyn, Bürger in der grosen Republik, deren Grenzen . . . mehr als die Grenzen eines Erdballs umfassen" (quoted by Hans-Jürgen Schings in *Die Brüder des Marquis Posa. Schiller und der Geheimbund der Illuminaten* [Tübingen, 1996], 190).

[77] Wilhelm Flitner, *Goethe im Spätwerk* (Hamburg, 1947), 198: "Das Ideal der Gesellschaft vom Turm führt über den Gegensatz des Adels und Bürgers hinaus, es bezieht sich aber auf eine neue gesellschaftliche Krise, die erst mit der französischen Revolution erkennbar werden konnte."

[78] *Ästhetische Briefe* 15: "Sobald sie demnach den Ausspruch thut: es soll eine Menschheit existieren, so hat sie eben dadurch das Gesetz aufgestellt: es soll eine Schönheit sein." This area of the work, Schiller writes to Goethe (9 November 1798) is by nature "frey menschlich."

[79] See Schiller, "Shakespeares Schatten." As Gert Sautermeister has put it, Schiller "hat sich von der deutschen Prosa bürgerlichen Lebens distanziert": G. S., *Idyllik und Dramatik im Werk Friedrich Schillers* (Stuttgart, 1971), 51.

[80] In *Bewußtsein;* cf. A. W. Iffland, *Theater* vol. 3 (Vienna, 1843), 54.

[81] Sautermeister, *Idyllik und Dramatik,* 206. "Über die Faktizität der dramatischen Gegenwart," Sautermeister continues, "richtet sich der Blick des Zuschauers auf die Vergangenheit und die Zukunft."

[82] A good example of such a sentimental "resolution" of problems is the final tableau of Iffland's *Reue versöhnt:* "Sie umarmen sich sanft in verschiedenen Gruppen" (*Theater* vol. 4 [Vienna, 1843], 122).

[83] We have seen how willing he is to disrupt the status quo and how impatient with "das ewig Gestrige." Cf. also Harald Steinhagen, "Schillers Wallenstein und die französische Revolution," *Zeitschrift für deutsche Philologie* 109 (Sonderheft

Schiller), 1990, 85 and 94, where Wallenstein is seen as a political idealist (or at least "akzeptabler Politiker") who is "zu früh gekommen." Gerhart Sautermeister, who is aware of the socio-political implications of the utopian "idyll" represented by Max and Thekla, sees Wallenstein as "der geschichtsmäßige Träger dieses Wunsches" (*Idyllik und Dramatik,* 81.) It is surely Max and Thekla who have been born "too soon."

[84] The play is a domestic action, set in a courtly milieu. A "schöne, freie Menschlichkeit" falls victim to courtly "Borniertheit und Gemeinheit." The Princess's tragic fate is also a victory over "das Gemeine und Schlechte" (NA 12, 340). Adelaide "fühlt immer als eine schöne Seele" and is at heart a natural "Bürgerin" with a "naives Gemüt," who wishes that she were not a princess, and Warbeck not (as she thinks he is) a prince (cf., *Warbeck,* III, "Eingehendere Entwürfe," 9).

[85] E.g. in his letter to Körner of 23 January 1797: "des Stoffes ist gar zu viel."

[86] G. Storz, *Der Dichter Friedrich Schiller* (Stuttgart, 1959), 309.

[87] See Schiller, *Sämtliche Werke,* ed. G. Fricke and H. Göpfert, vol. 2 (Munich: Hanscr, 1981), 1237 (note).

[88] DP I: 4, "Geworden ist ihm eine Herrscherseele."

[89] Schings (106) rightly designates Schiller's argument (*Briefe über Don Karlos* 2) that human rights were a burning issue in the sixteenth century as "anachronistic."

[90] Storz, 289.

[91] As Melitta Gerhard puts it, commenting on *Das Lied von der Glocke.* The intention is to evoke the ideal of humanity in its completeness and beauty; the impression made is somewhat mundane. See Melitta Gerhard, *Schiller* (Berne, 1950), 333.

[92] Friedrich Meinecke, "Schillers 'Spaziergang,'" reprinted in *Deutsche Lyrik von Weckherlin bis Benn; Interpretationen* I, ed. J. Schillemeit (Frankfurt/Main: Fischer, 1965), 107: "Aus der Bewegung des geschichtlichen Lebens . . . flüchtet sich der Dichter in eine ruhende Ewigkeit."

4: Herder, Goethe and the Romantic Tendency: *Götz von Berlichingen*

T**HE READER IS ENTITLED** to ask why, at this point, we are describing a chronological loop: *Wallenstein* was completed in 1799, *Götz* in 1774. The answer is: to preserve the appropriate *historical* order. This latter in turn derives from our basic principle, namely to examine the best examples of the type of play which is, in part at least, informed, in its structure, characterization, and in other ways, by impulses which can be described as historical rather than purely aesthetic. Changes in the way in which history is understood and approached therefore condition its arrangement and it is with Herder, in particular his "Sturm und Drang" treatise *Auch eine Philosophie der Geschichte zur Bildung der Menschheit*[1] that, in opposition to the position of the Enlightenment, a new approach which can be called, in broad-brush terms, "Romantic,"[2] makes itself felt. Short-term, apart from Goethe's play, the literary effects were not perhaps remarkable.[3] Goethe decided that he did not, after all, want to be a new Shakespeare, at least not along the lines sketched out in his and Herder's essays on the English dramatist; Schiller, as we have seen, remained, as an historian, under the influence of the Enlightenment. In the long term, however, we shall be tracing the effects of the 1774 revolution well into the nineteenth century. Not only do Herder and Goethe lay the foundation for the "vaterländisch" (patriotic) play, the whole question of the relation between present, past and future comes to be seen in a new light.

One is struck by the violence, sometimes virulence of the attack Herder makes on the Enlightenment in *Auch eine Philosophie*, culminating in a diatribe against the "mechanical" spirit of the modern age at the end of the second section (330–46). This is more than simply the standard response of the "Sturm und Drang" to what is perceived as the over-intellectualized[4] culture of "unser Jahrhundert." It reflects a belief that the ground must be cleared for the development of a new historical method, one informed by an awareness of time, and of the polar relation between past and present, a polarity between connection (through continuity[5] and the idea of an overarching "Absicht") and separation, the sense of a distinct "here" and "there."[6] Enlightened "pragmatic" history, as Herder sees it, "understands" the past, not by feeling its way into the individual "character" (301, 303) of a nation, but according to a pre-determined "word"; it picks over the facts and "crows" at the thought of its own superiority (349). Even Winckelmann gives a "caricature" of the Egyptians (292). When Herder makes the (on the surface) outrageously paradoxical remark: "In unserm Jahrhundert ist leider so viel Licht!" it is in the context of the distortion of truth that the tendency "sich am hellen, vortrefflichen Allgemeinen zu halten" (333), can produce in matters historical. The Enlightenment's view of the Middle Ages (and Herder is one of the first to attempt a rehabilitation of that period) is shown to be untrue when we see them, not in a historically neutral framework, but as a state of being, in time: "damalig," "in ihrem Wesen und Zwecken, Genuß und Sitten" (322). Being, one is tempted to comment, is truth, truth being. We must detach ourselves from them, or rather, them from ourselves, and make it impossible to abstract them from their historical context and "mit dem Maßstabe einer andern Zeit messen" (292). The same point is made in a more lapidary form in the "Classical" *Ideen zur Philosophie der Geschichte der Menschheit* (1784–91): History is "die Wissenschaft dessen, was da ist,"[7] that is, being, rather than "word." Herder has made his peace with the Enlightenment, but he has by no means reverted to its "pragmatic" criteria.

Awareness of history (history in everything, everything in history) is present in Herder from an early stage, and in a variety of contexts: for example, in his interest in folk-song and "national" literature,[8] and in his comments on language in the *Fragmente über die neuere deutsche Literatur* (1766–67). It is almost inevitable that the principle of what Grillparzer was later to call "Nationalität" should bulk large in Herder's thought. Just as history is for him simultaneously that of humanity as a whole and of individual nations, so language is common to all humanity, but each language is a "Nationalsprache," a treasure-house and vehicle for a people's character and history. A true student of language would need to be able to combine the disciplines of philosophy and history with that of philology (69–70). The idea of an encyclopaedic "Universalgeschichte der Bildung der Welt" is mooted in the *Journal meiner Reise im Jahre 1769.*[9] Both of Herder's treatises on the philosophy of history are informed by this polarity between the principle of individuality, which is cognate with that of nationality (a close parallel is drawn between the "Eigenheit eines Menschen" and the "Charakter einer Nation" [302]) and that of the unity of the whole: "das ganze Bild" [305]).

The sense of order is stronger in the *Ideen*, where the force and heat of the "Sturm und Drang" Herder, generated in no small measure by the need, as he sees it, to destroy the authority of the "trockne und kalte Vernunft" (285) of the *Aufklärung*, have subsided. But while it rejects the kind of rationalistically based generality favoured by a Montesquieu or Voltaire, *Auch eine Philosophie* is not an indiscriminate advocacy of disorder. Certainly, Herder seems to glory in multiplicity at times to the extent of creating deliberate confusion (or perhaps to confound "trockne Vernunft"!) as when he launches into a profusion of examples of the myriad peoples who appear on the stage of history (304–5), but if one has not "learned to see," then ". . . die Geschichte flimmert und fackelt dir vor den Augen, ein Gewirre von Szenen, Völkern, Zeitläuften" (305). The use of the expression "scene" is striking; indeed, the historical world is a stage, a "Schauplatz einer leitenden Absicht auf Erden,"[10] though we, as individuals with a limited vision, cannot see more than "Trümmer einzelner Szenen" (311), fragments of an historical epic drama ("unendliches Drama von Szenen" [353]) of which God is the author.

This work is rich in analogies and images, and another that appears frequently is that of the sea (with its constituent individual waves). The *Aufklärer*, for example, has a belief in individual perfectibility and reward ("Fortgang zu mehrerer Tugend und Glückseligkeit einzelner Menschen") and constructs a fiction ("Roman") to match (310); the observer who rejects this more facile optimism but has nothing to replace it, sees "Widersprüche und Meereswogen" (311). Herder, as we have seen, believes in a directing purpose. The individual human, a mere wave in the sea, cannot perceive it,[11] and as something inscrutable, it takes the form of a Fate whose way is "eisern und strenge" (358), but it is also "Providence" (313), since the Creator's purpose is after all the "Bildung der Menschheit." The "Sturm und Drang" does not reject the humanism and belief in progress of the eighteenth century, it simply gives it a different colouring, and is more at ease with the idea of individual tragedy. In this respect, Schiller certainly did absorb some of the lessons of "Sturm und Drang." As in the case of Schiller's Max Piccolomini, so here, this idea introduces into the historical pattern at least the implicit idea of the future, as well as past and present. Just as, in his discussion of folk-literature, the idea of a future regeneration accompanies his reflections on the history of German poetry,[12] so Herder hints at the future, however vaguely, in

Auch eine Philosophie, when he refers to the "Great Book" of God, which "über Welten und Zeiten gehet" (377) and to a "chain" which will extend he knows not whither (378).

If we try to formulate the form and structure of history, as Herder attempts to evoke it here, we are tempted, not least because of his own fondness for the theatrical metaphor (history, for example, as the "Bühne der Menschheit" [323]), toward something quasi-dramatic, but not Aristotelian: "Szenen, in deren jeder jeder Schauspieler nur Rolle hat" (352), that is, a loose assemblage of scenes whose unity is not made immediately obvious by their integration in "das Eine einer Handlung," such as is to be found in Sophocles (248). This last quotation is from Herder's *Shakespeare* and we must remind ourselves that the treatise on history and the essay on the English dramatist were worked out side-by-side in the period (ca. 1770–1774) in which Herder's influence on Goethe was at its height. The latter work, indeed, seems to have been finished first, though as far as the priority of ideas is concerned, it seems more likely that history imposed its pattern on drama, rather than vice-versa. As we hinted in the reference to Classical Greek drama cited above, history points Herder, in his discussion of Shakespearean structure (248–50), toward an alternative to that which is based on the (eminently dramatic) Aristotelian unity of action. The images of the godlike Creator and an infinitely multifarious, apparently chaotic creation, of the waves of the sea and of the discrete individual "scenes" in which characters are seemingly fate-driven, "blinde Werkzeuge" in a whole designed by "Vorsehung," recur:

> Wie vor einem Meere von Begebenheit, wo Wogen in Wogen rauschen, so tritt vor seine Bühne! Die Auftritte der Natur rücken vor und ab, würken ineinander, so disparat sie scheinen, bringen sich hervor und zerstören sich, damit die Absicht des Schöpfers . . . erfüllt werde. (248)

After all this, one is hardly surprised to find that this is not so much "Dichtung" (an aesthetic construct, carved out of the raw material of reality), as a process which parallels the continuous creation of the world: "Geschichte der Welt" (251). Herder's enthusiasm carries him so far that he declares that all Shakespeare's plays are "History im weitsten Verstande" (259). Whether this is an accurate description of Shakespeare may be questioned, but that is not what matters here. In however vague, and perhaps impractical a formulation, we glimpse here a model of a kind of play in which the construction is deliberately loose, the scope almost infinitely wide; in which the emphasis is on spirit — the spirit of a "whole event" (249: "Seele der Begeben-heit") — rather than the psychological processes of a group of char-acters enmeshed in an "action." The latter, insofar as it exists at all, is a pretext for the former: the real "plot" is that of history, with "so viel Ordnung und so viel Wirrung, Knote und Anlage zur Auflösung" (*Auch eine Philosophie*, 377). This is, of course, meant provisionally and provocatively, and taken literally, hardly likely to lead to the pro-duction of dramatically practicable plays. It is ironically appropriate that Herder should apparently have found himself constrained to write to Goethe, apropos of the first version of *Götz von Berlichingen*, that Shakespeare "[hat] Euch ganz verdorben."[13]

He was referring to Goethe's *Geschichte Gottfriedens von Ber-lichingen mit der eisernen Hand. Dramatisirt*, written in about six weeks[14] in 1771. The second version, *Götz von Berlichingen mit der eisernen Hand. Ein Schauspiel*, was completed in 1773. The change of description in the title, from "Geschichte" to "Schauspiel," probably reflects Goethe's feeling that he had strayed from the dramatic into the epic sphere, in particular in his development of the character of the vicious, but vibrant seductress and "Machtweib," Adelheid von Walldorf. Whether the second version, which we shall discuss, has moved so far toward the dramatic end of the scale as to cease to be epic, we shall see in due course.

That the play is entirely national ("vaterländisch") has long been recognized (e.g. by Ernst Beutler,)[15] and indeed was seen, as early as 1773, by the important "Sturm und Drang" balladeer Gottfried August Bürger: "Welch ein durchaus deutscher Stoff!"[16] It is also equally well-known, as indeed the characteristically extravagant enthu-siasm shown by Bürger in the same letter confirms, that the play is a document of contemporary relevance, full of the passionate, some-times rebellious, "free" spirit of the 1770s. One may doubt whether "deutsch" implied, in Bürger's case, a sense of community with the historical Götz. In general, "Sturm und Drang" dramatists see in ac-tions set in the past — Leisewitz's *Julius von Tarent*, or Klinger's *Simsone Grisaldo* for example — not history, but outlets for their own feelings.[17] Lenz sees *Götz*, rather as he sees Shakespeare's Histories, in terms of a "selbständige Existenz." Berlichingen is "ein antiker deut-scher Mann"; the first epithet suggests something almost as remote as Hermann, the second, here, has nothing historical or political about it, but represents the "Sturm und Drang" ideal of free, dynamic man-hood.[18] These qualities are present in Goethe's play, without question, but exclusive emphasis on them can obscure the fact that we are dealing also with a play that is deeply political and in its way, conservative,[19] and also historical in the spirit not only of Justus Möser, whose ideas on the "Faustrecht" it certainly mirrors,[20] but also in the more broadly philosophical spirit of Herder.

The influence of the latter[21] is clearly visible in Goethe's "Rede zum Schäkespears Tag" (1771), and the proximity of that oration-cum-essay, in its turn, to *Götz von Berlichingen,* soon becomes apparent. In rendering the sense of freedom which Shakespeare brought him, Goethe emulates Götz by declaring a "feud" against classicistic restriction: ". . . da ich sahe, wieviel Unrecht mir die Herrn der Regeln in ihrem Loch angethan haben . . . so wäre mir das Herz geborsten wenn ich ihnen nicht Fehde angekündigt hätte, und nicht täglich suchte ihre Türne zusammen zu schlagen."[22] That Shakespeare should be experienced as a representative and source of the spirit of Nature and freedom is of course a standard reaction of "Sturm und Drang" and we are in no way attempting, by concentrating on other aspects here, to deny this one, or belittle its importance. Indeed, it will prove to have relevance to our theme as well, in that not only the reality and spirit of the past, but also its relevance to "unser Jahrhundert," a Herderian phrase which Goethe echoes,[23] in other words, the future (as far as the characters are concerned), as well as the past and present dimensions, has a role to play. The most striking correspondence between Goethe's and Herder's perception of Shakespeare is, however, that in which we see what we have called the "form" of history, for which Herder has employed a quasi-dramatic analogy, transferred to drama itself and applied in particular to the question of dramatic action:

> Schäkespears Theater ist ein schöner Raritäten Kasten, in dem die Geschichte der Welt vor unsern Augen an dem unsichtbaaren Faden der Zeit vorbeywallt. Seine Pläne sind, nach dem gemeinen Styl zu reden, keine Pläne, aber seine Stücke drehen sich alle um den geheimen Punckt . . . in dem Das eigenthümliche unsres Ich's, die prätendirte Freyheit unsres Wollens, mit dem nothwendigen Gang des Ganzen zusammenstösst. (A 4, 124)

There is no denial here, any more than there is in Herder, of the unique validity and importance of the individuality, rather a recognition of the fact that the "whole," the world in which it exists, is beyond individual control. Exactly how "fatalistic" *Götz von Berlichingen* is, and how much of the hero's "freedom" is preserved, we shall have to consider later. For the moment, it is worth noting that just as he uses the Herderian expression "Geschichte der Welt," so Goethe

seems to echo Herder's phrasing in speaking of "die prätendirte Freyheit unsres Wollens."[24] And while there is little evidence of the Christian underpinning which, in Herder, complements the sense of "Fate"
with that of "Providence," we shall argue that Goethe is certainly
seized, in this play, of the idea of historical necessity. Götz has hitched
his wagon to stars (the Empire and the Emperor) which are on the
wane, and if he has a significance for the future, it is as a martyr, a man
who must remain true to his fine and honest nature and is rendered
infinitely vulnerable by that very fact, but who can serve as an inspiration to future generations.

The play's adoption of "open" form, its loose structure and cava-
lier flouting of "the rules," even in the less undisciplined second version,
is a commonplace of *Götz*-criticism and it accords, as was recognized
at the time (such as by Bürger, as we have seen) with the "free" mentality of the "Sturm und Drang." It is not entirely devoid of an element of "dramatic" plot — most notably in the personal relationship
between Götz and Weislingen — but the plot struggles, at times, to
make itself apparent in the welter of activity and movement, from
place to place, figure to figure. That there is more to this than a simple thumbing of the nose at classicism, we will attempt to show later.
For the moment, we are more concerned to show that the parts belong to a whole; there is an organic structure, one which is under-
pinned by imagery and symbol. This is not an action based on the
tensions between a closely integrated group of characters, but it is still
an action, the story of a life and a death, and the most helpful place to
begin is at the pivotal scene, in act III (headed "Saal," A 4, 715–17),
at which an apogee (Götz as free and active hero) has been reached,
and a decline (Götz as essentially passive victim) begins.

Götz has acted independently against the merchants of Nuremberg in what he regards as a legitimate quarrel or "Fehde," in accordance with the traditional procedures of the "Faustrecht," but the
Emperor has been persuaded to declare him outside the law and to
sanction the despatch of an Imperial force, a formal "Reichsexeku-
tion," against him. In the first part of the act, Götz had been victori-
ous in skirmishes with the "Reichsknechte," but now he has been
forced back into his castle of Jaxthausen. He is seen, with his fellow-
defenders, partaking of a meal which provides the most resounding
articulation of his spirit of freedom, and marks the beginning of his
destruction. His opening remark is characteristic: "So bringt uns die
Gefahr zusammen" (715). The little group is a society bound together
in amity and freedom, a microcosm of the Empire as Götz conceives it

should be (716–17). It is a society in which there are masters and servants, but where those who serve do so "edel und frey," and it has obvious similarities to the patriarchal society whose praises Herder sings in *Auch eine Philosophie*. At the same time, the little group is under threat, and though they may drink a toast to freedom, they are themselves, as Georg points out, effectively prisoners. The realities of history intrude. Goethe's audience should be aware of the discrepancy between the Empire as it is in the eighteenth century, when absolutism is established and the Princes are in control, and the vision that Götz propounds, and to make doubly sure, he changes what was a positive prophecy in the first version ("wird") into a conditional one ("würde") in the second.[25]

From this point on, just as the bottle of wine they are drinking is their last, and just as the Empire itself is described as "krüplich" (715), so the crippling of Götz, who is now a passive figure subject to manipulation by Weislingen, and whose iron hand is no longer a symbol of strength,[26] continues apace. Götz's vision of a healthy and happy Empire is clearly idealistic and idyllic, and Goethe is no doubt well aware that the audience will see it as such. Edward McInnes is quite justified in speaking of a "lack of understanding" (i.e. of the political realities of the historical situation) in Götz in this regard,[27] at least as far as a practical realization of this ideal in the foreseeable future is concerned.

What, though, of the "Nachkommenschaft" to which Lerse refers at the end of the play, which is watching it, and which is exhorted to understand Götz aright? There is clearly an element of mourning in our sense of the "degeneration,"[28] as Michelsen has put it, that destroys the physical Götz, but is Götz's image simply to be swamped in a passively elegiac mood? His actual defeat is inevitable in the circumstances, but the audience, as part of Lerse's "Nachkommenschaft," is placed in a position to ignore the Hegelian siren-voice that urges acceptance of "historical necessity" as Lukács understands it.[29] Götz's *moral* ascendancy is clear throughout and a subtle system of polarities, reversals and ambivalences illustrate how the philosophy of the "coming" age has distorted true values. The new system, that of "die Zeiten des Betrugs" (753), is perverting the ideals of strength and freedom, and of "Treue" (unswerving commitment to a person or cause), so that these qualities manifest themselves on the court side, in Adelheid and Franz, in a criminal form. Götz, as his portrayal of the Empire as it should be shows, wants order, but can be represented to the Emperor as a disorderly element. Eventually, he and Georg, the true "children" of the Emperor, are forced into the company of "robbers," in whom, ironically, the spirit of "Treue" survives.[30] The audience, alerted to its role as judge by the reference to the future generation, as by sundry other "prophetic" moments in the play,[31] will not be "reconciled" to Götz's fate. He will, in spirit, "rise again." Hence, perhaps, the suggestions of a parallel with Christ's Passion to which we shall come in due course.

The flesh of the historical loser is weak, but his spirit, as mediated by the historical experience, can still be potent. Möser, whose enthusiastic description of the sixteenth-century "Faustrecht"[32] helped to inspire Goethe, was well aware that the actual form could never be restored, but still saw some purpose in lauding and recommending its "Geist," by contrast with the rather flaccid atmosphere of the enlightened eighteenth century,[33] "unser *aevum*," as Goethe contemptuously calls it in contrasting the effetely classicistic present day with the "German" past in his hymn of praise to Gothic architecture, "Von deutscher Baukunst." Accepting that the precise form of Götz's vision of a free life cannot be realized, as indeed he himself seems half-aware, we can see a future relevance for it "im Geist," to quote his own words, for his "Enkel"(716) As Goethe writes in his "Epistle" to Merck:

> Und können wir nicht tragen mehr
> Krebs, Panzerhemd, Helm, Schwerdt und Speer,
> So ist doch immer unser Muth
> Wahrhafftig wahr und bieder und gut.[34]

Without straying outside the bounds of reality (as he does in the operatic *finale* of *Egmont*) to the extent that he undermines the sense of history, Goethe seems, by presenting Götz as a martyr who witnesses to the ideal of what we might call "constructive freedom," to be attempting to give him a spiritual after-life on earth, as well as in heaven, where he himself goes at the end of the play to enjoy "perfect freedom." For the living generation of the "Stürmer und Dränger," whose new valuation of imagination and emotion enables them to respond to the power of "spirit" in history, Lerse's call can indeed be effective. Lenz, for example, in his essay "Über Götz von Berlichingen," calls on the present generation to absorb the lessons of the play, "damit wir wieder Deutsche werden."[35] And it was not a totally disembodied spirit. While it was no doubt difficult to be inspired by the Holy Roman Empire as they saw it around them — it was, for eighteenth-century Germans, as for Götz,[36] still "Deutschland." It was the embodiment, however ramshackle, of German unity and there were even those, such as F. C. von Moser ("Vom deutschen National-geist," 1765) who clung to the idea that it might be made politically viable again.[37] We shall see later that the Empire and Emperor (Maximilian II) play an important part in the play's structure, and in giving it historical substantiality.

As we have said, the "Saal" scene marks the beginning of a decline, in which there is a sufficiency of echoes of, and (of course, not too explicit) parallels with the Passion of Christ. That the process should begin with what amounts to a Last Supper in which the last of the wine (whose symbolic importance has already been brought out in the "Brother Martin" scene in Act I)[38] is poured out and in which Götz seems to anticipate and accept his own death,[39] is significant. This is followed by a betrayal and a trial in which Götz is treated with the utmost disrespect and almost subjected to the ultimate humiliation, and though he is temporarily "freed" by Sickingen's intervention, we never feel that he can escape from the toils. In the final scenes, the suggestions of a Passion are quite strong. Instead of being granted a near-apotheosis in the style of Egmont, Götz appears as a broken man. He has been "nach und nach verstümmelt," his "Hour has come," and he accepts the will of God.[40] Outside, in the garden, he exhorts Lerse to take care of Elisabeth, recalling the words of the crucified Christ to "the disciple whom he loved."[41] There are even suggestions of Easter (and therefore of the future) in the setting in the garden, where Götz's spirit is lifted by the presence of Nature in spring, and where he finally breathes "himmlische Luft." We would argue that the symbolic (not, of course, allegorical) suggestion of what we have called "martyr"-status for Götz is not simply, as McInnes seems to hold, a step outside concrete history into the realm of "religiös-metaphysisches Bewußtsein,"[42] such as one might expect from, say, Zacharias Werner. While the outcome of the fight he has fought can be seen from one viewpoint as one of failure, it can also be seen as an historical equivalent of the biblical "good fight," in which the apparent outsider, however inevitable his defeat in the context of the "Geist der Zeit," as Herder would put it,[43] witnesses to a truth which can still have inspirational force for a future generation. The audience is to contemplate its own present, and possible future, as well as an elegiacally contemplated past.

However, the latter must not be assimilated to the former. The imperial constitution still holds, for Goethe and his audience, as the form in which "Germany" exists, and the task of finding a balance between unity and order and individual freedom is as urgent as ever. The historical experience demands a sense of change as well as of continuity. Götz may live in the spirit, but Goethe insists also on his pastness. He *is* "history." Even more decisively than his own death, the killing-off of Georg, his true spiritual son, has drawn a firm line between the late medieval world they inhabit, and the audience's present. The historical perspective, as we have said, separates as clearly as it connects and Goethe achieves this effect triumphantly in this play, much more so than in *Egmont*, by creating the sixteenth-century world in the state of "being" to which we referred in our discussion on Herder. This means a living, rather than a merely academic authenticity and Goethe's mastery of the language of the age of Luther, supported by the sixteenth-century source on which he was able to draw,[44] helped him considerably in achieving this aim. The sixteenth-century Holy Roman Empire is brought into a solid and concrete life, with numerous references to personalities and events, and the practical workings of the system.[45] The social scope of the work is truly panoramic — from Emperor to gypsy — and (more important) as loosely structured as the Empire itself, which is a correspondingly broad canopy under which everything happens.

In their actual happening, the "Szenen" (in Herder's sense) are relatively free-standing. Integration, insofar as the word applies, is thematic rather than dramatic in the sense of an Aristotelian "action." The sequencing of the scenes, and the management of the time-intervals, which we often have to supply for ourselves, is clearly intended to produce the "open" effect of "epic" theatre and involve the audience in an observing and calculating function.[46] Thus we learn in the "Jaxthausen" scene (678) that Götz intends to make "Hell hot" for the Mayor of Nuremberg and his citizens, "tomorrow, or the day after." This thread then disappears for some time, to re-surface suddenly when Götz and Selbitz are chance guests at a peasant wedding, at which the conversation turns quite naturally to the theme of the venality of lawyers ("Götz!" exclaims Selbitz, "Wir sind Räuber!": 692) and which the guests have to leave at a moment's notice because "Die Nürnberger sind im Anzug" (693). The wedding-scene functions as a pure vignette of "life," a door through which the hero can step out of the dramatic action which might have enclosed him, and enter into a world of historical action: a man living and being in his own time. In a similar way, the siege of Jaxthausen in act III is rendered in vignettes of pure "happening," whose vigour and vivacity the

eighteenth-century audience would enjoy, while being made simultaneously aware of the difference between Götz's "then" and their
"now." The bullet-making scene in particular, which is hardly dramatically integral,[47] with on the one hand, its precise detail, and on the
other, the "free" image of Georg clambering about on the castle-roof
removing the lead guttering while he is shot at from below, combines
an instantaneous vitality with an equally strong sense of past-ness.

The play does also, as we have said, have an action which is more
psychologically dramatic[48] and which centres on the "interesting"[49]
figure, in the parlance of the time, of Weislingen, and his relationships
with Götz and Adelheid. Weislingen, with his inability to find inner
peace and a settled relationship to the world around him, is in fact —
as a character — much more representative of the "Sturm und Drang"
Goethe than is Götz who, as most critics agree, lacks the substance to
be cither a Werther or a Faust. But this dramatic action is structurally
a kind of (only partially developed) inset into a panoramic whole of
"epic" action. Edward McInnes points out, quite reasonably, that the
psychological action is not integrated with the political theme, in
which Weislingen also plays an important part. The political confrontation, he says, lacks "a clear and representative general dimension,"
and he goes on to argue that this "inevitably brings about a sharp re-
duction of [the play's] historical importance."[50] On this point, we
must demur. It was a self-indulgence on Goethe's part to allow so
much scope to personal preoccupations in the delineation of Weislingen, as it had been in the first version to over-develop the figure of
Adelheid, but one doubts whether a closer dramatic integration would
have benefited the play historically or indeed in any other way, since it
would have run counter to the basic concept. *Götz* is surely conceived
as a "Haupt-und-Staatsaction," in the sense in which Goethe used this
expression in his essay to render the essence of the loose "Shakespearean" form which he was trying to create.[51] This term, which emphasizes the elements of (often lurid) adventure, usually in high places,
and of action in the sense of occurrence rather than integrated plot,
can be applied to any kind of storytelling, and indeed achieved greater
prominence in the narrative literature of the Baroque (e.g. the novels
of Anton Ulrich von Braunschweig)[52] than in the popular theatrical
form developed in Germany by Johannes Velten and carried on into
the eighteenth century by the Austrian J. A. Stranitzky. As a dramatic
form, with its emphasis on event, it had the advantage of helping to
create history as a living reality; as a formal historical narrative, it is more
likely to be the result of the pragmatic approach of the Enlightenment

("... der Herren eigner Geist In dem die Zeiten sich bespiegeln") as the hero, in the *Urfaust*, indicates to Wagner. The body, that is, rather than the spirit of history, not a living, but a dead past:

> Ein Kehrichtfaß und eine Rumpelkammer
> Und höchstens eine Haupt und Staats Acktion[53]

The "Shakespearean" development of the loose and open form is clearly not meant to be seen in this light, either aesthetically or historically. Its very looseness enables it to embody the "Ganzes" (in Herder's sense) of which Götz, as a single "Woge," or this episode, as a single "Szene," is a part. Its logic and unity, what enabled no less an authority than August Strindberg to call the play, in spite of its "seeming formlessness," a "firm unit,"[54] is derived from poetic and thematic sources as much, if indeed not more than from dramatic ones. Motifs of freedom and unfreedom (old, and potentially, new "German" strength as against debility, and honest, "alte deutsche Treue" [as Schubart calls it][55] as against "Betrug": betrayal, deception), underpin a network of relationships, part opposition, part affinity, between the characters. Thus, for example, Adelheid is Götz's moral antipode, but rightly senses an affinity with his energy and virility. This enables the plot-line to move from point to point without a clearly motivated transition in terms of dramatic action. The fact that Lerse's announcement of the favourable terms offered to end the siege is followed by Georg's song about the bird that escapes from the cage,[56] is a good illustration of this. That Götz is then betrayed and taken prisoner does not undermine, but rather ironically highlights the dominant theme of freedom. Nor are we taken "out of history" by this appeal to our sense of political morality. The spectator will be aware that in the age he can see "coming" before his eyes, which Götz is to name prophetically that of deceit,[57] the "getreuherzig" Berlichingen cannot win.

However, Goethe, politically always a reforming conservative, would surely have wanted it also to reflect on the possibility of a better balance between power and freedom in the present-day Empire. He certainly gives the Emperor and his political concerns — holding Germany together, giving it internal peace and harmony and fighting off the predatory foreigners — considerable prominence. The figure appears on stage on only one occasion, but his name is often on the lips, both of the proponents of the freedom of the knights,[58] and of those who wish to curb it, in favour of the authority of the territorial princes, most notably Adelheid, who comments on his indulgent treatment of Götz after the escape from Heilbronn: "Er verliert den Geist eines Regenten" (A 4, 728). Just as much as Götz, even more so, perhaps, from the historical point of view, the Emperor stands at the heart of the play as the point at which the lines cross, or the centre which diametrically opposed forces threaten to tear asunder. The historical issue, after all, is what the Empire is, should be, and will become. The prime weakness of the play as an historical drama is perhaps the fact, not that it departs from reality, but that the reality to which it points as a vehicle for a renewed "German" freedom and honesty, proved, despite the best efforts and intentions of thinkers and publicists such as von Moser,[59] Wieland and the older Goethe himself (e.g. in the social reflections of *Wilhelm Meister*), to be so little capable of self-renewal. Though it is fair to point out that no one, in the 1770s, was anticipating the French Revolution, let alone Napoleon.

Certainly, *Götz von Berlichingen* is not a revolutionary play in any political sense. Götz may be a disruptive element in the context of an Empire which the Emperor, the soul of a body whose limbs will not obey it, and which is therefore restricted to merely "speculating and wishing,"[60] finds it almost impossible to govern. *His* dream of an ideal order may be Utopian, but Weislingen is manifestly unfair in attempting to associate him with the idea of a "Schwindelgeist, der ganze Landschaften ergreift" (A 4, 695), and that he should be manoeuvred, finally, into the paradoxical situation of a leader of the Peasant Revolt is part of the play's pattern of decline, of his personal historical tragedy: the time is out of joint, and he has no chance of putting it right.

While Goethe, throughout his life, remained, in some sense at least, a realist, the Romantic generation that took up and developed much of what he had begun, particularly in his "Sturm und Drang" years,[61] had a natural tendency to transcend reality. This leads to the apparently paradoxical situation in which a generation that had an intense interest in the past, and was fascinated by theatre and produced a large amount of ostensibly "dramatic" literature, does not have a single historical drama of rank to show for its efforts. There are some undistinguished "Ritterstücke," such as Tieck's *Karl von Berneck* (and even a few fragments by Novalis!) which skate across the surface of the Middle Ages in the wake of Goethe's *Götz*, but there is nothing of note. Indeed, this surface, "factual" medievalism is not a truly congenial vehicle for the Romantic spirit. The deeper a play has its roots in Romantic spirituality and psychology, the less it lends itself to the purposes of historical, or any other drama. Romantic history, for all its respect for ancient monuments and documents (which it did much to make accessible), finds it all too easy and attractive, in its desire for "unmittelbare Herrschaft des Geistes über die Materie," for "Magie,"[62] to move from the temporal into the timeless. This is also a movement from fact into myth. The spirit, or "poetry" of the "Vorzeit" which cannot be achieved "in dieser Zeitlichkeit," is to be set free so that it can eventually help to foster the spiritual restoration (paradise regained) which is the aim of all "Romantisierung." This is an important part of the burden of the last of Novalis's *Hymnen an die Nacht*[63] and it is in the fragments of a plan for the Second Part of the same author's novel, *Heinrich von Ofterdingen*, that we have the clearest glimpse of Romantic "fulfilment," and a final triumph over time, a "Vermählung der Jahreszeiten."[64]

The particular predilection of the Romantics for the Christian Middle Ages when, as A. W. Schlegel sees it, "contemplation of the infinite annihilated the Finite" and "the poetry of Nature was poured out in unbelievable abundance,"[65] is of a piece with this tendency. There is many an echo of Herder's thought in Schlegel's criticism (which, characteristically, takes a consistently historical form), but he just as consistently wishes to push the ideas further than Herder or Goethe would have thought legitimate in seeking the "meaning" of history. His attack on the pragmatic school of the Enlightenment, in which he even quotes Faust's reproof to Wagner, develops into a demand for a "poetische Geschichte,"[66] one that conveys us beyond the limitations of time.

The choice, and treatment, of material by Romantic dramatists reflects this in its preference for the "poetically" historical, the mythical and mystical (the latter particularly in the case of Zacharias Werner). Ludwig Tieck's *Kaiser Octavianus* (1804) has, as Roger Paulin makes clear, strong echoes of Jakob Boehme and as a "celebration of poetry, fancy, romance,"[67] deserved the place which Tieck gave it at the head of his collected works.[68] Clemens Brentano, while he represents a second generation of Romanticism which is less inclined than that of Tieck and the Schlegels to disregard the claims of the material world, finds, in *Die Gründung Prags*, his congenial historical topic in the age when history, as "eine Seherin, eine Dichterin, eine Künstlerin,"[69] is still open to the transcendental and conducive to the free exercise of the imagination. The time in which his formally dramatic figures "move" is, correspondingly, "eine ideale Zeit."[70]

The practical consequence is that German Romantic drama does not offer a sufficiently substantial reality to stimulate the audience into the exercise of its sense of time in the way we have indicated. There are of course similarities with *Götz von Berlichingen*. Shakespeare was still a powerful influence, indeed, he was a lifelong preoccupation for the most important early practitioner of Romantic drama, Tieck, who also revered the work of the young Goethe. Freedom, and liberation from the restraints of Classical form, were still very much watchwords of the Romantic Movement. But the complementary influence of the Spanish drama, especially Calderón,[71] indicates a difference, a stronger cultivation of formal practices which militate toward a radical weakening of the real element in the action, which as even Friedrich Schlegel recognizes, drama must retain to some extent,[72] in favour of the cultivation of mood. It opens the text to a "spiritual" reality that is essentially timeless, so that the past, insofar as it plays a part at all, becomes not the past realized, but the past distilled into pure spirit. Tieck speaks in such terms in his comments on Kleist's *Das Käthchen von Heilbronn*. He takes the play as a "Gedicht" which has been "ganz als Volkssage behandelt," and is loud in praise of its "leichtere Art, welche Episoden zuläßt," and which "eben dadurch einen Durchblick erlaubt in die große, freie Natur."[73]

This idea of a "Durchblick," which presumably means a transparency in the Käthchen-von Strahl action which Kleist would hardly have intended, is totally characteristic of Tieck. In his own dramatic practice, he goes further. In the two plays,[74] both based on chapbooks, in which he can claim to be writing "historically" in the Romantic sense, his avowed aim is to make as much as possible of "reality," including that of a dramatically "present" medieval reality, disappear. As he puts it in the 1828 preface to *Kaiser Octavianus* (though commenting, in fact, on *Genoveva*), his aim, in these "dramatisations" of *Volksbücher*, is to destroy the reality which the theatre normally brings with it ("mich vorsätzlich von allem Theater und dessen Einrichtungen entferne[n]"), in order to concentrate entirely on "keine andere Wahrheit, als die poetische, durch die Phantasie gerechtfertigte."[75] His Romantic practice is even more radical in the second play than in the first. Thus, while he may or may not have been evoking a medieval "spirit," he was certainly not creating a dramatically viable reality, and was thus barring the way to any possibility of the historical experience as we have defined it. The same is true, to a greater or lesser extent, for all German Romantic drama that treats themes with any semblance of historical potential. That two great dramatists of the past, Shakespeare and Calderón, were heroes for Tieck and many other Romantics, un-doubtedly says much for their poetic spirit, but was of little use for their dramatic production, for they were not understood dramatically, and their influence contributed, as Sengle says, to a disintegration of German Romantic drama, for the most part, "in lyrisch-unverbindlicher Mystik oder in halbepischer Vergangenheitsdarstellung."[76]

That German national consciousness rose, in political and intellec-tual life, to an entirely new level of prominence during the Romantic period, is well enough established to require no special demonstration here. The end of the Holy Roman Empire, the need to re-think and rebuild in the German states, in particular Austria (to which we shall turn in our next chapter) and Prussia, had created a new set of condi-tions in which the beginnings which can be detected in Herder, in Goethe's "Von deutscher Baukunst" and *Götz von Berlichingen*, and other products of the "Sturm und Drang," developed apace. And they did so in tandem with a growth in interest in the past, a natural source of inspiration and nourishment for the mind that is seeking to redis-cover and develop its sense of identity. As Fritz Valjavec has put it: "Der von (der Romantik) angefachte Sinn für die deutsche und abendländische Vergangenheit kam auch der stolzen Besinnung auf die nationalen Eigentümlichkeiten unseres Volkes zugute."[77] This can be seen reflected in many aspects of German writing and thought during the period, from Wackenroder and Tieck[78] onward, and in the drama as well as in other fields. The question we must consider here is whether it can lead to a successful historical drama in the Romantic context, or whether it is of importance mainly as a preparation for what was to come in the post-Romantic period. When we remind our-selves that the most important requirement is the creation of an effec-tive link between a past and a present reality, we already begin to fear that the answer must be in the negative.

We have already noted the Romantic tendency to wish to tran-scend reality and the preference for the legendary is still present in what is probably the most important of the truly "vaterländisch" dra-mas of the Napoleonic period, Fouqué's *Der Held des Nordens*, a dramatisation of the Nibelungen legend which draws heavily on the Nordic, as well as the German version. Korff, while he recognizes the work's aesthetic inadequacies, devotes a long section to it on the grounds that it is a "legitime Vorstufe" of Wagner's *Ring*-Cycle.[79] This latter question we can (gratefully) leave aside, but Korff does make a case for discerning in it the powerful, if dangerous cult of a "Germanic" fate-ethic.[80] We must judge this, of course, in the context of the early nineteenth century, and relate the "heroic" spirit to contemporary events and moods, and Fouqué's friend E. T. A. Hoffmann who, while not himself a dramatist, had a strong interest in the theatre, is perhaps a better guide. In his *Neueste Nachrichten von den Schicksalen des Hundes Berganza*, he praises the work in somewhat fulsome terms, singling out Fouqué as a Romantic giant among non-Romantic pigmies: ". . . den, der mit seltner Kraft die nordische Riesenharfe ertönen ließ, der mit wahrer Weihe und Begeisterung den hohen Helden Sigurd in das Leben rief, daß sein Glanz all die matten Dämmerlichter der Zeit überstrahlte, und vor seinem mächtigen Tritt all die Harnische, die man sonst für Helden selbst gehalten, hohl und körperlos umfielen."[81] The Romantic celebration of the "poetic" spirit which transcends all everyday reality, and an awareness of the unheroic nature of contemporary German reality, could be said to be in balance in such a statement, but what is certain is that Hoffmann does not urge a practical comparison between past and present upon us. It is not easy to make the leap from the legendary land of the Nibelungs to modern times, and Fouqué does not really seem to do much to help us. A comparison with Hebbel, in due course, might be revealing.

Meantime, we can close this account with a brief glance at another minor, in this case perhaps even peripheral figure, Ludwig Uhland. As poet, as scholar, and as politician, Uhland was strongly attracted to the past, to the ages of chivalry and legend, but he was also one of, if not the most earthbound of the Romantics. His material is potentially Romantic, but he either could not, or would not master the style and general literary practice which truly frees the mind and creates the Romantic mood in which what he perhaps genuinely felt might have been effectively expressed. On the other hand, given the problematic nature of true Romantic feeling for historical drama in our sense, this limitation might have been a strength, had he possessed genuine dramatic talent. One can see the potential in a play like *Ernst, Herzog von Schwaben* (1817), but not the fulfilment. His "old" world is more authentic than, for example, Tieck's in *Sternbald*, or perhaps even Arnim's in *Die Kronenwächter*, but it does not live. His "patriotism" is certainly local (Württemberg is his "teures Vaterland"[82]) but he also has a strong sense of loyalty to a "German" whole.[83] The picture of heroic "Treue" which he paints in the play is certainly, in potential at least, more than just a museum-piece and certainly more easily transferable to modern conditions than the "Germanic" (if "gigantic") heroism of Siegfried and Brünhild. Indeed, in the concluding speech by Ernst's mother Gisela, Uhland could even be said to be pointing his audience, in prophetic mode, towards a modern application:

> Nein, leben, leben soll mein treuer Ernst,
> Fortleben wird er in dem Mund des Volks,
> Er lebt in jedem fühlenden Gemüt,
> Er lebet dort, wo reines Leben ist.[84]

One seems even to catch a faint echo of the ending of *Götz von Berlichingen*, especially when Gisela goes on to talk of a "himmlisch Zelt" where, no doubt, the dead friends and heroes will be able to breathe "himmlische Luft." But neither in the play itself, nor in the prologue which he wrote for a performance to celebrate the Württemberg constitution in 1819, did Uhland create a link powerful enough to carry the work as an historical drama in the full-blooded sense in which one can use the term of other "national" plays like *Götz* or Grillparzer's *Ottokar*, to which we shall turn our attention in the next chapter.

Notes

[1] Written in Bückeburg in 1773, published 1774. References to this text, and to other essays of the 1770s, will be to the edition by Wilhelm Dobbek, *Herders Werke,* vol. 2 (Weimar: Volksverlag, 1957).

[2] Thus H. A. Korff can describe Romantic "Germanistik," which he sees as the foundation of the historical novel, as "ihrerseits die Frucht jener großen Bewegung, die wir die romantische nennen und die zuerst in der Dichtung, nämlich mit dem Götz von Berlichingen, beginnt": cf. H. A. Korff, *Geist der Goethezeit,* 2nd ed., vol. IV (reprint: Leipzig, 1958), 358.

[3] For the sub-genre of the "Ritterstück" to which *Götz* can be said to have given birth, see Sengle 31–32. Klinger's *Otto* (1775) is an early example. Grillparzer paid homage to it in *Die Ahnfrau;* perhaps Hebbel's *Agnes Bernauer* can be seen as a late descendant: the subject had, after all, already been treated by Josef August von Törring (*Agnes Bernauerin,* 1781).

[4] "Kopf und Herz ist einmal getrennt," 337.

[5] Cf. 311: "Ein Streben aufeinander in Kontinuität."

[6] See 287–88: ". . . siehst du nicht, daß es mit dem dortigen Geist der Zeit, des Landes, der Stufe des Menschengeschlechts ganz anders ist?"

[7] Herder, *Ideen zur Philosophie der Geschichte der Menschheit,* in B. Suphan, ed., *Ausgewählte Werke,* vols. 4–5, book XIII (Berlin: Weidmannsche Buchhandlung, 1887–1901), 145.

[8] In "Von Ähnlichkeit der mittleren englischen und deutschen Dichtkunst," he finds that by contrast with the English, German literature lacks historical roots: "Bei uns wächst alles a priori" (*Werke,* ed. Dobbek, vol. 2 [Weimar: Volksverlag,

1957], 270). See also the "Ossian" essay: "Das menschliche Geschlecht ist zu einem Fortgang von Szenen, von Bildung, von Sitten bestimmt" (202).

[9] See Hans Reisiger, *Johann Gottfried Herder* (Hildesheim: Olms, 1970), 84.

[10] Cf. 313: "Schauplatz der Bildung der Welt."

[11] "Weiß ich, wohin ich mit meiner kleinen Woge komme?" 373.

[12] Cf. my article, "Historical ambivalence in Goethe and Scott," *New German Studies* 13 (1985), 168.

[13] Quoted by Ernst Beutler in *Der junge Goethe;* A 4, 1075. It is worth noting that Herder ducks the task of elaborating the theoretical basis of such a "Shakespearean" drama (257: "Aber ich bin kein Mitglied aller unsrer historischen, philosophischen und schönkünstlichen Akademien . . .").

[14] See Hanna Fischer-Lamberg, ed., *Der junge Goethe,* vol. 2 (Berlin: de Gruyter, 1963), 332. This edition contains helpful information on the composition, historical background, and the use made by Goethe of the original "Lebens-Beschreibung" of the sixteenth-century Berlichingen himself and of other sources. The text itself is quoted from the Artemis edition, vol. 4. The relationship between the two versions is also discussed in my article: "Historical Ambivalence in Goethe and Scott," 161–184 (cited as NGS).

[15] Artemis-Ausgabe, 4, 1074.

[16] Letter to H. C. Boie, 8 July 1773. Bürger was at the time engaged in composing his best-known ballad, "Lenore," which, like *Götz,* was known to and influenced Scott. "Dieser G. v. B.," he writes, "hat mich wieder zu drei neuen Strophen der Lenore begeistert."

[17] Leisewitz, says Werner Keller, has the intention "Personen und Vorgänge von der historischen Situation abzulösen" (J. A. Leisewitz, *Julius von Tarent,* ed. W. Keller [Stuttgart: Reclam, 1965], 83). Klinger, in *Simsone Grisaldo,* celebrates the great soul "auf dem hohen Gipfel meiner Selbständigkeit"; cf. H. Nicolai/M. Gras-Racic, eds., *Sturm und Drang* vol. 2 (Munich: Winkler, 1771), 1079.

[18] Cf. J. M. R. Lenz, "Über Götz von Berlichingen," in *Sturm und Drang,* vol. 1, 831 and 833. For Shakespeare, see the "Anmerkungen übers Theater," 859.

[19] Götz, after all, denies at Heilbronn that he is a "Rebell," and declares himself "Ihro Majestät treuer Knecht" (722).

[20] Cf. NGS, 165. See also Hans Reiss, "Goethe, Möser und die Aufklärung. Das Heilige Römische Reich in Goethes Götz von Berlichingen" in H. R., *Formgestaltung und Politik. Goethe-Studien* (Würzburg, 1993).

[21] Cf. also NGS, 165–68.

[22] A 4, 123. Goethe's lifelong tendency to embody thought in imagery shows itself in the use of the prison-metaphor in this passage and the same image is prominent in the text of *Götz von Berlichingen.* That Goethe's play could perform a similar function for his own contemporaries is evident, inter alia, from the letter by Bürger to Boie already referred to: "Frei! Frei! Keinem untertan als der Natur . . . etc."

[23] A 4, 125: "Und was will sich unser Jahrhundert unterstehen von Natur zu urteilen." Cf. also "Von deutscher Baukunst," A 13, 25: "und unser aevum?"

[24] Cf. Herder, 377: "So viele blinde Werkzeuge . . . die alle im Wahne des Freien handeln."

[25] Compare A 4, 593: "Es wird! etc." and 717: "Jeder würde das Seinige erhalten . . . etc."

[26] As it is when Brother Martin kisses it in act one (650). Götz himself eventually spells it out: "Sie haben mich nach und nach verstümmelt . . . etc." (751).

[27] Cf. Edward Mc Innes, "Moral, Politik und Geschichte in Goethes Götz von Berlichingen, " *Zeitschrift für deutsche Philologie* 103 (1984), Sonderheft, 15.

[28] Peter Michelsen, "Goethes 'Götz': Geschichte dramatisiert?" in *Goethe-Jahrbuch* 110 (1993), 46–47: "Götz als 'der Letzte' steht im Zeichen einer Degeneration der Menschheit."

[29] Cf. Michelsen's account (52–53) of the interpretation in Hegel's *Ästhetik*. As Michelsen points out, Hegel's proofs come from outside the text: "für das Stück trifft das nicht zu."

[30] A 4, 743: "O Kayser! Kayser! Räuber beschützen deine Kinder . . . Die wilden Kerls, starr und treu."

[31] Cf. NGS, 170–74.

[32] "Von dem Faustrecht," 1770.

[33] Cf. NGS, 165.

[34] See H. Fischer-Lamberg, ed., *Der junge Goethe,* vol. 3 (Berlin: de Gruyter, 1963), 28.

[35] J. M. R. Lenz, *Werke und Briefe,* vol. 2, ed. S. Damm (Leipzig: 1987) 639–40.

[36] E.g. A 4, 717: "Wollte Gott, es gäbe keine unruhige Köpfe in ganz Deutschland . . ."

[37] For Moser and Goethe, see D. W. Schuhmann, "Goethe and Friedrich Carl von Moser. A Contribution to the Study of Götz von Berlichingen," *Journal of English and Germanic Philology* liii (1954): 1–22. The sixteenth-century empire, says Gundolf, was close enough to the state of that of the eighteenth to relate easily to current conditions ("nah genug um alle gegenwärtigen Verhältnisse des Heiligen Römischen Reichs zu bestimmen"). F. Gundolf, *Goethe,* 2nd ed. (Berlin, 1925), 123).

[38] Cf. also NGS, 182, note 30.

[39] 716: "Wenn die (that is, die Freiheit) uns überlebt können wir ruhig sterben."

[40] Compare Christ's words to the disciples in Gethsemane (Matthew 26: 45) and his acceptance of God's will (verse 39).

[41] John 19: 26–27.

[42] McInnes 17.

[43] Cf. *Auch eine Philosophie,* 287.

[44] See Fischer-Lamberg 332–33 and notes, *passim.*

[45] For example the Coronation (605), the threat from the Turks (for example, 684), the "Reichstag" (661), the practice of "Visitation" (692–93), the situation of the "freyer Ritter" (660), Lerse's situation as "Reuters Knecht" (702).

[46] For audience-involvement, cf. NGS, 172, 174.

[47] In terms of "plot," we are being told that ammunition is running low.

[48] Benno von Wiese, for whom history in this play is a "foil" and a source of "nourishment" for the taste for "Drama als Guckkasten" derived from Shakespeare, sees the play as essentially a "psychologisches Charakterdrama" (*Die deutsche Tragödie von Lessing bis Hebbel,* DTV edition, [Munich: Deutscher Taschenbuch Verlag, 1983], 56–57).

[49] He is described as "interessant" by Adelheid's "Kammerfräulein" (679) on the basis of the "halb trauriger Zug" in his features: the outer sign of his inner complexity and disunity.

[50] McInnes 5.

[51] Cf. A 4, 124: "Wer eigentlich drauf gekommen ist . . . etc."

[52] Described as "Haupt- und Staatsaktionen" by Richard Newald in *Geschichte der deutschen Literatur* vol. 5, 4th edition (Munich, 1963), 364.

[53] A 5, 15.

[54] August Strindberg, *Open letters to the Intimate Theatre,* trans. and ed. W. Johnson (Seattle-London, n.d.) 47.

[55] Schubart, *Deutsche Chronik* (1774; reprint: Heidelberg: Schneider, 1975), 91. Schubart is repeating the complaint common among "Stürmer und Dränger" and indeed many "Aufklärer" against the influence of "Französismus."

[56] A 4, 717–18.

[57] 743: "Es kommen die Zeiten des Betrugs."

[58] In particular, of course, in the "Saal" scene in act III (715–17). Cf. also 654, 660, 662, 726 and (with bitter irony), 743: Götz: "O Kayser! Kayser! Räuber beschützen deine Kinder."

[59] Von Moser does not deceive himself as to the serious weaknesses engendered by "unsere Trennungen," but still maintains that the Germans are "Ein Volk, von Einem Namen, unter Einem gemeinsamen Oberhaupt" (*Von dem Nationalgeist*).

[60] An image from the original version (A 4, 593) which survives only in a truncated form in the "Schauspiel" (715).

[61] A. W. Schlegel, in the lectures eventually published as *Geschichte der klassischen Literatur,* sees him as ". . . der Wiederhersteller der Poesie in Deutschland" (A. W. S., *Kritische Schriften und Briefe,* ed. E. Lohner, vol. III [Stuttgart: Kohlhammer, 1964], 84).

[62] A. W. Schlegel, *Klassische Literatur,* 59. Cf. Friedrich Schlegel: "Die neue Religion soll ganz Magie sein. Das Christentum ist zu politisch und seine Politik ist zu materiell" (letter to Novalis, 2 December 1798).

[63] Cf. "Sehnsucht nach dem Tode," stanzas 3–6.

[64] See Novalis, *Schriften* (ed. P. Kluckhohn and R. Samuel), 2nd edition, ed. H. Ritter and G. Schulz, vol. 1 (Stuttgart: Kohlhammer, 1960), 355.

[65] *Vorlesungen über dramatische Kunst und Literatur, Kritische Schriften und Briefe* vol. V, Stuttgart 1966, 25.

[66] 53. For a good brief account of Romantic national and historical thinking, cf. Paul Kluckhohn, *Das Ideengut der deutschen Romantik* (Tübingen: Niemeyer, 1966) chapters V and VI. For the younger Friedrich Schlegel, see E. Behrens, *Friedrich Schlegels Geschichtsphilosophie (1794–1808)* (Tübingen: Niemeyer, 1984).

[67] Roger Paulin, *Ludwig Tieck. A Literary Biography*, 144. For Boehme, see 141–42.

[68] Cf. Tieck, *Schriften*, vol. 1 (Berlin, 1828).

[69] Clemens Brentano, *Werke*, ed. F. Kemp, vol. 4 (Munich: Hanser, 1966), 527.

[70] *Brentano, Werke*, 845.

[71] Well illustrated by the attention given to him in Hoffmann's *Neueste Nachrichten von den Schicksalen des Hundes Berganza*. Acknowledged by Tieck in respect of *Octavianus* in his prefatory remarks in the *Schriften* (I, p. xxxviii).

[72] See the article "Literatur" in the journal *Europa:* drama belongs to the "exoteric" branch of poetry, which remains within the "Verhältnis des menschlichen Lebens"; the genre in which the "esoteric" can flourish is the novel (Friedrich Schlegel, *Europa*, ed. E. Behler [reprint: Darmstadt: Wissenschaftliche Buchgesellschaft, 1953], I: 55).

[73] See H. Kasack/A. Mohrhenn, eds., *Ludwig Tieck*, vol. I, (Berlin: Suhrkamp, 1943), 387. "Nature," as used here, belongs to the realm of the "esoteric": cf. F. Schlegel, *Europa*, I: 55.

[74] *Leben und Tod der heiligen Genoveva* (1800) and *Kaiser Octavianus.*

[75] *Schriften* I, p. xxviii. Roger Paulin speaks of a "total surrender to mythical imagination" in *Genoveva* (118).

[76] F. Sengle, "Klassik im deutschen Drama," *Der Deutschunterricht* 5 (1987): p. 1.

[77] F. Valjavec, *Die Entstehung der politischen Strömungen in Deutschland* (Kronenburg-Düsseldorf: Athenäum, 1978), 337.

[78] E.g. in the cult of the Golden Age of Nuremberg and of Albrecht Dürer (Wackenroder's "Ehrengedächtnis unsers ehrwürdigen Ahnherrn Albrecht Dürers"; Tieck's *Franz Sternbalds Wanderungen*).

[79] *Geist der Goethezeit* IV, 268. Fouqué's drama is treated on 259–69.

[80] "Schicksals- d.h. Todesbereitschaft . . . das großartige und echt germanische Ethos" (267).

[81] E. T. A. *Hoffmann, Fantasie- und Nachtstücke*, ed. W. Müller-Seidel (Darmstadt: Wissenschaftliche Buchgesellschaft, 1971), 137.

[82] *Vaterländische Gedichte*, no. 3: *Uhlands Gesammelte Werke*, ed. H. Fischer, vol. 1 (Stuttgart: Cotta, n.d.) 84.

[83] For example Werner von Kiburg's set-piece speech in act II of *Ernst, Herzog von Schwaben*, in which the character portrays all the "Stämme" of Germany gathered together in unity and harmony, and speaks as "ein deutscher Mann": *Gesammelte Werke* vol. II, 32–35. While he does full justice to Uhland's local patriotism, Hugo Moser also shows him as a "Vorkämpfer der politischen deutschen Einheit" in Frankfurt: cf. Hugo Moser, "Ludwig Uhland" in von Wiese, ed., *Deutsche Dichter der Romantik* (Berlin: E. Schmidt, 1969), 478–79.

[84] *Gesammelte Werke* vol. II, 72.

5: The Emergence of Austria: Franz Grillparzer

SURVIVORS OF A PREVIOUS ERA, such as Goethe, may have disapproved, and even Grillparzer, who felt a sympathy for that era as a kind of spiritual home, associated "Nationalität" with "Bestialität" in a well-known epigram. But he could never have been in any real doubt that in the political world which began to take shape in Central Europe after the demise of the Holy Roman Empire, it had become necessary, if only as a defence-mechanism, to think in national terms, with inevitable consequences for historical thinking as well. Under the force of circumstances (i.e. Frederick the Great), Austria had been "created," under Maria Theresa and Haugwitz, as a centralized administration of the Habsburg dominions;[1] now, propelled by the circumstance called Napoleon, it had to be re-created as a political nation. The publicistic activities of Hormayr and Friedrich Schlegel's lectures *Über die neuere Geschichte* are among the most prominent examples of this effort during the Napoleonic period proper. This was to be, moreover, a form of nationhood which was a constant balancing-act, somehow finding an equilibrium between apparently irreconcilable opposites. It had to be simultaneously both German and not German, and its very existence precluded the proper fulfilment for a majority of its citizens of the idea (established by Herder and the Romantics) of a "Volk" as a national entity demanding political embodiment. The Slav peoples in particular had been inspired by this idea, and it bore fruit in various nationalist movements, not least that of the Czechs, which so annoyed Grillparzer who, ironically, treated episodes of importance in Czech as well as Austrian history in both the plays we shall be discussing, *König Ottokars Glück und Ende* and *Ein Bruderzwist in Habsburg.*

Francis I could call his Habsburg Empire "Austria," but he could not call forth a Habsburg *nation* by decree. Nor could even a manipulator as supple as Metternich cancel out the French Revolution or the Romantic Movement. Grillparzer, himself no lover of liberalism or Romanticism, saw that, as his essay on Metternich amply demonstrates.[2] That the nationalities were not going to become assimilated into an essentially "German" state became clear in 1848, when Palacký, in refusing to go to the Frankfurt Parliament, declared himself not a German, but "an Austrian of Slav nationality." The Schwarzenberg administration that followed the revolution set out, and failed, to create "[ein Band] das alle Länder und Stämme der Monarchie zu einem großen Staatskörper vereinigen soll."[3]

Even before that, the problem of reconciling opposites was apparent, and it can be seen in one of the prime examples of the "vaterländisch" Austrian patriotism of the Napoleonic period, Friedrich von Hormayr's *Österreichischer Plutarch* (1807–12). This work attempts to inspire an essentially Romantic heroic national fervour, while setting strict limits to the Romantic principle of individuality: Austria is a "Völkerverein" which accommodates great individual variety, but is united by a "Gefühl fürs grosse Ganze" which should override national individualism.[4] Grillparzer was to argue in similar vein when his *Ottokar* caused a furore among the Czechs, to whom he would concede only the status of a "Volksstamm" within a "Staatsverband."[5] During the war against Napoleon, nationalistic and Romantic influences were certainly about, and not only in the circle of Caroline Pichler, to which Hormayr belonged. "Wir haben uns als Nation konstituiert"[6] declared Stadion in 1809, playing the national-patriotic card on the resumption of hostilities, and the War Manifesto was composed by Friedrich Gentz, one of a number of German Romantic importations[7] which included Adam Müller[8] and Friedrich Schlegel, who with his lectures on history, strove to use history to lay a foundation for an Austrian national consciousness and ideology.[9] The immediate dramatic fruits of these patriotic enthusiasms are to be observed in productions like Heinrich Collin's *Regulus*, aesthetically unremarkable and strictly classicistic in form, but according to Friedrich Schlegel, "durchaus national und wahrhaft vaterländisch."[10] The potential for an Austrian historical drama is there and the young Grillparzer, who also had contact with the "Pichlerkreis," produced a patriotic fragment in *Alfred der Große* (1812)[11] and, stimulated by Hormayr,[12] conceived a project for a drama from Austrian history, *Friedrich der Streitbare*, which remained on his drawing-board for some time. It was not until about 1820 that he began to devote himself definitively to the theme of King Ottokar, but even on this medieval theme, as we shall see, the long shadow of Napoleon still falls.

"Austrian" patriotism had to wrestle with numerous complexities and seeming contradictions. An Austrian national feeling was desirable, even necessary, yet because a return to all-out eighteenth-century

Enlightened Despotism in the style of Joseph II was not practicable, the empire had somehow to contain nationalist ideas (largely "German" in origin) which, in their pure form, threatened to tear it to fragments, within a pragmatic, broadly "German" unifying framework. Because (after language), history was perhaps — in the case of the Czechs, certainly[13] — the most important thread in the texture of national consciousness, a writer who dealt with the past was likely to be treading simultaneously on ground of burning contemporary political relevance. We shall begin our preliminary survey of Grillparzer's historical and political outlook by examining his attitude to the principle of "Nationalität."

The famous epigram ("Der Weg der neuern Bildung geht / Von Humanität / Durch Nationalität / Zur Bestialität": [I, 500]) was Grillparzer's immediate response to some acts of cruelty in Italy in 1849. At the same time, it accords pretty well with his general view. He recognized (while himself holding on to many of the values of the Enlightenment and eighteenth-century humanism) that the nationality-principle was endemic to the political climate of the age of liberalism. However, he associated it with something of which he had an innate horror, namely disorder,[14] and realized that it represented a threat to the development of an Austrian civilisation which was in need of refurbishment, but basically sound and which, like the proponents of the "Siebzigmillionenreich," or a left-wing publicist such as Schuselka, he felt had to be rooted in a German culture.[15] But not the culture currently prevalent in "Germany," the "kleindeutsch" version, that is, in which Prussia was dominant. "Nationalität" was the product of an un-Austrian mentality. "Der Deutsche ist von der Schule her gewohnt, mit Verachtung des gesunden Menschenverstandes sich mit Worten zu begnügen," writes Grillparzer (III, 1142) and "nationality" is one such "word." It was associated, for Grillparzer, with a kind of selfish individualism ("Eigensucht"), which was seen as a foreign, "German" trait ("Eigensucht. Deutschland gewidmet": I, 578). He poured scorn on the proponents of "Winkel-Nationalitäten" in the Austrian Empire (III, 842), above all the Czech national revivalists, whom he saw as mystically dreaming "Germans" in Slav clothing.[16] Palacký's attempt to carve out a measure of autonomy for his people (in an article of 1849) called forth an impassioned tirade ("Professor Palacký," III, 1051–52) in which that worthy man was taken to task as a silly enthusiast, a "Germanized Czech" who, like the "Reichstag" (in a poem of the same year), "fails to see the quietly busy finger of God" and to appreciate the value of the Austrian tradition: "all, woran Jahr-hunderte gebaut" (I, 325).

True Czechs, Grillparzer feels, are sensible Austrians; they know ". . . daß jahrhundertalte Verhältnisse sich nicht auf gutdeutsch durch einen täppischen Enthusiasmus über Nacht aufheben lassen." They would be more than content with a German-based civilisation, pro-vided that it was an *Austrian* one, blessed with the "Bescheidenheit, gesunder Menschenverstand und wahres Gefühl" (III, 809) which made Grillparzer unwilling to contemplate living anywhere else. He comments on Viktor von Andrian-Werburg's *Österreich und dessen Zukunft*:

> Ebenso wird dem deutschen Prinzip, und damit dem Prinzip der Ein-heit die Oberhand verschafft, wenn man die Fesseln der Bildung auf-hebt. Die deutschen Provinzen werden durch ihren Zusammenhang mit dem gebildeten Deutschland dadurch eine solche Oberhand erhalten, daß alle diese slavischen und magyarischen Bestrebungen dagegen wie Seifenblasen zerplatzen werden (III, 1036).

We shall be returning to these matters, at least briefly, when we come to consider the major historical plays, and in particular *Ottokar*. For the moment, we wish to broaden the discussion somewhat and turn to the subject of history in general.

Grillparzer's well-documented horror of Hegel, and of histori-cism, with its obsession with "operative forces," in Popper's phrase, rather than individuals,[17] is not just a simple disagreement with a spe-cific individual over the nature of history. It is a part of his "Austrian" ambivalence towards "the Germans," for whose classical culture we have seen him show such veneration. Idealist philosophy in its extreme form grated on a mind that was in part at least formed by enlightened Josephinism. In a characteristic outburst in his diary (1845) against what he saw as a new wave of religiosity, he singles out as the chief fault of "the German" that: "Die Wirklichkeit [übt] eine geringe Macht über ihn aus" (III, 1143). The ultimate explanations and great abstractions, where objective Reason takes pleasure in self-contemplation, where one can write the history not of the past, but of the future,[18] left him cold, indeed chilled to the bone.

This does not mean that Grillparzer lacked a sense of history, a "Gefühl für Geschichte, Welt und Völker," as Hugo von Hoff-mansthal called it.[19] It is precisely this feeling that makes him so critical of Palacký's attempt to alter the Austrian status quo, and of the Prussian attempt to plan a new Constitution and "give" it to the people.[20]

There could well be a certain irony in his remark that the event would be "welthistorisch" (III, 1073), that is, both epoch-making and the product of an abstraction from history by a kind of Hegelian Reason. Grillparzer, whose natural conservatism is vividly, if a little one-sidedly brought out by Peter Stern,[21] confesses that he is no great lover of constitutions, but if there must be one, he prefers one that, like the English, has evolved through time in a natural way, and is a "necessary organism"; "God's work," rather than man's. As Julius puts it in *Ein Bruderzwist in Habsburg* (line 2828): "Die Zeit hilft selbst sich mehr als man ihr hilft," and Rudolf, in the same play, surely speaks for Grillparzer when he urges the Bohemian Estates not to put their trust in their own "Menschenwerk" (line 1639). But the Germans want something ready-made ("etwas Fertiges") and so must deduce it from history (not their own, because they do not have one, in the sense of a continuous development).[22]

What is "Geschichte"? It is a projection onto the universal scale of the natural laws of human life, in which we are interlinked and driven by "passions and errors," but at the same time it is a progression in time, in which change can be discerned, with the difference that it is not a simple series of building-blocks laid end to end, a sequence of "new ages." We use our reason to make what sense we can of, and learn what we can from, history, but we cannot distil it from events for analysis in the laboratory of pure reason. It takes place in the realm of Nature, of human "Dasein," whose "law" is "immerwährender Wechsel auf den alten Grundlagen" (III, 1009).

It is true that the only real "force" of history is, for Grillparzer, "die Macht der Begebenheiten" (III, 926), but this need not necessarily lead us to deduce a kind of blank, essentially meaningless, perhaps even Büchneresque "Fatalism," such as seems to suggest itself to Ulrich Fülleborn.[23] Grillparzer is here reacting to the uncongenial notion of "die Macht der Geschichte," the idea of an abstract, objectively rational force outside Nature. There is such a thing as an historical "Zusammenhang der Ereignisse" (III, 1076), but it is the pragmatic Austrian rather than the speculating Prussian (or his Slav surrogate) who possesses the key to it. These "Begebenheiten," as the diary-entry we have quoted (from 1857) makes clear, have not just an individual, but an historical "Wirkung," one which is continuous and links past with present ([they] "wirken noch jetzt, wenn auch niemand von ihnen weiß"). This is of a piece with Grillparzer's rejection of the attempts of nineteenth-century political theorists, or revolutionaries, to create an historical discontinuity, under the illusion that they, like the historicists, possess, in their "armseliges Wissen" a "natural magic" whereas the true magic is Nature itself ("weil die Natur allerdings für uns eine Magie ist.") We can no more simply discard the old than we can prevent the change to the new from occurring, as the inevitable growth occurs. To "understand" history by replacing the "impenetrable" events with "etwas Verständliches" (III, 384) is, as we shall see in the *Bruderzwist*, to align oneself with Nature, or "God" (almost interchangeable in this play).

Before we turn to the plays, we have first to come to terms with Grillparzer's own pronouncements on historical drama.[24] It is hardly surprising that with his almost classicistic appreciation of form, and his concept of drama as an artificial present in which attention is concentrated on character and action, what Peter von Matt calls "das aktuelle räumliche Gegenüber,"[25] Grillparzer should have felt some resistance to the tendency of history to intrude its own reality into that of the dramatist, disrupting his control of "strict causality" and demanding a loosening of form which brought with it a threat of the sprawl that he condemned in Romantic writers like Tieck and Fouqué. Perhaps this influenced Grillparzer's decision not to proceed with the plan for *Friedrich der Streitbare:* the notes and sketches he made suggest that he would have found it hard to prevent "epic" sprawl, and the domination of character by fact. *Ein treuer Diener seines Herrn* could easily have developed along historical lines, but eventually remained a drama of "character."[26] In the case of *Ottokar* and the *Bruderzwist*, however, we can speak of an attempt to reconcile drama with history. Baumann is over-influenced by Grillparzer's own statements in his dismissal of historical aspects and details as "Historienmalerei."[27]

Grillparzer first came up against the "epic" problem in a serious form in his work on *Das goldene Vlies* and the result, as he informs us in his *Selbstbiographie*, was that he found himself forced into the "schlechte Form" of the trilogy.[28] Drama is "eine Gegenwart," and the audience must not be compelled (or invited) to come out of that "present" (which Grillparzer is well aware is artificial) in order to be able to understand the action. This particular subject is not strictly historical, but Grillparzer goes on, in the same discussion, to dismiss the trilogy-form, which has "etwas Episches" about it, as "extremely faulty" in the case of Schiller's *Wallenstein* as well. The issue arises once more when Grillparzer comes to discuss *Ottokar*. He wishes it to be seen as a "Trauerspiel," not a Shakespearean History. Historical drama is a form which is "durchaus nicht empfehlenswert . . . Die Form des Dramas ist die Gegenwart": a "present," that is, in the sense of "Unmittelbarkeit der Wirkung." The reflective involvement, the "Mitgeschäftigsein" of the public fatally undermines the "necessity" which is a prime requirement of tragic drama (149–50). Clearly, as he looks back (the *Selbstbiographie* was begun in 1853), Grillparzer aims to come to terms with, and if possible reconcile a dichotomy which he feels lies at the heart of his play: it is surely significant that he claims that the very "loyal," that is, pro-Habsburg ending, which he imagined would ensure a smooth passage through the censorship process, had been dictated by "die dramatische Notwendigkeit" (152). He either cannot or will not see the political sensitivity of the subject, which struck the censors immediately and eventually caused a furore among the Czechs, which Grillparzer later describes with a lack of sympathy and comprehension which recalls his remarks on Palacký (162–65).

What concerns us principally is the fact that, while he has a strong interest in history and, as we have tried to show, an awareness of its presence in national life, Grillparzer seems to wish to deny it a presence in drama based on historical material. His generally rather dismissive attitude to Shakespeare's Histories is of a piece with this.[29] Even in the diary-entry (1825: III, 304–5), written apropos of *Ottokar*, in which he describes Shakespeare as a "master" of the genre, he emphasizes how easy it is, on grounds of the law of causality, to make him appear a bungler. "What a burden he must have found it!" writes Heinrich Laube, in his introduction to the 1872 edition of the *Complete Works*, commenting on the difficulties of dramatising a political action. So why did he not simply extrapolate the "dramatic" plot from history and deal with it in the standard classicistic form, as indeed he seems to have felt that Schiller could have proceeded in the case of *Wallenstein*?[30] Like Schiller, he surely took a conscious decision to deal with the material in an at least partially historical, and therefore also partially "epic," form.

He does seem, in the diary-entry referred to, to be groping towards some explanation in the concession that there could be such a thing as a "historische Tragödie," in which a certain "Inkongruenz" is not only justifiable, but requisite because if he is to be true to history, the dramatist must show "God," or Nature, as well as the hero, at work, and in the hint that he might himself be ready to venture into this "gefährliches Feld." But however indecisive the theoretical background, it can surely not be denied that there is an historical play, though hardly an unequivocal "historical tragedy," alongside the undeniable personal tragedy in *König Ottokars Glück und Ende*.

The figure of Otakar Přemysl II, King of Bohemia, the great antagonist of the founder of the Habsburg dynasty, had already suggested itself to Hormayr, and Friedrich Schlegel, as a suitable subject for patriotic comparison and contrast, and the obvious parallel with the battle against Napoleon would have been very much in their minds and those of their readers.[31] Kotzebue, as Grillparzer reminds us in the *Selbstbiographie*, had already portrayed him as a bloodthirsty tyrant in *Rudolf von Habsburg und König Ottokar* (1815).[32] That some of these resonances should not have attached themselves to the figure in Grillparzer's thinking is unlikely and from about 1818 onwards, he himself took up the theme of the conquering-hero figure, with the possible alternative theme of Hannibal in mind. The death of Napoleon (1821) triggered a poem in which there are thoughts which find echoes in the *Hannibal*-fragment of that year, and in the great confrontation in act III of *Ottokar*, to which we shall come in due course. We should make it clear at the outset, however, that while it was inevitable that the finished product (completed in 1823, though not performed till 1826) should be in many ways "historical," Grillparzer surely conceived it, and made every effort to carry it out, as primarily a tragic drama, and that it can quite legitimately be interpreted, as it often has been, as such. Our primary evidence for this assertion is the form; we shall certainly be arguing that this is put under considerable strain by what can be called "historical" (and broadly "epic") impulses, but this is a case of a potential "History" within a drama, not the reverse.

In view of the fact that he interprets the play very much as a tragedy centred on the King of Bohemia, one is surprised to see W. E. Yates describing its form as that of a Shakespearean History.[33] In conception and — largely at least — execution, the work is surely a *Hubris*-and-*Nemesis* tragedy, with Ottokar, as Yates rightly insists, as sole "hero." We saw Grillparzer grappling in his diary, albeit in very vague terms, with the feeling that the history of the subject, in which he had immersed himself, and which clearly interested him, deeply, was pulling him away from the strict necessity and causality that he felt was the essence of tragic drama, speculating that historicality in a play would require a certain motivational "Inkongruenz," such as he saw (and often criticised) in Shakespeare, and wondering whether to dip a toe in this Herderian "ocean of events" (87). Yet his finished play shows little or no sign of a willingness to loosen the discipline of a dramatic action derived from the interaction of characters, and rely on "history" (or simply, life itself) to act as a driving-force and provide the unity of a wide range of figures and events that often have no direct connection with each other. The play has a certain expansiveness, it is true, and there are stresses and strains on the complicated web of threads which all run together in the figure of Ottokar, but the web still holds together. Even Rudolf does not have the weight to "balance" Ottokar as a *dramatic* character.[34]

However, Rudolf *does* act as a counterweight in another way, namely as the principal conduit for history. Formally, the work may be a tragedy, in which his role is the not very rewarding one, dramatically, of representing Right. Viewed in terms of its overall effect, it is a hybrid, in which the duality of history and drama or, as Grillparzer formulated it on another occasion, of history and "poetry," "Begebenheit" and "Handlung,"[35] is reflected. At one level, this is a matter of the fascination of the medieval actuality; not so much the solid material detail, which by comparison with Scott, we may say is skimped,[36] but the political reality of the feudal Empire. At another, it is the nature of history — Austrian history, for Austria is a truly historical nation — in which continuity and change are intertwined, that comes to the fore and makes Rudolf seem, when, as we can sometimes hardly avoid doing, we think historically, *more* important than Ottokar, not only in his own time, but also as a modern-day presence. His "piety," that is, his openness to the voice of God, is of course appropriate for a man of the Middle Ages, but centering, as it does, on the ideas of "Recht" and "Ruhe," it has much of Josephinian deism about it and when eventually the scales fall from his eyes (line 1910) and he undergoes a Pauline conversion, it is to a post-heroic ideal, in which "die Welt ist da, damit wir alle leben."

A truly historical effect, as we have said, depends, not on the transparency of the past to the present, but on a perception of them as discrete, but interrelated realities. There is no doubt of the solid reality of the Middle Ages in this play. The "Deutschland" whose blood "rolls in [Rudolf's] veins" (line 1787) is the Holy Roman Empire and the personalities and institutions of the time (such as Richard of Cornwall [III, 1039], the Hansa [1044] and the practice of "Fehde" [1039]) and the full panoply of thirteenth-century legalities and fiefdoms, lend a dense medieval — that is, explicitly non-contemporary — texture to the whole. That the clash between Rudolf and Ottokar could be seen as exemplary history, with a clear modern applicability, had been established by Friedrich Schlegel in his lectures *Über die neuere Geschichte:* the "good" Habsburg Emperor is confronted by a Napoleonic antagonist: ". . . ein Schauspiel, wie die Geschichte nur wenige darbietet. Auf der einen Seite Tapferkeit, mit Milde und Weisheit gepaart, auf der andern Seite Heldenmut, aber ein stürmischer, herrschsüchtiger, leidenschaftlich grausamer, von Stolz verblendeter."[37] But Grillparzer does not wish to abstract from history into allegory. Bohemia, though raised at the end of the twelfth century to the dignity of a Kingdom which could choose its own ruler, is still a fiefdom, which has to be bestowed on Ottokar. We can no more simply abstract from him to Napoleon than we can from Rudolf to the Emperor Francis.

At the same time, to qualify for admission to our present discussion, the past must reach into the present. The question of the old Kingdom of Bohemia, and its "freedoms" (an issue to which we shall return in more detail in dealing with the *Bruderzwist*) was "dead history" for Grillparzer at this time, hence his scornful surprise and anger when the Czech nationalists (who could well have seen in it that "insulting" assumption of "German" superiority) took offence at the play.[38] The question of "Austria" (inclusive of the Napoleon-theme) was, however, a different matter and certainly no "loyal" afterthought. It is the most likely reason for some, at least, of the manifestations of a relative "epic" looseness in the play's formal fabric, especially in the Third Act. The introduction of Ottokar von Horneck (I, 1036–37) is the most blatant example. Yates calls it "dispensable":[39] in terms of dramatic composition, it is worse than that, for it drives a wedge through the "Gegenwart" of the dramatic action. But when we recall that it is essentially over "Österreich," an entity which exists, at the moment, as much in the mind as on the ground, that Rudolf and Ottokar are fighting — and it is striking how often the word itself occurs in this play — and that this is still a burning issue in the nineteenth century, then one might almost call it historically "indispensable." The case of the elder Merenberg is more subtle, but an extended account of his arrest can hardly be said to be dramatically necessary, whereas it furthers the Austrian theme, in particular in the opening speech, in which Merenberg identifies himself, first as "German" (line 1025: "der Deutschen äußerste"), then as an "Österreicher" (line 1357). More important still, Merenberg points us, in his prayer to God, to the future, and thus prepares the ground for the vision of the culminating lines of act V. The ideal Austria is associated with the God-given vision expounded by Rudolf (lines 1910–28): the true emperor will preside over a community of peoples living harmoniously together in peace and order, rather than asserting and imposing his "heroic" imperial will. A new age is replacing that of "der Gewaltgen Zeit."

Once again, we catch Napoleonic echoes, and while we know that Grillparzer was not completely enamoured of the un-heroic Metternichian Austria in which "die Welt [hat] nichts mit Großem mehr zu schaffen (cf. the poem "Napoleon," I, 145), we know too that he was even less so of the self-assertive "leader"-figure. The most important thing for us here is that Rudolf is opening a window of historical time within the dramatic "Gegenwart"; inviting us to consider a future Austria which is a potential, and historically "necessary" entity, and needs to be "created," in accordance with "God's will," so that Right and Order may prevail.

These are thoughts of peace in time of war, the reverse of the situation of the audience, for whom the "present" of the drama is a past, albeit with a present resonance. The "actual" Austria of the play is the war-torn chaos which has existed since the extinction of the Babenbergs, and is invoked as early as the second scene of act I, in which Margarethe, in lines of historical exposition which are but sketchily motivated dramatically ("Ich habe diese Krone nicht gesucht") describes how Magyars, Bavarians and Czechs "[hausten] mit dem Schwert in Österreich" (line 297). Here again, we see an historical rationale behind a speech which dramatically, looks like an unnecessary digression, and is indeed formally set apart as a visionary moment with biblical overtones. Margarethe is taken up to a Pisgah, a high place (line 319), rather as Rudolf is by God (lines 1904–6), and shown a panoramic, and not entirely realistic, "picture" of Austria. We do not, of course, need to prove authorial intention in order to posit an effect, but it is hard to imagine that there is no symbolic, or historical intention on Grillparzer's part, especially when we take into account the play's expression, not only of his interest in history, but of his historical vision, which comes down in great measure to the role of God in history, or perhaps one could even say, God *as* history.

This is neither the medieval/Baroque idea of *providentia*, nor some kind of Hegelian teleology. History is for Grillparzer, to repeat, "what happens": the "Begebenheiten," in the pattern which the human mind ("Verstand") gives them in order to make sense of the world, a pattern basically of the interaction of old and new, a constant movement conditioned by continuity and change. This is the natural order of things and for Grillparzer, the child of the Josephinian Enlightenment, the word "God" stands for the inner principle of that order. Even in the medieval context of the action, where the concept is, inevitably, clothed to some extent in the vestments of the church, its essentially non-religious function is discernible. That Rudolf stands on "God's side" is made apparent in act one (the Ambassador's speech, 1001–2), and it is also the side of "Right" (shown in his support for Margarethe). In the first of his two great speeches in act three (I, 1039–40), God — or the natural and necessary course of history — is said to be on *his* side. There is even talk of "miracles" (lines 1796–97), but it is not a supernatural power that draws men to him and away from Ottokar, but his adherence to the principles of "Ruh und Recht," enunciated at the beginning and end of the speech. There is already here a recognition that while the continuity of the old is being asserted in Rudolf's demand for "Recht," for the "return" of Austria to the Empire, one cannot but think that something new (in the thirteenth-century context) is being asserted in the call for "Ruhe," something that, in the nineteenth century, needs to be re-asserted vis-à-vis the challenge of Napoleon. The old argument of "Fehde" (the legitimate quarrel), which is adduced by Ottokar (and which still had some validity for Goethe's Götz von Berlichingen), is swept aside: "Hier aber gilts nicht Fehde; Ruhe, Herr!" (I, 1039). After he has demonstrated that Ottokar has lost the battle, Rudolf launches into a second speech, in which he attempts to win over his antagonist with what is certainly a moral, but also an historical argument. Ottokar is urged to discern "God's hand" (line 1891) and His "holy will" (1892) in the course of events and this is not simply a matter of the victory of right over wrong. Rudolf is in tune, not with a heavenly, but an earthly "world to come," a post-heroic age in which the Right of Conquest no longer applies. Mankind stands "am Eingang einer neuen Zeit" (lines 1914–20).

Ottokar, the tragic hero, experiences a moral, but not an historical enlightenment in the final act (lines 2825–74). It is true that he now recognizes the supremacy of the "Herr der Welten" (line 2832), whose name he takes into his mouth in the first act only in order to take it in vain, but whether he accepts that this "Lord of the Worlds" has decided for Rudolf and against him politically as well as morally (compare Rudolf's use of the phrase, line 1793) is by no means clear. He certainly does not abandon the fight and having lived by the sword, dies by it as well, "with harness on his back." The personal tragedy, the part that reminds us of *Macbeth*, has re-asserted itself, but the dual nature of the work also asserts itself in the duality of its ending. Grillparzer does not finish on the "natural" (personal) tragic ending (line 2967), but adds a festive and prophetic conclusion, showing the triumphal foundation of the Habsburg dynasty and opening a vista into the future (the audience's present), with an ironic echo of the ending of the first act (where it is Ottokar who is hailed as ruler of Austria and German Emperor). Even though Ottokar is not alive to experience this, it can still be called in some measure a "tragic" irony in the "closed" context of a dramatic action. The spectator (in the time of the drama) feels it for him. At the same time, that same spectator has to call on his historical consciousness as a nineteenth-century observer, to experience it to the full. And in that context, the personal questions; responsibility, guilt and so forth, bulk less large than others which take us beyond the tighter and narrower network of causality which lies at the root of strict "tragic necessity." Aesthetically, the "epic" problem re-emerges here, and we would need to re-define the word "tragic" (as seems to be implied in some of Grillparzer's own pronouncements, especially in connection with Shakespeare), in order to speak with confidence of a truly "historical tragedy." The *Bruderzwist* takes us a few steps closer to such a form.

Ein Bruderzwist in Habsburg (begun in the mid-1820s, but not completed until early in 1848) ends, notoriously and famously, with Mathias's cry "Mea maxima culpa," ironically complemented by a "Vivat Mathias" from the street outside. It is useful to begin by asking whether, and if so in what sense, this is a "tragic" guilt, and the *Bruderzwist*, as, among others, Bruce Thompson says it is, an "historical tragedy."[40] That there is responsibility, even guilt in history, and that the Thirty Years' War, in whose shadow, thanks to the historical awareness of the audience, the whole action lies, can legitimately be described as a "tragedy" for "the whole Empire,"[41] may be conceded. But is that kind of tragedy, and that kind of guilt, truly dramatic — that is, the guilt which ties the tragic "hero" to the tragic catastrophe in what is at least the aesthetic equivalent of a causal link?

Grillparzer himself raises the question of responsibility and guilt on a number of occasions, in connection with both action and inaction. In the conversation between Thurn and Schlick in act IV (II, 425–26), the former enunciates a view which we might call historically, rather than dramatically tragic. One may have a specific, perfectly moral *individual* purpose in setting a course of events in train, but that process ("die Tat") is like a runaway horse, and if it produces results that were not desired, then: ". . . kein Trost von Zweck und Absicht, All was geschehn das hast du auch gewollt" (lines 2223–24). The guilt of inaction lies, of course, ultimately, or at least principally, with Rudolf. His aim, he says to his Chamberlain, Wolfgang Rumpf, has been to maintain the "Zünglein an der Wage" (line 1421) in equilibrium. Now, he feels himself forced to act, and fears the worst;

the breakdown of order, and civil war. He rejects one kind of guilt, but accepts another:

> Leiht mir nicht eure Schuld; wenns etwa Schuld nicht,
> Daß ich vertraut, ein schwacher Sterblicher, kein Gott. (1426–27)

History (what "happens") belongs to God (it is "deines Reichs": line 1464)[42] and beyond human control. Within the limits of his own "Amt" (1467), he admits to a mistake, and thus, to responsibility, in having trusted various people to act in a certain way. There is an implication that guilt is diffused over a wide range of "villains," to use Thompson's term;[43] not only Klesel and Mathias, in this instance, but even Rumpf, who failed to inform his master that "the house was burning" (1417) must bear some responsibility. A diffused guilt is not a dramatic guilt, in the sense in which we have seen Grillparzer speak of dramatic causality. He himself, in his Testament of 1848, demanded that this play, and *Libussa*, neither of which he published, should be destroyed as "leblose und ungenügende Skizzen."[44] No doubt, his own depressed state contributed to this decision, but it is possible that the pure dramatist in him felt that in both, the general, perhaps even quasi-religious, aspects outweighed the personal to too great an extent, and that in their different ways, both plays were more "historical" than he would have wished. That is pure conjecture; what can be asserted is that we have here a work — and a very successful one, in spite of its author's misgivings — which is as nearly historical, perhaps even as nearly Shakespearean, as is possible within the limits of Grillparzer's aesthetic *credo*.

The form of the play reflects this diffuseness. It has not entirely renounced the basis of dramatic unity, namely the inter-relation of all who participate and all that happens through the network of an integral action focussing on a centre (in this case, Rudolf), but it has slackened the tension of that network very considerably. Cäsar, for example, is Rudolf's natural son, but he engages our interest more as "der freche Sohn der Zeit" (line 1345) than in the somewhat contrived relationship with Prokop's daughter who, with a touch of self-conscious classicistic symbolism, is named Lukrezia. The formal "hero" does not appear in act II, which is set in Mathias's camp, and in which we seem to feel the wind of history, or "events," or "God's will," blowing the characters hither and thither as the Greeks and Trojans are blown in the *Iliad*. Nor is he present in act V, in which his death is reported, and under the nominal "control" of Mathias, events take their course and civil war draws inexorably closer. The time-scale has certainly been radically compressed,[45] but interestingly enough, the most striking of these adjustments to time, the premature involvement of Ferdinand with Wallenstein, while "unhistorical" as fact, has a powerful historical effect by conjuring up, as nothing else could, the image of the Thirty Years' War, and that not only as the "voice from the crowd" which predicts its exact duration (line 2849).

Ironically, the Wallenstein of the play, who stimulates our historical consciousness, seems to lack any sense of history himself. He is completely what Ottokar is with only partial success, and Mathias, with his "leeres Heldenspiel" (2313) only dreams of being: the man of "Gewalt" rather than "Gewissen" (cf. lines 2731–36), single-mindedly intent on imposing his "own" will, and taking no account of "fremde Meinung oder Tadel" (line 2734). He has the quality which Rudolf, in whom that sense is especially keen, ascribes, perhaps unfairly, to mankind as a whole: he "lebt nur im Augenblick" (line 2302). When he says "Die Zeit entscheidet" (2757), he is referring to the compulsion of the present moment. He is naturally attracted to Ferdinand, who, like him, believes in the principle of a single will ("ein Wollen" [2736]) in government and whose drastic solution to the problem of Protestantism has so frightened and horrified Rudolf (cf. II, 363–64).

Insistence on one's "own" will and convictions ("Eigendünkel," "Eigensucht," "Selbstsucht"), whether in the mind of the reactionary, or the reformer, appears time and again as the direct antithesis of the way of "God" (which could be paraphrased for this play as the true path of "Nature" in this world). We are dealing with existence in the here and now: The motto Rudolf has devised for his "Friedensritter," "Nicht ich, nur Gott" (line 1221) is a way of saying that man should try, not to "make" history, but to flow with it. It is in achieving the stillness (not lifelessness) of Nature (star, stone, plant, animal, and tree), which symbolizes mastery over "den eignen Willen," that perception of truth and the basis of right action lies (II, 362: lines 411–17).[46] The spirit which animates the Bohemians who extract from him his agreement to the Letter of Majesty, Rudolf sees as the anti-historical spirit of "Eigennutz" (1717);[47] even their religious convictions derive from self-assertion, "Menschenwerk"(1641).

For the innate conservatism of Rudolf's position, which one cannot but think is also Grillparzer's, even though he certainly cannot be said to endorse all that the emperor says or does, is not a denial of history. Rudolf himself is living in history; he may have an insight into the "Ganzes," the "All" which represents a transcendent truth and "order," but he is not, like Libussa, a part of "das Hohe" which, as Kascha says, has departed from the earth with her (*Libussa*, line 2512; II, 343). The "eternal stars" afford him a presentiment of an "order" which in an ideal form, can be said to dwell "dort oben" (line 428), and towards which he, as "ein schwacher, unbegabter Mann" (421), feels a humble reverence. He is not a seer from a higher dimension revealing eternal religious truths, but a mere man trying to live in harmony with the true spirit of Nature and of history. The "All" with which he believes the house of Habsburg to be in harmony (line 1282) is in essence that of the continuity of history, the line through which the past is part of the present, and the present part of the future. Addressing the Bohemian delegates, he uses the eminently "historical" metaphor of the bridge:

> . . . Ist doch der Glaube
> Nur das Gefühl der Eintracht mit dir selbst,
> Das Zeugnis, daß du Mensch nach beiden Seiten:
> Als einzel schwach, und stark als Teil des All.
> Daß deine Väter glaubten, was du selbst,
> Das ist die Brücke, die aus Menschenherzen
> Den unerforschten Abgrund überbaut . . .
> Und deine Kinder treten künftig gleiche Pfade,
>
> Ist eure Satzung wahr, wird sie bestehn . . . (II, 405)

It is not their "Menschenwerk," their own individual "improving" (line 1640) of what now exists that will decide the issue of change, but the "truth" which lies in the natural order and historical process and which works through peaceable, rather than forcible means. Grillparzer uses the analogy of a tree weighed down by a stone which, in its traditional emblematic application, signifies that virtue is advanced by adversity ("crescit sub pondere virtus"): he, no doubt, is thinking of a dualism of progression and retardation.

However, change there must be; the old time must give way to the new. Rudolf, as he is generally closer than the others to the law of Nature, is also closer to the workings of the historical process, which is itself continuous and unending. The fact that "das Alte scheidet und das Neue wird" is in itself "stets dasselbe" (2273–74). The majority of men are unaware of this process, as they are of the continuity and flux of Time, but Rudolf has recognized, one assumes even before the play begins, the new age, "die Zeit, die wildverworrne, neue" (line 321) which thrusts its way into his solitude in the figure of its "pupil," his son Cäsar. Here we cross from the realm of the timeless, from the philosophy of history, in which Rudolf is a character with a wisdom and awareness that transcends his own present, to that of "events," of practical reality, where men make decisions and decide outcomes, and where he is simply the historical Rudolf II of Habsburg, the head of the Holy Roman Empire in the early seventeenth century.

In an historical drama, as we have more than once had occasion to reiterate, the history must be real and the old, old. Obviously, Rudolf's thinking informs, and is expressed in connection with his behaviour as a dramatic character, and in this, he is to a great extent a vehicle for Grillparzer's own thinking which, as we shall see, is directed as much towards the nineteenth-century present as the past. But he is also given a very solid existence as the real early seventeenth-century figure, with his Spanish background, and his fascination with the "wonders" purveyed by such as John Dee (line 1324), "The Queen's [i.e. Elizabeth I's] Conjuror," a "dunkler Ehrenmann," like Faust's father,[48] whose presence has distracted Rudolf from pressing business such as the recrudescence of Hussitism among the Bohemians and the activities of Mathias and Klesel (cf. II, 395–98). Dee was, among other things, an astrologer, and this is perhaps the most revealing of all the aspects of the seventeenth-century reality presented, from the point of view of Grillparzer's method of communicating this action as "history," in which "die Zeit" (a word which occurs in this play with a frequency which must in itself stimulate historical consciousness), includes present, past and future dimensions.

As we saw in the case of Schiller's *Wallenstein*, so here, the dramatist has tempered superstition with a more "modern" cast of thought. One of the key speeches on the subject (II, 361–62) arises out of the question of Rudolf's "belief" in the stars. Ferdinand, the strongly orthodox Catholic, has dismissed astrology as "finster," and "Schein," which presents an opportunity for Rudolf to leap to his own defence, expounding the doctrine of "God and Nature," with which we are clearly meant to have at least a measure of sympathy. Yet both are "right" to a degree. As modern observers, Grillparzer and his audience, like Schiller and his, would have agreed with Ferdinand, and we have seen how reluctant Schiller was to include, in the interests of historical authenticity, material which could undermine the tragic dignity of the work and how, in the process of smoothing away its "barbaric" edges, he robbed it of much of its historical force. Grillparzer does not have such aesthetic qualms, and has his hero withdraw into a world of mystery and mystification, bringing the speech to an end in a gradually thickening fog of incoherence, and finally, total silence (lines 434–39). This is not the past raised (as in Schiller) to a symbolic level at which we can almost forget that it *is* past, but the very seventeenth-century world of unenlightened thinking and religious dispute which gave birth to the Thirty Years' War, the true catastrophe of the play as "historical tragedy" which, though it is here merely a cloud on the horizon, has a more real presence in this play than it does in Schiller's work. The conditions of the year 1848, replete with the threat of "Bürgerkrieg" (a not infrequent motif in this play, as in Schiller's), cannot but have played a part in sharpening its impact.

The notion of time, in particular in the form of "the [changing and labyrinthine] times"[49] is a very real presence in this play, a factor which must surely help to loosen the grip of the dramatic present on the spectator's mind and make it more predisposed to see and follow connections outside it, if the dramatist is minded so to direct its attention. And Grillparzer is so inclined, more so indeed than in *Ottokar*. One aspect in which this is apparent is the way in which the prophetic spirit appears, voluntarily or involuntarily, in the words of the characters, and points toward a future, which, for the audience, is either the past (the Thirty Years' War), or its own present (the imminent danger of revolutionary upheaval in, perhaps even the disintegration of, the Austria of the 1840s). This interplay of present and future begins even before Rudolf appears, when Klesel refers to Ferdinand as "the future emperor" (line 180). His aim, as a character within the dramatic action, is of course to spur Mathias on to forestall such an eventuality, but by a neat historical irony, our knowledge of what actually happened after 1618 — that is, of the *historical* Ferdinand — is also activated. Ferdinand remains, throughout the play, the "künftiger Kaiser," and the spectre of the coming civil war haunts the text. In a sense, the event which is yet to come is more important than any which actually occurs in the play. When Rudolf speaks of "Bürgerkrieg" in act III (line 1675), he is thinking, of course, of his resolve to avoid a war — a civil war within the "noble house" of Habsburg! — with Mathias, but while the lapse in that resolve which in fact brings about his ruin is crucial for the individual, more narrowly "dramatic" tragedy (which is effectively ended in act IV), nothing he could have done would have averted the eventual lethal "Bürgerkrieg." He can know nothing of this, but we know, and our knowledge, thanks to this reference, is projected back into the action of the historical tragedy. This constitutes the "true tragedy,"[50] but if

that is in a sense the case, it is only because we are enabled, nay encouraged to think historically, and the more explicit prophetic visions
of the War placed in the mouth of Rudolf (lines 2254–64) and then,
as the mantle passes in act V, of Klesel (2664–67, 2695–700), continue and strengthen this tendency. The last-mentioned reference, indeed leads directly to the appearance of Wallenstein as man of action
and military "hero," and the report of the Defenestration of Prague.

The trigger for the Thirty Years' War was, of course, conflict between Catholic and Protestant, with Bohemian Protestantism playing
a particularly prominent role in the early stages. This conflict is faith-
fully chronicled, and Grillparzer makes particularly effective use of the
Letter of Majesty in act III. This document is both the crystallisation
in specific, concrete form of the real historical conflict, and, like the
goblet in *Die Piccolomini*, a symbolic object. Grillparzer endows it
with symbolic force through the image of the "wild verzehrend
Feuer" that Rudolf can feel emanating from it, and while the religious
issues are not lost in the discussion, the main emphasis lies on the political, in a way eminently conducive to reflections about the state of
Austria in the *Vormärz*, threatened by liberalism and nationalism.
What bothers Rudolf most in the Protestant campaign for an officially
recognized freedom of belief is the threat to God-given, natural order,
the spirit of self-oriented "Aufruhr" (line 1190), which seeks its own
"rights" while disregarding the safety and stability of the whole, with
which he feels the document, and those who press it on him, are im-
bued. At a time when there was a very vocal "Young Austrian" opposition, when Viktor von Andrian-Werburg (writing earlier in the
1840s) senses the "imminente(r) Notwendigkeit einer durchgreifen-
den Systemsänderung" and from the safety of exile, a radical like Josef
Tuvora speaks of "action" rather than evolution,[51] the contemporary
relevance to its own present of the political reflections contained here,
and elsewhere in the play, must have struck, and been intended to
strike, the audience.

It was in Bohemia that the Thirty Years' War began, as a Bohemian rebellion against Habsburg authority. The national tensions
between Czechs and Germans which had in the fifteenth century been
a contributory factor to the Hussite uprising were certainly less severe
at this time,[52] but had become acute again in the nineteenth century.
Grillparzer had had a taste of them in the aftermath of *Ottokar* and in
the 1840s, the Czechs, together with the Magyars, could be seen as
representing a serious threat to Austria's political unity, the principal
instrument of whose preservation was the Habsburg dynasty. The fact

that the word "Österreich" is less prominent here than in *Ottokar*, and that the play focuses, from the title onward, on the role of the dynasty, does not mean that the Austrian theme is any less important, but perhaps reflects the fact that here, it is not the creation, but the preservation of Austria that is at issue. Both the seventeenth- and the nineteenth-century situations resonate in the *Bruderzwist*. Hussite echoes are more prominent than in the earlier play. "Der Huß ist tot, doch neu regt sich sein Glaube," warns Julius (line 1314) and this fact is closely linked to the spirit of "Aufruhr" (1331). In Act III, when Rudolf is being alerted to the dangers that surround him, we learn (1434) that Mathias has gone to Tabor, a name forever associated with rebellious Hussitism, and Prokop, Lukrezia's father, rejects the simple designation "Protestant" and declares himself an Utraquist (1360).[53] Rudolf's bitter reply, "Warum des böhmischen [Glaubens] und nicht des deutschen?" has a political, as well as a religious significance, and by going on to link religious division with war and death, he implicitly expresses his view of the historical role of his dynasty.

"Maximilians unweise Söhne" (line 124): thus Klesel, a less than pleasant character, but the shrewdest politician in the play, characterizes the three representatives of the House of Habsburg that we meet in the *Bruderzwist*. Rudolf sees that the best hope of avoiding disaster lies in the avoidance of any action that might trigger an explosion, but this does not mean complete inaction, and he fails to act in time, and then acts when it is too late. This results in the accession of Mathias, the bungling would-be "hero," who is utterly incapable of handling the problems he has inherited and helped to create, who is superseded, even before his death (in the year following the end of the play) by Ferdinand II, the man of conviction and "Gewalt," who knows exactly what must be done and will use whatever force is necessary to get it done. The end-product, as we know, will be a savage civil war lasting thirty years. It is hardly an impressive record, and Rudolf himself, who is given a theoretical political wisdom, even if Grillparzer does not cleanse him entirely of the "politically ineffectual" character as a ruler, in the words of R. A. Kann,[54] of the factual historical figure, admits as much. Speaking of himself as well as the Archdukes Maximilian and Ferdinand, who agreed to place power in Mathias's hands, he concedes: "Wir habens gut gemeint, doch kam es übel" (line 2287) and what follows, if it falls short of radical criticism, is at least an admission of responsibility. Only Mathias, he goes on, deserves outright condemnation, since he alone acted out of "Selbstsucht"; yet that same Mathias must now enjoy undiluted power, since only in that way can the Habsburg dynasty, which "unites all the parts into a whole" (2324), continue in existence to fulfil — eventually — its mission. As emperor, he has been "das Band, das diese Garbe hält" (1163), now Mathias must take over that task. The "Königtum" is much more powerful than the inadequate individual; it needs the latter, of course, in order to exist, but it can remain untainted by those inadequacies. We cannot believe that Rudolf thinks Mathias capable of solving the problems facing him, but the binding authority of the dynasty will be even more necessary after whatever disaster is impending, has occurred.

The Habsburg theme, then, combines present, past and future. Its (idealized) spiritual foundation is harmony with the "Geist des All" (1282), which is also the spirit of the natural historical process: it neither anticipates, nor accompanies "the new" (1281), but imitates "Den Gang der ewigen Natur" (1284). For that reason, Rudolf says to Julius, in another of the play's prophetic moments: "Mein Haus wird bleiben immerdar" (1279). Julius has just urged him to take account of the needs of the individual, present moment, and our first reaction, not by any means unjustified, is to censure Rudolf for dodging the issue by switching categories and temporal dimensions to talk of the universal and eternal. But it is precisely this duality of dimensions which makes the Habsburg theme so eminently historical, as the theme of kingship in Shakespeare's Histories is historical. An analysis of what happened (in the seventeenth century) can by this means stand alongside reflection on what is happening or may happen in the nineteenth, and on the imperative requirement, among all this disorder, for a core around which order can crystallize and survive. The often acknowledged fact that the *Bruderzwist* is, as Thompson says, "one of Grillparzer's least dramatic plays"[55] is a defect only if we see it as an intended *dramatic* tragedy. It is certainly more dramatic in form than a Shakespearean "History": it presents a group of convincing characters in action and interaction, but if there is a personal tragedy, it is a subordinate part of an historical one. The absorbing interest lies in this case in the fact that history is not a vehicle for the characters, but they a vehicle for history.

Notes

[1] Ernst Wangermann, *The Austrian Achievement. 1701–1800* (London: Thames and Hudson, 1973), 15. The mercantilist Hörnigk had already pointed out, in 1684, that there was an "Austria" that could be considered as "eine kleine Welt in sich selbst" (cf. P. W. von Hörnigk, *Oesterreich über alles, wenn es nur will,* ed. G. Otruba [Vienna: Bergland, 1964], 51–52).

[2] "Fürst Metternich" (1839) in Grillparzer, *Sämtliche Werke,* ed. P. Frank and K. Pörnbacher, vol. III (Munich: Hanser, 1964), 1022–34. In a separate entry (1839–40), Metternich is called the "Don Quixote der Legitimität in Europa" (1035). Unless otherwise stated, Grillparzer is cited from this edition, identified by volume and page number.

[3] Quoted in Rudolf Kiszling, *Fürst Felix von Schwarzenberg. Der politische Lehrmeister Kaiser Franz Josephs* (Graz-Cologne: Hermann Böhlaus Nachf, 1952), 52.

[4] Cf. K. Adel, *Josef Friedrich von Hormayr und die vaterländische Romantik in Österreich* (Vienna: Bergland, 1974), 72–73.

[5] "Selbstbiographie" in Grillparzer, *Ausgewählte Werke,* ed. O. Rommel, vol. X, (Vienna-Teschen-Leipzig: n.d.), 164. For Schlegel, Austria represents the idea "eines freien und friedlichen europäischen Staaten-und Völker-vereins" (*Über die neuere Geschichte,* 261).

[6] Quoted from Ernst Joseph Görlich, *Grundzüge der Geschichte der Habsburgermonarchie und Österreichs* (Darmstadt: Wissenschaftliche Buchgesellschaft, 1970), 181.

[7] It was Gentz, the "deutscher Pedant" who, according to Grillparzer, infused the idea of system into the "mousseux" of Metternich's thinking.

[8] E.g. his *Elemente der Staatskunst* (1810).

[9] Friedrich Schlegel, *Über die neuere Geschichte* (1810–11). Gentz praised the "Austrian spirit" of these lectures (see Schlegel, *Werke. Kritische Ausgabe* ed. E. Beher (KA), vol. 7 [Munich-Paderborn-Vienna: Schönigh, 1966], lxxxviii). Hormayr's *Plutarch* was hailed by Schlegel as a "Nationalwerk" (121). For Hormayr's relation to the drama, see further Sengle 88.

[10] See Sengle 86.

[11] This was an "historical drama" of the type in which the audience were invited to recognize contemporary figures in a nominally "past" action (Alfred was in fact the Archduke Johann). See Maria Steiger, "Grillparzers Alfred der Große und die Zeitgeschichte," *Euphorion* 17 (1910): 149–52.

[12] Cf. Josef Nadler, *Grillparzer* (Vienna: Bergland, 1952), 73.

[13] This was so even before Palacký's *History of the Czech People* (vol. 1, 1836; the crucial "Hussite" volume in 1850) began to exert its inspirational influence to the full. The Hussites in particular became a source of pride and comfort for a national consciousness which was often severely bruised, and the theme features prominently in the historical plays and novels of Alois Jirásek. As late as 1897, on the occasion of the fiasco of Badeni's language-ordinances, the poet J. S. Machár, in a bitter lament entitled "The Warriors of God" (the title by which the Hussites were known), urges the Czechs to "shave off their Hussite beards" and accept the

role of lackeys. See further my article "The Uses of History: German and Czech Perspectives on the Hussite Hero in Habsburg Austria" in *Strathclyde Modern Language Studies* x (1990): 5–18.

[14] "Für die Freiheit aber ist da nichts zu lernen wo der Begriff von Ordnung fehlt" (III, 1076). Shades of Octavio and Max Piccolomini!

[15] "In diesem alten, baufälligen Gebäude wohnen viele sich halb fremde Menschen und die jetzt herrschende Influenza der Nationalität begünstigt, ja fordert heraus zu Spaltungen und Parteien" (III, 1041: unpublished appeal to the people, 1848). Those who favoured the "großdeutsch" solution to the question posed by 1848, that is, the incorporation of the whole of the Austrian state into a new Empire, felt, like Bruck, Schwarzenberg's close ally, that Austria was "a German state" (cf. Heinrich Ritter von Srbik, *Deutsche Einheit. Idee und Wirklichkeit vom Heiligen Reich bis Königgrätz* [Munich, 1935; reprint: Darmstadt: Wissenschaftliche Buchgesellschaft, 1963], 380). For Schuselka, cf. in particular his "Ist Oesterreich deutsch?" (1843). For a reformed Austria, the exiled Liberal can answer his own question resoundingly in the affirmative.

[16] He fancied that he noticed a touch of this "German influenza" even in Hormayr's *Vaterländischer Almanach für 1823:* "Er fängt nämlich an, philosophisch generalisierend . . . zudem noch altritterlich und mystisch zu werden" (III, 1012). Instead of a sound, "pragmatic" historian like Johannes Müller, Hormayr now seems to take the likes of Fouqué, Friedrich Schlegel, and even Zacharias Werner as models.

[17] K. R. Popper, *The Poverty of Historicism* (1957; London: Routledge, 1961), 45. For Grillparzer, see the diary-entry of 1860 (III, 1157–58). Gerhart Baumann speaks of Grillparzer's "Witterung für die Gefahr des Historismus." (*Franz Grillparzer. Sein Werk und das österreichische Wesen* [Freiburg-Vienna: Herder, 1954], 119). Cf. also Olaf Christiansen, *Gerechtigkeitsethos und rhetorische Kunst in Grillparzers "Ein Bruderzwist in Habsburg"* (Uppsala: Almqvist & Wiksell, 1980), 44 and my article, "Grillparzer, Shakespeare and Historical Drama," *German Life and Letters* 44 (1991): 208–20.

[18] See the epigram "Historiker."

[19] Cf. Hilde Bürger, ed., *Hugo von Hofmannsthal und Harry Graf Kessler. Briefwechsel,* (Frankfurt am Main, 1968), 155.

[20] "Preußische Konstitution" (1844): III, 1073–77.

[21] "History is [for Grillparzer] a stage, a setting for changes, and each change is for the worse": J. P. Stern, *Idylls and Realities. Studies in Nineteenth-Century German Literature* (London: Methuen, 1971), 23.

[22] III, 1074–76.

[23] U. Fülleborn, *Das dramatische Geschehen im Werk Franz Grillparzers* (Munich: Fink, 1966), 161.

[24] A full account in W. N. B. Mullan, *Grillparzer's Aesthetic Theory. A Study with Special Reference to his Conception of the Drama as "Eine Gegenwart"* (Stuttgart: Heitz, 1979).

[25] P. von Matt, *Der Grundriß von Grillparzers Bühnenkunst* (Zurich: Atlantis, 1965), 38. For a succinct statement of Grillparzer's views on "presentness" and

"causality" in drama, see his essay: *Über den gegenwärtigen Zustand der dramatischen Kunst.*

[26] See my article "History or Drama? The Curious Case of Grillparzer's 'Treuer Diener'" in *Quinquereme* 11 (1988): 129–45.

[27] Baumann 115–16.

[28] "Selbstbiographie," 104.

[29] For a more detailed discussion of Grillparzer's relation to Shakespeare, see my article "Grillparzer, Shakespeare and Historical Drama," *German Life and Letters* 44 (1991): 208–20.

[30] Cf. the comments in the "Selbstbiographie," 10.

[31] Hormayr presents Ottokar as self-assertive and destructive, Rudolf as constructive ("bauend") and working with the grain of Nature. Ottokar is a "tragic," Rudolf an "epic" subject: see Adel 76–77. Schlegel (*Über die neuere Geschichte,* 23) draws a similar contrast. Much the same contrast of temperaments appears in his comparison of the "true" emperor, Charles V, and the "false" type (clearly, Napoleon), who aims at a material "Universalmonarchie" (300). A similar thought may have gone through Grillparzer's mind during the period of his work on *Ottokar.* He notes in his diary, in 1820: "Napoleon wäre in kein Kloster gegangen" (III, 976).

[32] See Sengle 88.

[33] W. E. Yates, *Grillparzer. A Critical Introduction* (Cambridge: Cambridge UP, 1972), 101–7.

[34] *Pace* Walter Silz, against whom Yates argues convincingly, 111.

[35] Diary-entry, quoted by von Matt, 3.

[36] In the opening scene, for example, Grillparzer does not seem to be much concerned, even assuming he knows the answer, as to the difference between a partisan and a halberd.

[37] Schlegel, KA 7, 237.

[38] See particularly "Selbstbiographie," 162 ff. "Nicht minder verletzend," says Palacký in his "Idea of the Austrian State" (1864: German version 1865), "ist ein anderes Sofisma, welches wir Böhmen häufig hören müssen: ihr seid eine noch allzuwenig gebildete Nation . . ." (F. Palacký, Die *Oesterreichische Staatsidee* [reprint; Vienna: H. Geyer, 1974], 28). Later (72–73), Palacký hurls the example of the Hussite Wars in the face of the arrogant Germans: The Hussites, of course, were anything but "dead history" for Grillparzer, but they meant something very different (cf. the discussion of the *Bruderzwist,* 133 above).

[39] *Grillparzer,* 105.

[40] Bruce Thompson, ed., *Franz Grillparzer — Ein Bruderzwist in Habsburg* (Glasgow [Scottish Papers in Germanic Studies], 1982), xiv. Ottokar is described in similar terms (xvi) and in a note (1824), Grillparzer describes the idea that Rudolf sees both that disaster is coming and that it cannot be stopped as "für die Tragödie, ein grandioses Motiv seiner Untätigkeit" (II, 1259).

[41] W. E. Yates 238.

[42] And it follows that history is also beyond the dramatist's control. Cf. III, 304: "Das Letzte der historischen Tragödie aber ist Gottes Werk, ein Wirkliches, die Existenz."

[43] Used of both Klesel (xxiv) and Ferdinand (xxvi).

[44] Quoted on II, 1257.

[45] See the historical table, II, 1257. Rudolf, for example, granted the Letter of Majesty in 1609. Rudolf died in 1612: before we are told of this, Wallenstein has already reported the Defenestration of Prague (1618) to Ferdinand.

[46] One is reminded of the moral of *Der Traum, ein Leben:* true happiness resides in ". . . des Innern stille(r) Frieden."

[47] Cf. Rudolf's remarks to Ferdinand, II, 359–60: ". . . Eigendünkel war es, Eigensucht, Die nichts erkennt, was nicht ihr eignes Werk."

[48] Cf. Thompson's note, 93 (line 1322 in this edition). Dee (1527–1608) was an alchemist, astrologer, and mathematician who enjoyed Elizabeth's favour and was sometimes used as a secret diplomatic agent. He was not, in fact, a Scot.

[49] From Rudolf in act I ("die Zeit, die wildverworrne, neue," line 321) to Ferdinand in act V ("Aus den Wirren In denen labyrinthisch geht die Zeit" (line 2463).

[50] W. E. Yates 238. Act V is seen as necessary "to bring out the whole perspective of the action."

[51] Viktor von Andrian-Werburg, "Über Österreich und dessen Zukunft" (1843–47) and Josef Tuvora, *Briefe aus Wien* (1844), excerpted in Madeleine Rietra, *Jungösterreich. Dokumente und Materialien zur liberalen österreichischen Opposition 1835–1848* (Amsterdam: Rodopi, 1980), 422 and 407 respectively.

[52] Cf. Karel Krofta, *A Short History of Czechoslovakia* (London: Williams and Norgate, 1935), 73.

[53] The Utraquists (so called because they took Communion in both kinds, "sub utraque specie") differed from the more radical "Taborite" group to which the great Hussite general, Žižka, belonged, in that they did not want to break completely with Rome. They eventually subdued the Taborites and in the sixteenth century, came under strong Lutheran influence, which contributed to a growing alienation of the Czechs from the Habsburgs (see Krofta 64–65). It may not be insignificant that Lukrezia's father bears the name of Žižka's successor as military leader of the Taborites, Prokop the Bald!

[54] R. A. Kann, *A History of the Habsburg Empire 1526–1918,* 2nd ed. (Berkeley: U of California P, 1977), 4. Rudolf's belief that "mein Name herrscht" (line 1166) is shown in the conversation with Heinrich Julius to be naïve, and his philosophy of harmony with "God and Nature," to be tenable in absolute terms, but impractical and inadequate in the world of "das Einzelne, die Gegenwart" (line 1278).

[55] Bruce Thompson, ed. xxxi.

6: "Non-Austrian" Historical Drama: C. F. Hebbel

THERE SEEMS TO BE a contradiction in the title of this chapter: after all, Hebbel lived and worked in Vienna from 1845 onward and Austria, over the centuries, has displayed an almost legendary skill in importing and assimilating talent from without. But Hebbel was not one to be assimilated; he once described himself as a "Nicht-Oesterreicher"[1] and the label of "North German"[2] adheres to him wherever he goes in the South; Bavaria (as we shall see in the case of *Agnes Bernauer*) or Austria. One has only to juxtapose him with Grillparzer to justify their separation as historical dramatists. The one abhorred Hegel; the other was influenced by, or at the very least, had a strong affinity for, him. Insofar as his work is "national" at all (that is above all in his "Nibelung" trilogy), Hebbel's "Deutschtum" is closer to the Prussian than to the Austrian model, and it gained him precedence over Grillparzer in the affections of the Prussian *Reich*.[3] Grillparzer did not like *Die Nibelungen;* Treitschke, who was to become "the ideologist of a pro-Prussian power-state with a national-imperialist mission,"[4] praised it.[5] This discussion will be resumed in detail in due course: for the moment, we are concerned to justify the distinction between the "German-ness" of the environment out of which Grillparzer's dramas arose, and that of the Germany which Paul Joachimsen has called "extra-Austrian,"[6] and in which Bismarck could call Austria a "worm-eaten galleon" and Vienna "no longer a German city."[7]

In spite of Restoration and Metternich, there was no way back, after Napoleon, to the Germany of the Holy Roman Empire, and in spite of the power of Romantic myth-making, no way forward to fulfilling the desire for German unity that the War of Liberation had awakened, through the slogan "Kaiser und Reich" and the evocation of the glory of the Hohenstaufens.[8] Blood and iron and the Prussian "Machtstaat" as "dogmatised," in Joachimsen's phrase, by Hegel,[9] looked, even then, a better bet than Romantic longing, though it might perhaps be argued that the two were united in the attempts of poets and artists to link the new Prussian "Reich" with the Barbarossa legend.[10] Whatever the significance of its role in the German

Confederation and the exact aim of Metternich's policy,[11] Austria possessed its own separate history and identity and as we have seen, writers like Grillparzer could feel themselves to be both German and not German, while Hebbel never ceases to think of the community to which he belongs as "deutsch." We shall concentrate in this chapter on the period *preceding* the Austro-Prussian War and the foundation of the "Deutsches Reich," as German literature in the latter part of the nineteenth century was dominated by the non-dramatic genres, at least until the advent of Hauptmann. There was no lack of nationalism in the Germany of Bismarck and of "Weltpolitik," only of presentable dramas to embody it. There was a "Schillerpreis," but after Hebbel, although many plays were written, none were of a calibre sufficient to live up to that title. Paul Heyse, himself a co-laureate with Ernst von Wildenbruch, gives a list of names among whom only that of Emanuel Geibel (in addition to the two mentioned) survives even in the literary histories.[12]

Many of the plays written during this period were on subjects taken from history, and themes that could be called broadly Germanic featured prominently among these. This trend was naturally intensified after the foundation of the Prussian "Reich," but even before the triumph of Bismarck, from Arndt and Jahn (*Deutsches Volkstum*, 1810) onward, there are many signs — not least in a whole string of prominent and talented historians[13] — of the development of a German national consciousness that was likely to find fulfilment in the arms of Prussia rather than of Austria. Hohenzollern became the heir of Hohenstaufen, a development already hinted at very strongly in Grabbe's *Kaiser Friedrich Barbarossa*.[14] But Wilhelmian Prussia was unable to inspire a "patriotic" drama of better quality than Wildenbruch's mediocre attempt at a "charismatic apologia" (Ketelsen) for the Hohenzollern state, *Die Quitzows* (1888).[15]

As our title indicates, our principal subject here is Hebbel, but there are two playwrights whose literary importance requires recognition, and in some of whose work at least, the question of a "historical" content can be said to arise, namely Georg Büchner and Christian Dietrich Grabbe. There were, of course, many others who wrote plays with an historical subject[16] or, as in the case of the "Nibelungen" theme, a legendary one with a very strong "Germanic," and therefore historical resonance (e.g. Emanuel Geibel's *Brunhild* [1857]). This example we can afford to leave out of our study (with a grateful reference to Sengle), but we shall have occasion more than once to note the prominence of the theme in the nineteenth century. The existence of Wagner's *Ring*-cycle, even if it does not fall properly within our terms of reference, cannot be left entirely unmentioned, and it is on Hebbel's treatment of the saga that we shall eventually conclude.

Büchner may have said that in *Dantons Tod* (1835), he was simply "a writer of history,"[17] and it could well be that this was a mere smokescreen. In any case, the positive "historical" aspect — that is, the experience of history as a real past — seems to be confined to the element of factuality. As is well-documented, he makes thorough use of Thiers and Mignet, and often has the historical characters speak in their own recorded words. Although we recognize the events and principal actors in the drama of the French Revolution, still very much a burning issue for the contemporary audience, the true life of the work lies elsewhere: on the one hand, in breaking through the barriers of stylized and idealized "Classicism," and on the other, in the metaphysics, rather than drama, of history. History, that is, in terms, not of the community of past and present in time, but of the meaning, or meaninglessness, of human activity and endeavour. Robespierre and St Just attempt to convince themselves that there is some teleological point,[18] some Hegelian reason,[19] in what they are doing. But while the instinct to search for meaning is there, reality remains impenetrable, and it can hardly be denied that Danton's pessimism prevails in what appeals as more a debate than a drama.[20] With the coherence of reality goes that of any written history, either in narrative or dramatic form, for we can hardly interpret the famous formulation "Fatalismus der Geschichte,"[21] echoed, for example in Danton's remark to Julie in the night-scene (II, 5: "Puppen sind wir . . .") as an expression of belief in the reality of a Greek Fate or a Baroque "Verhängnis," let alone a "Weltgeist." Indeed, it could be said that Büchner is not so much writing *of* history, as writing history *off*. Some might argue that an anti-historical statement is still an historical statement of a kind, but it is hardly one likely to lead to an historical drama, in that it seems to deny the possibility of history as action.

Writing, as was Büchner, in a period of disappointment for nationalists and liberals alike, a time "voll Halbheit, albernen Lugs und Tandes," as the hero phrases it in *Napoleon oder die hundert Tage* (1831),[22] Grabbe is fascinated by the phenomenon of "greatness," in particular the highest pitch of desire and ambition, and fixes on figures from legend (Don Juan and Faust)[23] and history (Hannibal, the Hohenstaufens, Napoleon) who can be seen as incorporating it. He certainly seems to have been concerned with "Germany" as a political and cultural idea and potential reality, its past, present, and possible future. We shall see this reflected in the Hohenstaufen plays, but even in them, we sense that the concept of history which predominates in him is that of history as an abstract process and this is probably what he has in mind when he expresses the aim of saying "etwas über den Geist der Geschichte."[24] This is a "history" that is manifested in individual people and time, but the appreciation of whose real meaning and substance, which is essentially philosophy, lifts us out of that world. "Past" and "present" are largely irrelevant, and the possibility of an historical drama, at least as we have defined it, is reduced. What distinguishes Grabbe from Hegel is that whereas the latter experiences history as demonstrating the "freedom" of man, as he arrives at the insight that the "I" (the conscious, thinking mind) is "der Boden für alles . . . das gelten soll,"[25] Grabbe feels that history itself is, to use Sagarra's phrase, "a thrilling but pointless spectacle";[26] not the meaningful existence of man, on earth and contained in time, but existence cancelled and made meaningless by Time as a destructive, ever-turning wheel. Napoleon himself is no more than "the little flag on the mast" of the Revolution,[27] which meanders on without plan or purpose, while for the "Volk," the brute "machine" of history,[28] or one might almost say, simply "life," goes on through its endless cycles. The accidental drowning of Friedrich Barbarossa, or the sudden death from a stroke of Henry VI on Mount Etna, may be seen as a "terrible and tragic fate,"[29] and there are certainly frequent references to fate in both of the Hohenstaufen dramas, but it is a terror which arises out of a feeling of meaninglessness. The context for the sense of utter negativity that makes Heinrich wish he had "never been born," has already been set in the preceding scene, in which a master and his man view the landscape over which succeeding waves of history have swept. The Emperor, says the latter, is "terrible"; "Wird sterben," is the reply, "Unsre Saaten wachsen immer wieder."[30] In a sense, these are *anti*-historical dramas. Whereas Hegel sees "world history" as a meaningful (if sometimes tragic) process, and Treitschke can talk, after the Battle of Sedan, of "Reason (speaking) in History,"[31] Grabbe seems to imply that in the unending sequence of days and years, no one, not God, nor even "Fate" disposes. "History," then, is the brute force of events, essentially shapeless and devoid of teleological continuity. As von Wiese says, "alles Ideelle bleibt für Grabbe in die Wirksamkeit der Geschichte [the material, factual world] verflochten und ist nur Funktion, nicht aber metaphysische Ursache der Vorgänge."[32] This seems to rule out the idea of a transcendent "Fate," but as in the case of Schiller, where History is "fast überirdisch," still allows von Wiese to talk in more or less metaphysical terms of "Schicksal," and of "Geschichtskräfte."[33] A sense of community between a real past and present seems unlikely to arise in such circumstances.

In the two plays, *Kaiser Friedrich Barbarossa* and *Kaiser Heinrich der Sechste* (1829 and 1830 respectively), which make up "Die Hohenstaufen," at least the bare bones of a national historical drama, as we understand the term, are present. The Hohenstaufens had considerable contemporary resonance, for both Austrian, and for "kleindeutsch," Germans. Schuselka castigates the Grillparzerian epigone Otto Prechtler (*Die Kronenwächter* [1844]) for having celebrated the Habsburgs at the expense of the true tragic theme of the "Verfall der deutschen Weltmacht," and Naumann celebrates Raumer as a "Reichsgründungsschreiber."[34] Grabbe had ambitions to create a "Nationalschauspiel" by portraying a "brilliant" epoch of German history in some six to eight Hohenstaufen plays,[35] and if we move from the realm of abstraction to that of individual reality, it is the case that in these plays, he is presenting German history to a German audience. We have, in embryonic form, a panorama in which, from a base in the High Middle Ages, we can look back to a "Vorzeit" in which we can descry the figures of Wittekind,[36] indeed, of the Nibelungs themselves, and forward to the nineteenth century.

The principal heroes are certainly representative of the urge to "greatness," the "Wille zur Macht," but the "German" quality of themselves and the men they lead is heavily and repeatedly stressed. The substantiality of the old world of the Hohenstaufen Empire is established by many a solid detail, and by visually impressive scenes such as the great procession (18) and the "Lustlager" at Mainz (77) in *Barbarossa*, and the Hagenau "Reichstag" in *Heinrich der Sechste* (169). Most important of all, perhaps, is the fact that the spectator is sometimes encouraged to see this theme historically, that is, in terms of a continuity stretching potentially even to the present rather dull days, and possible brighter ones in the future. We have already mentioned the Hohenstaufen-Hohenzollern link in *Kaiser Friedrich Barbarossa*, and it is worth pointing out that — through the "prophetic" technique so often used in historical drama — Grabbe has evoked the image of Frederick the Great and possibly even Frederick William III.[37] Barbarossa has a "presentiment":

> Ich ahns, daß *andre* Friedriche mich einst
> Ersetzen, sei's aus meinem Hause, sei's
> Aus eurem! (48)

In addition to the idea (chimera) of world-domination, there is a "German" project, that occupies the forefront of the minds of both Hohenstaufen emperors. The potential is evident from the several celebrations of Germany and the Germans in both plays,[38] including a motif that will assume greater importance later, the idea of Germanic heroism and "Treue," with its echoes of the Nibelungen legend. We are already reminded of the figure of Hagen, by the "hehrer, großer Tod" of Wittelsbach (58), and the motif of the *Nibelungenlied*— which Grabbe saw as a truly "nationelles Kunstwerk"[39] — is introduced with the appearance of Heinrich von Ofterdingen (then thought to have been the author of the medieval epic). Hagen is "der wilde, doch treue Knecht," and the spirit of the Nibelungs is alive in Barbarossa:

> Hätt ich nicht Hohenstaufens Größ erblickt,
> Nie wäre Nibelungen mir geglückt. (82)

There is even a link between the German theme and the issue of German unity, as much alive at the time of the "Bund" as it had been when Guelf and Ghibelline (still used by Hebbel, in his diary [31 December 1848], as symbolic for German disunity) were at each other's throats: "Ist Deutschland einig," says Barbarossa, ". . . So ists der Erde Herrin" (59). There is even a prophetic hint in the Archbishop of Mainz's comment on Henry VI's plea that the Imperial Crown be made hereditary (188), which would, of course, have weakened the power of the princes. The idea is "riesenhaft," says the cleric, but at the same time, it is perhaps not such a megalomaniac chimera as the striving for "Weltherrschaft." It is, rather, untimely: "die Zeit [ist] für ihn [den Entwurf] zu klein, zu unreif" (189).

Hebbel's reflections on the drama and on history are liberally sprinkled with concepts and terms (such as "Idea," "World Spirit," "collision," "world-historical individual"[40]) which, whether they were acquired through direct study or simply as part of the general climate of thought within which Hebbel fought his way forward, can certainly be described as in broad terms, Hegelian. Hebbel was most certainly accessible to this kind of speculation: as he himself says in his Diary for 1855, in connection with his relationship with Friedrich von Uechtritz, "die ungeheuren Probleme des Lebens" lay very close to his heart.[41] We do not really need to go in depth into the question of Hebbel's exact relation to Hegel, which has exercised critics over the years, and arises in pretty well every serious study of his drama. That there was a debt of some kind seems irrefutable. The latter had died in 1831, but through his own writings, and to some extent those who felt his influence, not only philosophers, but also nationalist historians like Johann Gustav Droysen, a leading light in the pro-Prussian and anti-Austrian group in the Frankfurt Parliament,[42] he exerted a powerful influence on political and historical thinking in the nineteenth century. (The case of Marx will be dealt with separately, because in our context, it arises separately, out of strict chronological order.) J. P. Stern's formulation seems reasonable: "There is some evidence that he (Hebbel) owed to Hegel the overall scheme within which his plays are located and their plots resolved."[43]

Hegel, if not the founding father, then the central pillar of historicism (interpretation of the world as the outcome of history, as development and change whose central core and dynamic is spiritual ["geistig"] and meaningful),[44] sees history as anything but a "blind medley of contingencies," as it seems to appear in Grabbe and Büchner; rather, it is a "rational development"[45] with absolute Reason as its ultimate content. His is, in Nipperdey's formulation, a "philosophically constructive" historicism.[46] Not that the facts can be disregarded: it is in and through them that history occurs, but in themselves, the facts of what Hebbel (whether directly influenced by Hegel or not) calls "die materielle Geschichte" are a "Wust," an unweeded garden.[47] Their true content and meaning is not individual, but general, and can be apprehended only "through general concepts."[48] Collisions between the individual and the general are inevitable, even though the ultimate "subject" of history, the "Weltgeist" works, as it must, through individuals, their passions and desires.

Hebbel calls drama "die höchste Geschichtschreibung" insofar as it combines the individuality of its characters (without which it is not dramatic[49]) with depiction of "die großartigsten und bedeutendsten Lebensprozesse" in which individuality is, of course, transcended, processes that require insight into the "decisive historical crises."[50] This brings to the fore a question central to his philosophy of life and his dramatic practice: the potentially tragic relation of conflict between the individual and the general[51] that seems to reach some kind of resolution only within the framework of a philosophy of history. Certainly, this question is also central to Hegel's historical thought, but Hebbel's own temperament and experience, with dualism and dialectic built into the basic structure, would surely have brought it to the forefront in any case. His talent, as he himself said "was kindled in contact with history."[52] He experienced life in terms of "Kampf" and

"Gegensatz," the often tragic outcome of individuation,[53] a process full of tragic choices, often between two goods. This "Dualismus des Rechts," he saw as the "law of drama" and of history.[54]

"Ich glaube," Hebbel wrote in his diary[55] on completion of *Herodes und Mariamne*, "einen Fortschritt gemacht zu haben." One could argue the case for this assertion from several points of view, but the successful incorporation, in symbolic form, of history into drama is perhaps the most important of them. The idea of an impending historical change is certainly raised in the audience's mind by Meister Anton's famous "Ich verstehe die Welt nicht mehr" in *Maria Magdalene* (1843), but the sense of a distance, and continuity, between two points in historical time, can hardly be said to have been evoked by simply portraying a generation-gap. Anton does not yet belong unequivocally to the past, and the play is a *bürgerlich*, and not an historical, tragedy. In *Herodes und Mariamne*, the spectator, who may or may not have Josephus at his fingertips, can still be relied on to be aware of, and informed about the Bible and the Christian context, and frequently has his attention drawn,[56] even before the Three Kings appear, to the impending irruption into the world of a culture that links his own present with the dramatic present of the characters, whose past-ness he simultaneously recognizes. The "historical" aim is to make quite clear to the audience the dialectic of the cultural values of the day (Jewish and Roman) and the coming culture of "humanity" ("a new form of the Idea," as Sten G. Flygt puts it[57]), which Hebbel's contemporaries could see as compatible with their own. At the same time, the general historical theme was missed, Hebbel himself tells us,[58] by many and it is certainly less prominent than it might be, mainly by virtue of the intensely dramatic clash of personalities, the "sex-conflict," in Edna Purdie's phrase,[59] at the centre, and to some extent also by the tight-knit and almost "Classical" form (for example, in observance of the unity of place), which helps to concentrate the audience's attention on the psychological action in the dramatic present.

This action is set in a wide-ranging and rich geo-political context, but this is a somewhat distant circumference, whereas the bright light is focussed almost exclusively on the centre, a fact which could be said to make the play Hebbel's dramatic masterpiece, but dilutes somewhat its impact as history. Herod's relation to Mark Antony and Octavian does, of course, impact on the drama by motivating the "Blutbefehl" through which Mariamne's "humanity" is offended, and the fact that Artaxerxes has been employed as a human clock is related to the issue of the human being as a free individual rather than a mere object or chattel. But the very centrality of the idea makes them seem like factors in an historical equation of the "necessary" variety, rather than part of a living historical world, connected to us through a temporal continuum. Hebbel sketches in the background efficiently in the time and space he can spare for this task, but it is not enough to overcome the gap created by such a remote and distant milieu. When he brings in detail of a *German* medieval world in *Agnes Bernauer*, the mere mention (for example of Cologne Cathedral) is enough. The link on which the sense of continuity, or "community" as we have phrased it, depends in *Herodes und Mariamne*, is an abstraction. Consequently, the experience of history that the play provides (as opposed to its dramatic effect) has an abstract quality reminiscent of *Ein Wort über das Drama* or the preface to *Maria Magdalene*, which cast a shadow from which Hebbel would have been glad to escape, but which, not without some justification, followed him as far as *Die Nibelungen*, as the (unpublished) preface to that work demonstrates.

Hebbel had a strong sense of "German-ness" which transcended the inner divisions of the Confederation. He felt the humiliation ("Deutschlands Schmach," as he called it) that "Germany" had suffered in 1850 in the dispute with Denmark over Schleswig-Holstein, as "ein persönliches Leid"; it made him aware of "das natürliche Band . . . was den Menschen mit seinem Vaterland verknüpft."[60] Germany was for him a cultural unity: in a review of a performance of Goethe's *Faust* (1850), he waxes eloquent in pan-German mode about "das wunderbare Gedicht, das alle Eigenschaften unseres Nationalcharakters abspiegelt" and which gives rise to an "erlaubtes Selbstgefühl."[61] His devout wish was that it should also achieve political unity, the issue which had been raised by the battle against Napoleon and had come very much to the forefront again with the 1848 Revolution. This seems evident from his observation of current events in his Diaries.[62] In an entry dated 21 December 1851, he notes, apropos of the inability to agree of Prussia and Austria, "die beiden Herzkammern" (18 February 1853), that the Germans can work together in war, but not in peace: "Unglückliches Volk, das die Arbeit gemeinschaftlich verrichtet, aber nicht in Frieden miteinander essen und trinken kann . . ." On 31 December 1852, he observes: "In Deutschland ist alles beim alten, doch wird mir versichert, daß wenigstens die Zollvereinigung zustande komme. Gott geb's, es wäre ein Anfang!" "Nur die Einheit Deutschlands," he writes in 1857, "führt zu seiner Freiheit als Nation."

Interestingly, Purdie links the absence in *Agnes Bernauer* of the "sex-conflict" which dominates *Herodes und Mariamne*, with a generally less dramatic effect: a "dominant impression of logic."[63] Certainly, while it has some episodes of high dramatic intensity, the work has in general a less intensely dramatic, a looser and more nearly "epic" *structure*, extending over a much longer time-span, with more frequent changes of scene, and incorporating, rather than simply referring to, the more general historical reality in which the characters move, with what Theodor Poppe has rightly called a "farbiges Leben"[64] that recalls Goethe's *Götz*. This is hardly the result of concentration on the "necessity" of the "collision" of individual and state.[65] Nor of the decision to create a "tragedy of beauty,"[66] a "modern Antigone," deviating from tradition, and from Törring's "Volksschauspiel," in order to produce a work that was both tragic and, as he put it in a conversation with the King of Bavaria, "streng [that is, philosophically] historisch."[67] The fact is that the philosophical Hebbel is showing himself to be also a "German" Hebbel, and an "historian" in a different sense; the thread of "life" is intertwined with that of "logic." He has to resuscitate the old "Reich," which is the foundation for the central pillar without which the "necessity" of the play would crumble into dust, namely the principle of civil order and which, as Ernst knows, will crush Albrecht's almost inevitable rebellion, whether or not the latter is supported by Ludwig of Ingolstadt.[68] Just as a princess in Bavaria is a princess "im Heiligen Römischen Reich," as the "Kastellan" at Vohburg puts it (III: 7), so disorder in Bavaria is disorder in the "Reich"; the two are concentric circles and Ernst's authority depends on that of the ultimate centre, the Emperor. His confidence that Albrecht will be brought back to order rests on the fact that "der Kaiser hat seinen Adler schon fliegen lassen" (V: 6).

Hebbel remarked, in a letter to the theatrical director Franz Dingelstedt, that he wished to erect "a cross" over the grave of the recently deceased and buried Holy Roman Empire.[69] Hebbel is too much of a realist to share the Romantic desire to make it "arise," in the terms of Tieck's prologue to *Kaiser Oktavianus*, "in its old splendour," as the dramatists who attempted to resuscitate the Hohenstaufens were perhaps trying to do, in plays for which Hebbel showed scant regard. These "Hohenstaufenbandwürmer," as they are described in the preface to *Maria Magdalene*, had destroyed the unity of Germany,[70] and at that time, indeed, Hebbel seems to have shared Ludolf Wienbarg's doubts (expressed apropos of Uhland) whether German history could be "even a vehicle," let alone an inspiration, for the dramatist.[71] But the Holy Roman Empire had been, however inadequately, the political embodiment of the German nation, in whose reality and potential unity Hebbel certainly believed. And Hebbel admitted that modern Germans were still connected to the Middle Ages, which the Romantic poets and scholars had endowed with a revived contemporary relevance, by "many a thread."[72] In the *Preface* itself, Hebbel had pointed to Shakespeare, in his Histories, engaging with things that "still lived in the consciousness of his people," and, while rejecting the Hohenstaufen plays, endorsed their *aim* as "highly important and capable of realisation" and pointed to Wilibald Alexis's historical depiction of German *life* as a way of achieving it.[73]

He conceived the old Empire as dead and in its grave, but it was not inert; not incapable of reaching out through its relics and affecting the nineteenth-century dramatist. In an interesting letter to Maria, Prinzessin von Wittgenstein of 2 October 1858, Hebbel uses a similar image in describing a relic of Polish history he has been shown in Cracow. Such things are "Särge der Zeit," but the coffin-image is not meant negatively. Things like this have, he says, "mich von jeher magisch gefesselt." They are containers and preservers of a life which has gone and will not return ("nie wiederkehrender Zustände"), but one with which some sense of historical community is clearly still possible, rather as Ernst, in *Agnes Bernauer*, can feel a community of purpose as he addresses the picture of the dead King Ludwig: "Du sollst mir die Hand geben, wenn wir uns einmal sehen" (act III, scene 1). Each has worked for the welfare of the state. This latter principle plays a crucial role in *Agnes Bernauer* and it is not just the state as an abstraction, but the German state as a working political organism which has, for example, to give its sanction to the "Zunftbrief" which allows guild-members to attend the grand ball in Augsburg (cf. I: 15). As Hebbel says in the letter already referred to, a national history which lacks integral continuity, has to cede the centre-ground to the "menschlich" action, but the Empire "steht dahinter wie ein ungeheurer Berg mit Donner und Blitz." The Emperor on earth and God in heaven, "menschliche und göttliche Ordnung," as Ernst says, anticipating the words of the imperial herald (V: 9 and 10, 567 and 568), stand ready to pronounce judgement, as they already have upon Agnes, and it is to these powers that Albrecht eventually bows.

The absence of a true political unity, and the reality of rivalries and infighting between the constituent members of a loose framework like the "Reich," or the "Bund," were to be regretted, but it was within such a framework that all Germans (including even the Bavarians) were "deutsch," in the 1850s as in the fifteenth century. References, for example, to the possible reconciliation of Guelf and Wittelsbach through Albrecht's projected marriage with Anna of Brunswick,[74] could be meaningful in the nineteenth century as well: Hebbel himself (Diary, 31 December 1848) refers to the old rivalry of Guelf and Ghibelline in commenting on German disunity. Ernst, who has asserted the superior moral, as well as physical power (the "Gewalt des Rechts": V: 10, 569) of the greater whole over the individual, claims in the same speech to represent "das ganze Deutsche Reich," and subsequently uses the symbol of the banner to evoke the idea of "das deutsche Volk" (570). True, Albrecht expresses to his father his wish to kneel "nicht vor Kaiser und Reich, aber vor dir" (572), distinguishing, perhaps, between brute "Gewalt" and the "Gewalt des Rechts." To his own moral sublimity as an individual, Ernst has added the authority of the Whole, which is not just a Bavaria which is "in drei Teile zerrissen, wie ein Pfannkuchen, um den drei Hungrige sich schlugen" (II: 1, 505), but the whole German nation. Only if we think of this greater whole can we see in the judgement that is relayed to Agnes by Preising ("Die Ordnung der Welt gestört . . . etc.": V: 2, 557) a force which does something, at least, to counteract the objection to the subject-matter voiced by Otto Ludwig, and endorsed by Theodor Poppe, namely that it "[liegt] zu weit von der Weltgeschichte ab" to be a suitable theme for an historical tragedy.[75]

It may be that not enough has been done to satisfy all critics, but it cannot be denied that Hebbel set out to lay the foundation for the crucial role to be played by the Empire in the early stages. It embodies not just power, but Law. As is shown by the Mayor's remark in act I scene 15, its authority was necessary to validate the Augsburg "Zunftbrief" (500). Still in the first act, when Albrecht formally announces his (in essence revolutionary) intention to marry Agnes, Törring exclaims: "Denkt an Kaiser und Reich!" and Frauenhoven pronounces him "mad" (I: 18, 504). As soon as Ernst becomes aware that Albrecht has in fact made this radical break with the ruling social and political principle, at the end of the tournament scene in act III, the Empire comes back into play, and the latent "German" theme comes to the fore. It is only in the Empire that a concrete political reality that corresponds to the concept "deutsch" can be found. We have already been made aware of the potential conflict in Albrecht between "Italian and German blood" (II: 1, 505) and it is the latter that eventually prevails. A passion, which, while valid in itself, becomes subversive, must in the end be subordinate to the principle of order. We cannot help recalling that the revolutions of 1848 are but a recent memory.

It could be that, by becoming a play that is "deutsch" — and it is much more so, in language and substance, than Otto Ludwig's "Agnes Bernauer" fragments[76] — as well as a "Trauerspiel," this work can afford its audience, alongside the "world-historical" tragic "logic," of Agnes as a "sacrifice to Necessity" (V: 10, 571), an historical experience of a more *substantial* nature than one based on the "Idee," which requires that we abstract from reality in order to gain access to it. We have already remarked on the fact that, by contrast with the feeling of intense, almost "Classical" concentration of time and place in *Herodes und Mariamne*, we gain here an impression of dispersal reminiscent of *Götz von Berlichingen*. Certainly, the extreme looseness of structure in the latter, its hectically varied and abruptly shifting sequence of sometimes free-standing "Szenen," is not reproduced here. Hebbel's planning is clearer and more dramatically integrated, yet the two works have important traits in common: both are structured around a dualism, acted out by a triangular configuration of central characters (Götz-Adelheid-Weislingen; Ernst-Agnes-Albrecht), and the broad pattern of the action shifts between the opposed mileux of the first two in each case. There is in each a sense, not all that common in Hebbel, of movement in time and space; it is worth noting that in the case of *Agnes Bernauer*, Hebbel gives no indication at all at the head of his text of the location of his action, and a long and indeterminate period of time for its duration.

Mary Garland rightly observes that this kind of indication of time is "a notable innovation" and points to the emphasis on "the reality of a historical past,"[77] though she seems to wish to restrict this spectacle and "colour" to a humble subordinate role, as indeed is not infrequently the case with plays whose subject is taken from past periods. But in this case, the many references to medieval personalities and institutions, detailed set-pieces such as the ballroom scene in Augsburg (I: 15) and even more notably, the tournament-scene (III: 13), for both of which Hebbel describes the set he requires at considerable length, and the appearance of the herald of the Empire, preceded by the banner, and the Papal Legate, with the lighted candle (V: 10), surely build up the sense of a real, living and working, but *old* world, to a much greater extent than is required by dramatic considerations alone. In this latter scene, and in that in which Preising reads out part of Agnes's death-sentence (IV: 3), formal fifteenth-century language, inset into what is not notably archaic dialogue, acts as a further reminder that the world in which these characters exist dramatically, itself exists no longer, unless it be in historical time.

This is more than *casual* colour; the main action, which takes place in a dramatic "present," is set in a living framework which is demonstrably removed in time from the present in which the audience lives. It shows the past in that "state of being"[78] to which we referred in our discussion of Herder and *Götz*, and because we feel that it is past, it arouses a sense of time. Kaspar Bernauer's connection with the "Vehm" (II: 3; "Auch in Augsburg ist Westfalen") is another echo of *Götz*, though in this case, it is a potential rather than an actual reality. The medieval mentality is shown at work in a less spectacular example when Bernauer dilates to Knippeldollinger on his "sure method" for identifying a disfigured corpse ("So soll man drei Tropfen seines Blutes nehmen . . . etc.," I: 9, 495). The effect of the superstition and hocus-pocus is to make us aware of the gulf that lies between him and us, as he is of that between himself and the author of the book he has borrowed (494). At the same time, we are aware that we, and they, exist together in history. Hippocrates, Kaspar Bernauer the fifteenth-century barber-surgeon, and modern medicine (at whatever point in time we locate it) are part of a continuum, as are medieval castles such as Vohburg (III, 7 and 8), Regensburg panelling, and stained glass at Cologne cathedral.[79] Törring's reference (511) to Wolfram von Eschenbach and Heinrich von Ofterdingen remind us that since the Romantics, medieval literature was back on the national agenda, and continued to be topical right up to the "Reichsgründung." Hoffmann von Fallersleben's "Deutschlandlied" gave "new life," as Joachimsen tells us,[80] to a poem by Walther von der Vogelweide; Simrock's "Nibelungen" translation came out in 1827, and in 1870, he produced his *Lieder vom deutschen Vaterland aus alter und neuer Zeit*.

Ernst is particularly aware of his position in an historical continuum. We first see him (III: 1) in a study whose walls are hung with reminders of Bavarian history, and he then proceeds to reflect on his relationship with a "dead" past ("Nun! Sie sind tot!") that obviously still has relevance for him, and with the future (embodied in his son Albrecht). In his final appeal to Albrecht (V: 10, 570–71), he widens the scope of the continuum by shifting the perspective from "Bavarian" to "German": the Banner of the Empire is used, not only as a political, but also as an historical symbol: ". . . das deutsche Volk hat in tausend Schlachten unter ihm gesiegt und wird noch in tausend Schlachten unter ihm siegen." This awareness communicates itself, of course, to the audience as well.

Fouqué's *Der Held des Nordens* had already demonstrated the potential inspirational role that the Nibelungen story could play in the development of German national consciousness — Korff, indeed, considers it "the most important" of the medieval texts from this point of view[81] — and although Hegel saw no historical basis for such a role,[82] others thought differently, in particular in the period leading up to the crisis between Austria and Prussia, when, as Nipperdey says, the "German question" was the most pressing political topic in the life of the Confederation.[83] The Nibelungen story in particular, and the Germanic past in general, became even more influential, and potentially "historical" in their dramatic effect, after the victories of 1866 and 1870 had seemed to confirm the greatness of the present, and the anticipated future, of a Germany united under Prussia. The most influential German historians became infected with the nationalistic bug (Droysen, the young Mommsen, even Ranke) and the seeds of "Weltpolitik" and of associations like the Pan-German League, were being sown. Wagner's *Ring* inevitably had some influence, but more immediately germane to our investigation would be works by lesser talents like Wilhelm Jordan, Felix Dahn or Detlev von Liliencron. Jordan's *Die Nibelunge* (1867–68 and 1874) was held in high regard as a "hoher Sang von deutscher Art und Stärke." As Theodor Storm, himself not immune to the power of the *Nibelungenlied*, observes, the "mighty" quality of this work lay in the theme, not the poetry, but Jordan's success illustrates the appeal of the theme.[84] Dahn, who was also an exponent of the "Wotan Cult,"[85] and whom Class praises as the "Vertiefer deutscher Gesinnung,"[86] celebrated the Germanic past in poems, stories, and dramas.

That the "Nibelungen motif" was a congenial channel for what Ursula Jespersen calls "neuzeitliches Nationaldenken"[87] is no surprise. Jespersen is referring to the historical play *Knut der Herr* by the "Wahlpreuße" Detlev von Liliencron (1844–1909). This centres on the murder of a medieval Prince of Holstein in circumstances that recall the murder of Siegfried by Hagen, and Liliencron weaves the *Nibelungenlied* into his tale of heroism, betrayal and revenge through Tuk Ebbson's attempt to warn the victim.[88] Nor is it surprising that the celebration of "Nibelungentreue" (cf. Dahn's *Deutsche Treue*, 1875) and suchlike Germanic-heroic virtues has since then become suspect. As G. A. Wells points out, what was (as late as 1932!)[89] Hebbel's most popular dramatic work, one in which he invested a great deal of himself,[90] eventually more or less disappeared from the German stage, in large measure as a result of the "Ruch der Germanentümelei."

This is understandable when we recall that in Josef Weinheber's "Die deutschen Tugenden im Kriege," the "old loyalty unto death" is sworn "dem starken Mann, Dem Führer,"[91] or when we read in a History of German Literature published in 1937 that the German *Volk* is to be seen as "der wahre Erbe des Germanentums, seines nordischen Blutes."[92]

Hebbel can hardly be held responsible for the evil and destructive turn that German national feeling took in the Nazi period, but nationalism itself does provide a certain thread of continuity. He himself "was not incapable of chauvinistic tones on the subject."[93] He was no Wagner or Julius Langbehn, obsessed with the concepts of "deutscher Geist"[94] or "Germanic ideology,"[95] but as we have seen, he was by no means devoid of "German" feeling. Hebbel certainly introduces the "world-historical" dimension with the idea of a new, Christian form of the "Idea" (represented by Dietrich von Bern, i.e. Theoderic), which is about to supplant the essentially pagan heroic ethos represented by the Nibelungs. These latter are anything but "gute Christen" (cf. Hagen's ironic remark in *Kriembilds Rache*, IV: 11). However, he is also writing in a more substantially historical sense, in that he is explicitly presenting Germans of the past ("deutsche Eichen," *Rache* III: 8) to Germans of the present, and celebrating their "Mut" and "Treue."[96] As he wrote to Maria, Princess Wittgenstein, he felt that characters should always be "rooted in their nationality" and that his various "German" plays, including *Agnes Bernauer* and the *Nibelungen*, contained "die germanische Welt in ihren verschiedenen Entwicklungsstufen."[97] He felt that the *Nibelungenlied* was the German national epic,[98] and in his epigram "Auf das Nibelungenlied," celebrates the "Recken, die *unsere* ältesten Schlachten Durchgefochten (my italics)."[99] He saw his role in this undertaking not so much as original creation, rather as "mediation between the poem and the nation."[100] A world that is remote and dead, indeed whose death is graphically portrayed, is still, then, very much alive for the German author and audience of the Confederation. It is interesting that Hebbel should have had the feeling, in gauging the audience's response to his work, that "it was as if it were not the past, but the future that was being talked about."[101]

The world of the *Nibelungen* is that of heroic legend, albeit on the brink of history proper. A consistent "realism," psychological or otherwise (as in Geibel's *Brunhild*) would weaken its true historical potential, in terms of its effect on an audience. In Hebbel's diary-entry dated September–December 1861, the tragedian's desire for a "rein menschlich," "naturally" motivated action has to compromise with the "fundamental" presence of myth. So, as he later wrote to Dingelstedt (31 March 1866), he set out to re-create dramatically the "bas-relief" figures of the epic, endowing them with "genug, aber nicht zuviel Eingeweide." A totally (and merely) "human" motivation would indeed be, as Purdie seems to believe is in fact the case, "small and inappropriate."[102] The "grimmiger Hagen" and "das rächende Weib," in the language of Hebbel's epigram, are inwardly driven by forces they cannot control or halt, but which give them a somewhat greater-than-human stature. Hagen, because he must, takes the whole guilt of the Nibelungs on his shoulders, and Kriemhild, who wishes to spare at least Giselher, cannot do so.[103] In these two figures in particular, we feel a similarity and a difference, a Germanic humanity, but one that inhabits an heroic Germanic past, in a twilight area which is a spectrum stretching from the edge of myth (Brunhild and Siegfried above all) to the realm of firm, factual "history" (Attila and in particular, since the future belongs to Christianity, Dietrich von Bern). In that we can talk of all the characters in terms of time, they are all "historical" in our sense of the word.

The greatest difficulty with our last statement might seem to be presented by the figure of Brunhild (whose role Hebbel carefully keeps within bounds: the crux of the trilogy is, after all, the struggle between Kriemhild and Hagen). Her origin lies in a frozen time beyond time ("Wohl steht die Zeit hier still") and immune to change ("Und wir sind unveränderlich": *Siegfrieds Tod* I: 2, 668), but these expressions in themselves raise the question of historical time, even if by a (necessary) contradiction, for one wonders how Brunhild comes to have *any* concept of time and change! The point is, surely, that she enters the world of living time, and starts the clock of history, the domain of tragic collisions. Siegfried seeks to complete the transition for her by "killing" the "Erbin der Valkyrien und Nornen" (Hagen, in *Tod* II: 8, 684), and certainly makes retreat into that world impossible, though it is still capable of having an impact. Even Gunther shows awareness of it.[104] Siegfried has, in his adventure with the dragon, taken at least a step in the opposite direction[105] and it is fitting that with his death, both he and Brunhild should fade into a background of misty memories, rather as the gold, the other main "mythical" element in the plot with its association of an eternal curse of blood-guilt,[106] remains sunk in the Rhine. The "morning-time" of the world, which Kriemhild conjures up when she imagines herself going with her child to live among the animals (*Rache* I: 4, 745), is long past, just as the ancient Germanic heroic ethic embodied in the clash between Kriemhild and Hagen is about to give way to a more "Christian" one.

But the past has not been erased, and we have seen that the Nibelung theme had a powerful present resonance in nineteenth-century Germany. The play has a dual historicality. The heroic dramatic action *has* its past (the "mythical" dimension), and its future. Hebbel originally intended to give more prominence to the former in what eventually appeared as the "Nixenbrunnen" scene (*Rache* IV: 15), but although the passage dealing with Siegfried's legendary birth and the conflict of the two brides was, as Annina Periam puts it, "later stricken"(!),[107] enough remains in Dietrich's account of what he overheard to give a powerful symbolic picture of an historical process stretching both backward and forward from the dramatic moment into the misty extremes of the temporal spectrum. The mythical and national strand does seem to play second fiddle here to what von Wiese calls "das Entwicklungsgeschichtliche": one senses a subliminal Hegelian dialectic in the way in which "alt und neu . . . blutig ringen" (Hebbel, 809). Periam seems to feel that the purpose of the nixies' prophecies was to "heighten Dietrich's significance,"[108] but it is more likely that Hebbel was interested in opening up temporal "perspectives."[109] Hagen's remark in the "pilgrim" episode (*Rache* IV: 21–22) that "die Welt verändert sich," Kriemhild's declaration of a "Weltgericht," and Etzel's renunciation of power in favour of the true Christian, Dietrich, in the final scene, are clear enough indications. But to imply, as von Wiese does, that Germanic history is completely "thrust into the background" by World History,[110] is to exaggerate. In the end, Hebbel's most grandiose, and perhaps most practically effective (because symbolic) dramatic evocation of "Weltgeschichte" stands alongside an evocation of Germanic heroism, raised to mythic status, which can be called truly "vaterländisch," if no longer innocently so. Additionally, leaving aside the question of whether it is benign, this effect could well be more historically potent in the nineteenth century by virtue of the fact that it is derived from a pre-historical subject, one that is *not* anchored in a German history that is in the phrase of Hebbel's 1843 diary-entry, "resultatlos," and therefore capable of evoking a sense of discontinuity.

Notes

[1] In "Berichte aus Wien an die Augsburger Allgemeine Zeitung," quoted by Mary Garland in *Hebbel's Prose Tragedies* (Cambridge: Cambridge UP, 1973), 221. He refused in 1863 to participate in a project for an Uhland-monument, "weil ich kein Österreicher bin und mich also in speziell österreichische Dinge nicht mischen [darf]": Diary-entry no, 5033 in *Hebbels Werke* vol. X, ed. Theodor Poppe (Berlin: Bongs Goldene Klassiker, n.d.), 311.

[2] E.g. David Heald: "this austere and even perverse North German poet": in "Hebbel's Concept of Realism," *New German Studies* 1 (1973): 151. A "typical North-German," Hannsludwig Geiger calls him (in Hebbel, *Sämtliche Werke* vol. 2 [Berlin-Darmstadt: Tempel, 1961], 1129).

[3] Cf. G. Wallis Field, *The Nineteenth Century. 1830–1890* (London, 1975), 16: "In Wilhelmian Germany he was ranked higher [than Grillparzer] and partly as a consequence of the reaction against things Prussian and north German, his reputation since the Second World War has declined."

[4] Cf, Karl Dietrich Bracher, *The German Dictatorship. The Origins, Structure and Consequences of National Socialism* (1969), trans. Jean Steinberg (Harmondsworth: Penguin U Books, 1973), 25.

[5] Cf. Eda Sagarra, *Tradition and Revolution. German Literature and Society 1830–1890* (London: Weidenfeld and Nicolson, 1971), 163.

[6] "das außerösterreichische Deutschland": Paul Joachimsen, *Vom deutschen Volk zum deutschen Staat,* second edition (1920), revised and ed. J. Leuchsen (Göttingen: Vandenhoeck und Ruprecht, 1956), 69.

[7] See A. J. P. Taylor, *Bismarck. The Man and the Statesman* (1955; London: Grey Arrow, 1961), 190 and 76 respectively.

[8] As in Grabbe's Hohenstaufen plays, or Rückert's *Kaiser Heinrich der Vierte* (1845).

[9] A. J. P. Taylor 74. The Hegelian theory of the state may have had its revolutionary implications, but it was, says Joachimsen, "fürs erste . . . eine neue mächtige Klammer für den preußischen Staatsbau" (75).

[10] "Statues of Barbarossa and Kaiser Wilhelm I," R. H. C. Davis tells us, "were placed side by side to symbolize the 'fact' that where one had left off, the other had begun." See R. H. C. Davis, *A History of Medieval Europe. From Constantine to St Louis* (1957; London: Longman, 1968), 315.

[11] This policy, says Taylor, "stimulated, in the minds of both Austrian and non-Austrian Germans, the idea of the Austrian Empire as a half-German, or even a non-German state" (A. J. P. Taylor, *The Course of German History,* 57).

[12] See Heyse's letter to Theodor Storm of 21 November 1884, in *Theodor Storm-Paul Heyse. Briefwechsel* vol. III, ed. C. A. Bernd (Berlin: E. Schmidt, 1974), 98.

[13] Treitschke's nationalism is, of course, a byword, but Theodor Mommsen's assertion (1865) that a "categorical imperative" entitles the nation to "inflict every wound" to achieve its end would, as Hans Kohn says, "have perplexed Kant"

(*The Mind of Germany. The Education of a Nation* [1960; London: Macmillan, 1965], 184).

[14] Especially toward the end of act II, scene 2. Cf. also II. 3, in which, after the death of Wittelsbach, Hohenzollern is entrusted with the "Reichsfahne," and IV. 1, when Beatrice crowns him after victory in the tournament.

[15] Uwe-K. Ketelsen, *Literatur und drittes Reich,* 2nd ed. (Vierow bei Griefswald: S-H Verlag, 1994), 103 (and note 35). The dying seventeenth-century soldier bequeaths to the Hohenzollerns "das Erbtheil . . . Deutschland! Deutschland! Deutschland!" Wildenbruch, the would-be Prussian Schiller, can manage only what Soergel calls a "muddled enthusiasm" (*Dichtung und Dichter der Zeit* [Leipzig: R. Voigtländer, 1928], 76). Sagarra speculates that the Hebbel who produced the *Nibelungen* might have gone on to become "the national poet of the Empire, a much better Wildenbruch" (163).

[16] Raumer's history of the Hohenstaufens (6 vols, from 1823) made a strong impact. Grabbe, as we shall see, wrote two Hohenstaufen plays; Immermann produced a *Kaiser Friedrich II* (1828) and Ernst Benjamin Raupach, as Hans Kohn informs us, "wrote a cycle of not less than sixteen plays called "Die Hohenstaufen," popular enough in their day to call forth an overture from the young Wagner (cf. Hans Kohn 129).

[17] In a letter (28 July 1835) quoted in John Reddick, *Georg Büchner. The Shattered Whole* (Oxford: Oxford UP, 1994), 60. As Edward McInnes points out, Büchner goes on to suggest that he is bringing history to life "as an immediate present," in other words, *not* writing history, nor indeed "historical drama" in any meaningful sense. Cf. Edward McInnes, "Scepticism, Ideology and History in Büchner's *Dantons Tod*" in *For Lionel Thomas,* ed. D. Attwood, A. Best, and R. Last (Hull: U of Hull, 1980), 55.

[18] As McInnes says (57), the belief of Robespierre and St Just in the Revolution is "essentially teleological."

[19] Cf. Rodney Taylor, *History and the Paradoxes of Metaphysics in Dantons Tod* (New York-Berne: Peter Lang, 1990) especially chapter 5.

[20] It is hard to see the "dialectical totality" to which Taylor refers (251), with Hegel and Schopenhauer as the two poles.

[21] The "gräßlicher Fatalismus der Geschichte"; quoted by most critics, for example, Walter Hinck: "Georg Büchner," in von Wiese, *Deutsche Dichter des 19. Jahrhunderts,* 205.

[22] C. D. Grabbe, *Napoleon oder die hundert Tage,* act V, scene 7, in Grabbe, *Werke,* ed. A. Bergmann, vol. 2 (Emsdetten [Westf.]: Verlag Lechte, 1963), 457. Grabbe's plays are quoted from this volume.

[23] Cf. his *Don Juan und Faust* (1829).

[24] *Werke* 2, 186.

[25] Hegel, *Philosophie der Geschichte,* quoted by Rodney Taylor 175.

[26] *Tradition and Revolution,* 152.

[27] "Nur das Fähnlein an deren Maste": Letter to his publisher, Kettembeil, 14 July, 1830.

[28] Cf. Kurt Jauslin, "Nackt in der Kälte des Raumes. Emblem und Emblematik in Grabbes historischer Maschine," *Grabbe-Jahrbuch* 9 (1990): 46–70. Coherence is foreign to this world; it is one of "sich wiederholende(n) Kreisläufe" (56).

[29] Diephold: "das schrecklichste, das tragischste Geschick"; *Werke* 2, 238.

[30] *Werke* 2, 234.

[31] Quoted by Kohn 163.

[32] Benno von Wiese, *Die deutsche Tragödie von Lessing bis Hebbel,* 470.

[33] von Wiese, *Tragödie,* 479. For Schiller, cf. 217.

[34] Cf. Franz Schuselka, "Politische Dramen" (1847) in M. Rietra, ed., *Jungöster-reich* (Amsterdam: Rodopi, 1980), 189, and Naumann, *Mitteleuropa,* 38.

[35] Helga-Maleen Gerresheim, "Christian Dietrich Grabbe" in B. von Wiese, ed.: *Deutsche Dichter des 19. Jahrhunderts* (Berlin: E. Schmidt, 1969), 187.

[36] When Jordanus Truchsess, through the symbolic object of the drinking-horn, makes "all the memories of the past awake" (85).

[37] A. J. P. Taylor points out that while "the idea of a Prussian leadership of Germany, when consciously formulated in 1848, still came with a shock of surprise," the way "had been unwittingly prepared throughout the preceding generation" (*The Course of German History,* 57).

[38] E.g. 47: "Ein herrlich Volk sind meine Deutschen" and 79: "Mein Deutschland ist doch wunderschön" (Barbarossa), the latter echoed in Henry the Lion's hymn of praise to Germany in *Kaiser Heinrich der Sechste* (154: "Sieh erst die Alpen ragen . . . etc.").

[39] Cf. "Über die Shakspearo-Manie," *Werke* IV (1966), 35.

[40] In commenting on the historical "superficiality" of Schiller's *Don Carlos;* Diary 25 December 1843. The portrayal of Carlos falls between the stools of "individual truth" and true (historical) tragic greatness, in which the "highest power" intervenes between the "world-historical individual" and his "world-historical purpose."

[41] Diary 1855.

[42] For an account (from the Austrian viewpoint!) of the pro-Prussian, and "kleindeutsch" tendency in the Frankfurt Parliament and Droysen's "spezifisch norddeutsches Wesen," see Heinrich von Srbik, *Deutsche Einheit. Idee und Wirklichkeit vom Heiligen Reich bis Königgrätz,* vol. 1 [Munich, 1935; reprint: Darmstadt: Wissenschaftliche Buchgesellschaft, 1963], 366–68. Srbik speaks of the "Hegelscher Beisatz" in Droysen's thinking. See also Thomas Nipperdey, *Germany from Napoleon to Bismarck* (Dublin, 1983), 458. Hegel's view of historical necessity certainly helped to lay the foundation for Prussia's assumption of German hegemony and it is hard to disagree with Taylor's view that even Marx and Engels would have had to acknowledge him as their "master" in this regard (cf. *The Course of German History,* 60).

[43] J. P. Stern, *Idylls and Realities* (London: Methuen, 1971), 24.

[44] For a detailed exposition of historicism, see Nipperdey 441–46.

[45] As formulated by W. T. Stace in *The Philosophy of Hegel* (London: Macmillan, 1924), 438 (para. 633).

[46] Nipperdey 449.

[47] In *Ein Wort über das Drama; Werke,* ed. G. Fricke (Munich: Hanser, 1952), vol. II, 276–77. Hebbel's works are cited from this edition.

[48] Cf. Herbert Marcuse, *Reason and Revolution. Hegel and the Rise of Social Theory* (London: Routledge, 1941), 224–29.

[49] He criticizes Schiller for presenting "nur Symbole, statt individueller Charaktere"; Diary 25 December 1843, *Werke* (ed. Poppe), IX, 404. This is the element of "psychological realism" which, as G. A. Wells says, is "not to be set aside," even in *Die Nibelungen:* cf. G. A. Wells, "The Enigma of Hebbel's Nibelungen," *New German Studies* 13 (1985): 157.

[50] *Ein Wort,* 276–77. Cf. the reference in the Diary (1843) to the "Grundverhältnisse, innerhalb derer alles vereinzelte Dasein entsteht und vergeht" (*Werke* II, 439). Individuation, says Sten G. Flygt, is, for Hebbel, "a sin against the Absolute": Sten G. Flygt, *Friedrich Hebbel's Conception of Movement in the Absolute and in History* (New York: AMS P, 1966), 2.

[51] Cf. entry No, 2224 in the Diary for 1843: "Das Leben ist eine furchtbare Notwendigkeit . . . etc." Tragedy, says Hebbel, "annihilates the individual life in the face of the Idea."

[52] ". . . entzündete sich an der Geschichte"; Diary 1852, quoted by Heald 16.

[53] See in particular his poem "Das abgeschiedene Kind an seine Mutter."

[54] Cf. his review of Gervinus's *Geschichte des neunzehnten Jahrhunderts* (1862), in *Hebbels Werke,* ed. Poppe, vol. 8, 480.

[55] 14 November 1848.

[56] E.g. by references to Galilee and Galileans, including the ironical Biblical echoes in Herodes's remark (I: 1): "Aus Galiläa kommt mir nichts als Gutes!" (cf. John 1, 46: "And Nathanael said unto him, Can there any good thing come out of Nazareth? And Philip said unto him, Come and see," and 7, 41 and 52: "Shall Christ come out of Galilee? . . . out of Galilee ariseth no prophet.").

[57] Sten G. Flygt 46.

[58] Diary, 19 April 1849: "Herodes und Mariamne wurde gegeben . . . Das Verwirrende lag für die Masse der Zuschauer in dem zweiten Moment des Dramas, in dem historischen, dessen Notwendigkeit . . . sie nicht begriffen."

[59] Edna Purdie, *Friedrich Hebbel* (1932; Oxford: Oxford UP, 1969), 171.

[60] See his letter to Felix Bamberg of 31 August 1850.

[61] *Hebbels Werke,* ed. Poppe, 8 Teil, 171–72.

[62] As against Grillparzer, he sees Austria and Prussia as "One Nation," and tends to review the situation each New Year's Eve: 31 December 1848: "Das Jahr ist wieder herum. Es hat Deutschland eine Revolution gebracht; ob mehr, soll sich erst zeigen. Alle Erbfehler unserer Nation stehen wieder in voller Blüte; hie Guelf, hie Ghibelline! Mich wundert nur, daß in dem Körper eines Deutschen Einigkeit herrscht . . ."; 31 December 1849: "Im allgemeinen dieselbe Unsicherheit der Zustände . . ."; 31 December 1850: "Deutschland liegt zerrissen und zerschlissen da, wie immer . . ."

[63] Purdie, *Hebbel*, 171.

[64] Introduction to *Agnes Bernauer* in *Hebbels Werke* (ed. Poppe) 4 Teil, 10.

[65] Hebbel notes in his Diary (24 December 1851) in connection with this play: "Nie habe ich das Verhältnis, worin das Individuum zum Staat steht, so deutlich erkannt, wie jetzt." For the "necessity" that subordinates the individual to the state, see Ernst's description of Agnes as "das reinste Opfer, das der Notwendigkeit im Lauf aller Jahrhunderte gefallen ist" (V: 10). It is interesting to note that when he was in Munich in 1852, Hebbel failed to convince the old King Ludwig of this necessity (letter to Christine, 8 March 1852).

[66] "die Schönheit von der tragischen . . . Seite," Diary, 30 September 1851. Cf. Preising's remark to Agnes (V: 2): "[die angestammte Majestät] ist unzertrennlich mit ihm [Albrecht] verbunden, wie die Schönheit, die ihn fesselt, mit Euch."

[67] Letter to Christine Hebbel, 3 March 1852. For the "Antigone"-theme, cf. particularly Mary Garland 225–29.

[68] "Ludwig von Ingolstadt, oder wer für ihn spricht, das Reich steht hinter mir, mit Acht und Aberacht, weh dem, der seine Ordnung stört!" (III: 13: *Werke* I, 538).

[69] Letter to Franz Dingelstedt, 12 December 1851.

[70] *Werke* II, 301. In the same place, Hebbel describes German history as a "Krankheitsgeschichte." In a remark (apropos of *Genoveva*) in the Diary for 1843 (No. 2415), Hebbel emphasizes the disjointed nature of German history, which made the modern German unable to feel himself as the product of an organic process, and condemned the Hohenstaufen Emperors "die zu Deutschland, das sie zerrissen und zersplitterten . . . kein anderes Verhältnis hatten als das des Bandwurms zum Magen."

[71] Cf. *Ein Wort über das Drama; Werke* II, 280.

[72] The main merit of *Faust*, he remarks in the review already referred to, is its brilliant depiction of a "Mittelalter . . . in dem die Welt einmal steckte und an den sie sich noch mit so manchem Faden verknüpft fühlt."

[73] *Vorwort zu Maria Magdalene, Werke* II, 300–301.

[74] By Ernst (III: 6) and Preising (III: 10), *Werke* I, 525 and 532.

[75] See Poppe's Introduction to *Agnes Bernauer, Hebbels Werke*, Teil 4, 11.

[76] *Der Engel von Augsburg* (1856) and *Agnes Bernauerin* (1859).

[77] Garland 230.

[78] Cf. chapter 4.

[79] Scene 8, p. 527. And indeed, the foundation-stone for the work to complete the cathedral had been laid as recently as 1842!

[80] Joachimsen 63.

[81] H. A. Korff, *Geist der Goethezeit*, IV, 259 ("die bedeutendste Aufgabe").

[82] It was a past that, for him had been "completely swept away": there was no continuum (quoted by Kohn 115).

[83] The "major topic"; cf. Nipperdey 627.

[84] See Storm's letter to Keller of 18 February 1879. ("Und diesen Kerl nennen Literaturgeschichten einen gewaltigen Epiker!") For Jordan, who was an admirer of Hebbel's, see Wells 143. The poem was written, as Peter Sprengel tells us, very much with Jordan's preoccupation of German unity and unification in mind. It was advertised as "ein Born deutscher Kraft und heldenhafter Gesinnung." Cf. P. Sprengel, *Geschichte der deutschsprachigen Literatur 1870–1900. Von der Reichsgründung bis zur Jahrhundertwende* (Munich: Beck, 1998) 220 and 221.

[85] Kohn 162. Wildenbruch also toyed with these themes.

[86] Class, *Deutsche Geschichte,* 391.

[87] Cf. Ursula Jespersen, "Detlev von Liliencron" in Benno von Wiese, ed., *Deutsche Dichter des 19. Jahrhunderts,* 513: The theme offers ". . . das Nibelungenmotiv in einer Variante, die das Einbeziehen neuzeitlichen Nationaldenkens erlaubte." Wildenbruch, "durch und durch Preuße," also sees historical drama as a vehicle for national consciousness: cf. Sengle 182. See also Sprengel 443–44.

[88] Cf. D. von Liliencron, *Dramen (Sämtliche Werke,* vol. 14) (Berlin-Leipzig: Schuster und Loeffler, n.d.), 63 and 66. The pagan-Christian contrast is also echoed (in the figure of King Niels) and the character of the "Mannweib" Ulvilda who "frightens" Knut (64) is not unreminiscent of Brunhild.

[89] Edna Purdie 212. Class showers praise on the *Nibelungenlied,* stressing in particular the "strength" of Siegfried and the "düstere Größe" of Hagen. Hebbel's version is for him "ein gewaltiges Bühnenwerk" (*Deutsche Geschichte,* 62 and 389). For the importance of the "Germanic-pagan" tradition in the development towards Nazism see Dietrich Bracher, *The German Dictatorship,* 46–47.

[90] Cf. the diary-entry dated 17 December 1859: "nie hat mich ein Werk . . . so angegriffen."

[91] Quoted in Ernst Loewy, *Literatur unterm Hakenkreuz,* 2nd edition (Frankfurt/Main: Europäische Verlagsanstalt, 1967), 153.

[92] Loewy 63 (from a book by Walther Linden).

[93] See G. A. Wells, "The Enigma of Hebbel's *Nibelungen,* " *New German Studies* 13 (1985): 143.

[94] Cf. in particular Wagner's essay "Was ist deutsch?"

[95] See Fritz Stern, *The Politics of Cultural Despair. A Study of the Rise of the Germanic Ideology* (New York: Doubleday, 1965). Though Stern does seem to wish to link Hebbel with his countryman Langbehn (132n.). For Langbehn, cf. also Ketelsen 128–47.

[96] Cf. Hildebrant's speech to Kriemhild: "Rührt dich denn nichts? . . . etc." (*Rache* V: 11).

[97] Letter of 2 December 1858: ". . . man glaubt so wenig an Menschen, die man nicht in ihrer Nationalität wurzeln sieht . . . etc."

[98] Letter to F. T. Vischer, 1 June 1862.

[99] *Werke* I, 66.

[100] "Vermittlung des Gedichts mit der Nation." Diary-entry 3 October 1856. See also Hebbel's letter to Hermann Marggraff of 5 April 1862, in which he calls himself the "Sprachrohr des alten Dichters."

[101] Letter to his wife Christine, 2 February 1861: "Eine Aufmerksamkeit und Totenstille als ob nicht von der Vergangenheit, sondern von der Zukunft die Rede wär(e)": quoted by Poppe in *Hebbels Werke,* vol. 8, 11.

[102] Purdie 233.

[103] Cf. *Rache* IV: 4. Giselher: "Wir können ja nicht anders." Kriemhild: "Kann denn ich?"

[104] E.g. *Rache* II: 11, 773 ("Und wenn die Norne selbst . . .").

[105] In bathing in the dragon's blood, Siegfried not only "goes beyond the bounds of nature," as Hebbel wrote to Hermann Hettner (31 December 1859), he goes beyond the bounds of historical time as well.

[106] Cf. Hagen, *Rache* I: 2 (742): "Die Nibelungen haben ihren Vater Um Gold erschlagen . . ." and Volker's "visionary" account (*Rache* IV: 1, 791–92).

[107] Annina Periam, *Hebbel's Nibelungen* (New York: Macmillan, 1906), 209.

[108] Annina Periam 211. Wells (150) sees the scene as "unnecessary to the action": to the *dramatic* action, that is!

[109] Hebbel notes in his Diary (22 November 1859) that he has just finished act II of the *Rache:* "Die Prophezeiung der Meerweiber, die eine furchtbare Perspektive für die Zukunft eröffnet und Siegfrieds Geburt, die ein mystisches Licht auf die Vergangenheit wirft, dürften gelungen sein . . ."

[110] *Die deutsche Tragödie von Lessing bis Hebbel,* 630.

7: The Modern Age: Schnitzler and Brecht

ES GIBT KEIN DRAMA MEHR." This saying by Iwan Goll[1] is, in one sense of the word, manifestly not true: there is no lack of plays in German after the onset of the Modern Movement; many on themes taken from history, and among these, works whose "modern" credentials are indisputable. One thinks of Dürrenmatt's treatment of the Anabaptist theocracy in Münster (*Es steht geschrieben* [1947], recast as *Die Wiedertäufer* in 1967). Goll's remark makes sense, however, if applied to the idea of drama as it had existed since Aristotle: a coherent action between defined characters, located in a known reality. If "character" and "reality" become unstable and subjective notions, drama in its classic form comes under threat. One can see the fault-line developing between Ibsen and Chekhov.[2] Historical drama is probably more at risk than most other kinds, since the "historical" quality is linked with the idea of objective factuality, but insofar as such twentieth-century plays are indisputably "modern" (as distinct from, say, Hochwälder's *Das heilige Experiment*) they are a-, if not un-historical. The ambivalence, from the 1890s onward,[3] of the concept "reality," and its psychological internalisation, militate against the realisation of past actuality in the objective form essential to the "historical" effect. Elisabeth Brock-Sulzer says of *Es steht geschrieben* that it presents "nicht das Bild einer geschichtlichen Welt, sondern eine Welt eigenen Gesetzes." Dürrenmatt himself, in laying the foundation for his idiosyncratic conception of "Komödie" in an appendix to *Die Wiedertäufer*, denies that dramatic reality is any longer possible. Bokkelson (John of Leyden) ". . . wird in eine Fiktion verwandelt, wird zum 'Theater.'"[4] There is no room here for a sense of community between real past and present.

Expressionism aims to break with history and achieve a radical spiritual renewal. Georg Kaiser's *Die Bürger von Calais* (1912–13) begins with a strong sense of historical reality (the physical reality of Calais and its harbour), but moves progressively further away from the actuality of the period to a ritualistic, quasi-religious portrayal of the potential, at least, of the "New Man" who, as Martini has said, is "timeless."[5] The Marxist would demand realism: it is interesting to note that a Marxist historian of literature finds *more* realism in Kaiser's *Gas*-trilogy![6] Dürrenmatt, as he develops his philosophy of comedy, distances himself from history. In his "ungeschichtliche historische Komödie" *Romulus der Große* (1949/58) he plays with the idea of history, by exploiting the difference between what we see (that is, Odoacer as a civilized man of peace!) and what we know. Bockelson, in *Die Wiedertäufer*, escapes the fate of his historical prototype, and is absorbed into the world of "theatre."

With the work of such as Wildenbruch, Sengle sees the history of historical drama as "abgeschlossen."[7] Naturalism is at the same time the ultimate in "realism," and the opening of a door into a new, and more complex world, in which "reality" is a concept much harder to grasp. For those in the 1890s who would have seen the signs of the new age appearing, to be "anchored in history," as Sprengel puts it, was to be anchored in reality as traditionally understood, to make oneself as safe as one could within a "Schutzburg vor . . . der Moderne."[8]

Hauptmann's *Florian Geyer* (1896) did represent, as Sengle indicates, an impulse toward a "new, more lively form of historical drama" in the image of Naturalism.[9] It cannot be simply brushed aside: it presents a past age as a vividly realized theatrical present, in which robustly drawn characters, speaking an authentic-sounding "old" German, live and have their being. Like *Die Weber*, it gives "the masses" dramatic presence, but as historical drama, it was without issue. In Hauptmann's own case, it points, not so much to the historical, as to the mythic, even mystical domain, and the vagueness of its concept of a political "German nation," whose "tragedy" and "betrayal" the fate of the hero symbolizes, makes it hard for the reader or spectator to pin it down historically. While Wildenbruch's *König Heinrich*, in the same year, had a resounding success with an audience that, rightly or wrongly, could see a relationship with the era of Bismarck, Hauptmann's play was an equally resounding failure on the stage.[10]

There is much less of a sense of community than is the case with its most obvious predecessor, *Götz von Berlichingen*. Hauptmann, it seems, had a misty idea of the Reformation as a Great Renewal, an "elemental" phenomenon, in Kurt Lothar Tank's words,[11] and while *Geyer* was planned as the more "material" part of a (never realized) greater whole, we already see the hero here visualizing himself, not as a political martyr, but as a John the Baptist-figure in the context of the Kyffhäuser-legend: "Dem Barbarossa will ich den Weg bereiten."[12] While we cannot unequivocally brand Hauptmann a Nazi (though he

has been called a "Quisling of the Inner Emigration"),[13] it is understandable that there should have been a renewal of interest in the play
during the Nazi period.[14] Its rather wild, unfocussed energy, which is
of a piece with the tendency toward the mysterious and irrational that
was always a key factor in his make-up, does leave the door open for
such a development. With the ending of the kind of certainty that
Wildenbruch and his audiences shared, history, and in particular, history with a national dimension, became increasingly uncertain and in-
secure ground for the dramatist. Fritz Martini considers that: "Das
Geschichtsdrama aber ist in unseren Zeiten in einen schlechten Ruf
gekommen. Drama und Theater können sich auf die Geschichte nur
einlassen, wenn sie eben als Geschichte aufgehoben ist."[15]

Special circumstances could provide a platform for the occasional
recrudescence of the historical drama proper, albeit in a somewhat
muted form. The First World War prompted some to search for inspiration in history. In Paul Ernst's "neo-classical" historical plays, Sengle
says, "[ist] das formale und ideelle Element derart übersteigert, daß
die Wahl des Geschichtsstoffs ohne Bedeutung bleibt."[16] A play like
Preußengeist (1914/5) is hardly worthy of close analysis here, but its
patent attempt to glorify the "heroic" spirit of the Wilhelmian
"Reich" through a link with the assumed "Preußentum" of Frederick
the Great, a by no means isolated example of historical drama as
propaganda,[17] cannot be totally ignored. The same war caused Hofmannsthal to find himself as a patriot and to seek, and find in Austria's
past, an "Austrian Idea." One feels its imminence, in what Joseph
Redlich called a "Land der ererbten Müdigkeiten und Halbheiten" in
which the signs of approaching catastrophe were becoming ever more
frequent, the "Vorverstehen" to which the author himself referred in a
letter of December 1914,[18] fully reflected in Arthur Schnitzler's "dramatic history" of the Napoleonic period, *Der junge Medardus* (1910).
The shadow of an approaching war looms even more menacingly over
Brecht's *Mutter Courage und ihre Kinder* (1938/9).[19]

As Hofmannsthal's Prologue to Schnitzler's *Anatol* so poetically
indicates, there were some at least who saw that to be Austrian in a
fin-de-siècle Vienna still presided over by Emperor Franz Joseph, was
in itself to be in a sense history: "Rokoko, verstaubt und lieblich," yet
simultaneously aware of the un-reality of this reality, the fact that it
was "Theater." Schnitzler, certainly, is an acknowledged master of the
half-lights, and graceful, yet unsettling mixture of moods of turn-of-
the-century Vienna, but he was by no means out of touch with its social, and political, realities. In the letter to Elisabeth Steinrück to

which we have already referred, he strenuously denied that he had
turned his back on contemporary Austrian life. Schnitzler was concerned with the problems of the present, the depths of the human
psyche, the reality of reality, and so on, in addition to his personal
preoccupations with death and time, in a modern context. But the
present included the real society, and country, in which he lived.

Schnitzler's first novel, *Der Weg ins Freie* (1908), is a thorough
and serious examination of the Austria of his day, including its politics:
the failure of electoral reform to cure what Karl von Grabmayr called
the "Unnatur" of Austrian parliamentary life, the fragility of Austrian
liberalism and indeed Old Austria, for which the "deutschnational"
Linz Programme of 1882, the rise of figures like Lueger and Schöne-
rer, whom Stadler links to Lagarde in his hostility to non-Germanic
peoples,[20] could be seen as symbolic.[21] In spite of his antipathy to
politicians and their simplistic generalities and slogans,[22] there is sufficient evidence that even before the war, Schnitzler felt an interest in
the social and political affairs of his homeland. It may be that, as a
man of Liberal convictions, he could see no clear path in the world of
practical politics, but the thesis of the totally a-political Schnitzler,
"abseits jeglicher Politik" in Felix Salten's phrase,[23] does not hold. It
was the part of him that felt as an "Austrian" that prompted Schnitzler
to write *Der junge Medardus*. This is by no means the only play of his
which is set in the past (one thinks for example of *Der Schleier der
Beatrice, Paracelsus, Der grüne Kakadu* and *Der Gang nach dem Wei-
her*), but it is the only one that convinces as historical drama. If we
take the other plays just mentioned, we find, even in the *Kakadu*,
which takes place among the febrile atmosphere of a Paris in which
the Old Regime is on the brink of collapse, as it might also be said to
have been in modern Austria, that there is little historical substantiality. While we are in theory well aware — since we have read our history
books — of the nemesis which waits outside for the aristocrats, it is on
the "modern" questions of reality and identity, the almost Pirandello-
esque oscillation between "Sein" and "Spielen" within the theatre-
cum-"Spelunke," that the main emphasis lies.[24]

Der junge Medardus is set in the year 1809, the year of Austria's
premature attempt to unite the German nation (still more of an idea
than a reality) against Napoleon; a mixture, then, of the heroic and
the foolhardy or plain incompetent, but also the darkest hour before a
coming dawn. (The audience would have been well aware of this, of
course, and if it took the criticism on board, and perhaps made the
application to its own present condition, could also have glimpsed a

flash of hope for itself.) It is the period of the uprising in the Tyrol (which Vienna encouraged and on which it then turned its back), Napoleon's entry into the capital, the triumph of Aspern (described by Kann as "Austria's finest hour")[25] and the disaster of Wagram, and the signing of an ignominious peace, all in the space of about five months. Napoleon himself never appears as a character, but is always a presence and a preoccupation. The main actors are the middle-class citizens of Vienna, centring on the Klähr family, and an invented family of aristocratic French émigrés, the Valois, who nurse the fond dream of a Restoration, and whose plotting against Napoleon, indeed whose whole existence, is "theatrical" and pointless. Even this invention, justifiable on the grounds that the real-theatrical dualism runs through the play as a thematic thread, Schnitzler nevertheless felt himself called upon to defend as historically legitimate — that is, not disruptive of the sense of historical reality. It fitted in, he claimed, with the "Atmosphäre der Zeit und menschliche Möglichkeit."[26]

The principal dramatic thread, running in tandem with the "epic" thread of events, is the theme of heroism, at both the national and the personal level, and this turns out to be a broad and ironically complex spectrum. Vienna's truest, and most genuinely "Austrian" hero is its profoundest sceptic (Medardus's uncle, Jakob Eschenbacher). Medardus, its most idealistic seeker after a genuinely heroic act, eventually finds it, not by *doing* his "deed," but by resolving to "die for it"[27] in order to make it his own at last, having spent most of the action in a daze, wandering in a labyrinth of false "realities" imposed on him from outside by conventions and "words."[28] This makes him the war's "oddest"[29] hero.

But then, Austria itself was an oddity: a political entity with a long history, but no national identity. Schnitzler himself called it "ein sehr wunderbares und sehr kompliziertes Land."[30] This was as true in the early twentieth century, as it had been in the early nineteenth. It was an anomaly: a country with a sophisticated culture, but a socio-political structure dating from the *ancien régime*. As a "nation," it was something of a pantomime-horse, governable only by an effectively autocratic bureaucracy. Everyone knew this could not go on, but no one knew how it could be brought to an end. The Liberal system was exhausted and the role of the modern mass-parties was distorted by the national question, with a "deutschnational" tendency arising to complicate the issue still further. As far as the existence of Austria as a nation was concerned, as Joseph Redlich put it, "hopelessness was everywhere the mood and keynote of all the elements in national and social life which were excluded from a direct share of power."[31]

"An Taten war man in Österrreich nicht gewöhnt," says Hantsch,[32] and when Aehrenthal's administration more or less stumbled into the annexation of Bosnia and Herzegovina (1908), it was an act that brought war considerably closer. It was avoided on this occasion, but there were already voices from within, especially that of Conrad von Hötzendorf, the Chief of the General Staff and "one of the foremost gravediggers of the Habsburg Monarchy,"[33] prophesying war against Serbia. These were abetted from without by the solidarity of the new generation of German politicians such as Bülow, now willing, apparently, as Bismarck had not been, to sacrifice the bones of their Pomeranian grenadiers in an Eastern adventure and ready to swear "Nibelungentreue" to their Austrian brothers.[34] The atmosphere was stifling, and even a liberal like Schnitzler felt a momentary sense of relief when the war actually broke out, and was temporarily able to use the word "Vaterland" as if it were a real personal experience, not a conventional generality.[35]

He soon came round, though, to the view that the public patriotism, with its heroic rhetoric, was false, and reverted to his pre-war position, in which it was easier to love Austria as an individual, and real, "Heimat," than as a generalized, and abstract, "Vaterland." This seems to be prefigured, not just by Bernhardi's unheroic withdrawal from the public sphere, but by Medardus's eventual self-emancipation through self-sacrifice (though the process is convoluted), and above all by the case of Eschenbacher. There was, as we have seen, something unreal about the "official" Austria of Schnitzler's day, and his awareness of that is reflected in our play, but there *is* a real Austria, and a real Austrian heroism, which needs to be disentangled from the pretence and self-deception that surround it. A principal purpose of Schnitzler's portrayal of the citizens of Vienna as they — and their patriotic preconceptions, fed by Gentz's Romantic manifesto, and by the rousing songs of Collin — are confronted by the brutal reality of Napoleon, is to do just that. Eschenbacher does not believe in the rhetoric and consistently ironizes it, but he does his civic duty. He sacrifices himself, not for some abstraction, but for his sister and her family. When the volatile Viennese, whose moods, from patriotic defiance to the desperate call for the White Flag, are all unreliable, but "all genuine,"[36] decide that he is a national hero who deserves a marble monument, his sister remarks truly: "Es liegt wohl schon zu viel Erde auf dem Grab, sonst möchten wir ihn schon lachen hören. Der Jakob und ein Monument!" (DW 2, 179).

In a sense, though, the play itself is a monument. It certainly does not lack its authentically "modern" side, with its portrait of its main "hero," which is an investigation, not only of *a* character, but also of the ideas of character as such, and of "meaning" in life. There are certainly impressionistic and possibly Machian[37] overtones about Medardus, who is simultaneously a hero, and a "fool"[38] whose will, unlike Helene's[39] is at the mercy of impulses and stimuli.[40] But also, as Etzelt points out, of events, of the "Lauf der Dinge" and "in times like these," as General Rapp replies, the title of fool can be "ein Ehrenname . . . wie ein anderer" (DW 2, 215).

Rapp's words are surely a pointer towards an historical understanding of the action in other "times like these." Medardus does have a brief episode in which he is able, like some other Schnitzlerian characters, to escape the time and the reality of the physical world and live in those of the mind, almost the world of feelings and atmospheres inhabited by Anatol, in which all that matters is the moment of "Glück," but he knows that this "cannot last."[41] Medardus is also a man "of his time": the era of Romantic idealism,[42] which helps to explain the quasi-religious exaltation he feels at the flag-dedication ceremony.[43] It is a time in which the political forms and attitudes of the *ancien régime* are beginning to lose their solidity, one in which the concept of "nation" is beginning to enter the vocabulary of those who previously thought in terms of more or less personal quarrels between dynasts. Above all, the idea of a "German" national community, transcending other more incidental boundaries, is in the air, indeed, has been deliberately raised by the Archduke's manifesto, to which Kribbling explicitly refers. Although it is pointed out that the Germans are by no means united against Napoleon, Kribbling's "Es wird sich ändern"[44] is prophetic for an audience that knows that the War of Liberation is to come. And the solidarity of the greater "German nation," in spite of 1866, is surely also an issue in the pre-war hothouse atmosphere within which this play appeared.

However, there had been an 1866, and Austria had had to seek a separate way and become a "Vaterland" in its own right, a fact that confronted us in our dealings with Grillparzer. The theme of the North-South, Prussian-Austrian divide still resonates in Naumann's plea for a united (that is, in some sense German)[45] "Mitteleuropa."[46] Hofmannsthal, writing in time of war, keeps the distinction between Austrian and German, in an essay in which, significantly, he goes back to Grillparzer as the archetypal Austrian. Grillparzer, we recall, distinguished between the Austrian and non-Austrian German on the grounds that the latter found his relation to present actuality complicated by the fatal fascination of abstract ideas and what Schnitzler might have called "die großen Worte."[47] Hofmannsthal, who is certainly interested in promoting Austro-German solidarity, says something not so very dissimilar. The Austrian can respond to the present directly; the German needs to relate it to an idea:

> Es ist nicht die dunkle Tiefe, durch welche der österreichische Geist den Kranz erringt, sondern die Klarheit, die Gegenwart. Der Deutsche hat ein schwieriges, behindertes Gefühl zur Gegenwart . . . er ist hier und nicht hier, er ist über der Zeit und nicht in ihr . . . [the Germans] ringen um den Sinn der Gegenwart, uns ist er gegeben.[48]

In terms of this essay, Medardus is the more "German," and Eschenbacher the more "Austrian" of Schnitzler's heroes. The contrast between the heroism and patriotism of these two, which is one of the principal structural pillars of the play, helps to give it a national-historical dimension. The Eschenbacher whom Berger praises, at his grave, as an Austrian patriot was first and foremost, as Frau Föderl says, what he himself had exhorted Medardus to become: "ein Mann" (DW 2, 176, 178); someone who refused to see the world through the glass of some conventional formula. Eschenbacher would, indeed, have rejected the cliché-reaction, used even of a little child killed by accident (DW 2, 198), that he had "died for his country." Yet he is as much of a loyal patriot as anyone else, if not more so and by "standing at his post"[49] and showing up the false heroic rhetoric of so many of his fellow-citizens,[50] he can also be said to act as an image of true, positive Austrian heroism: reality rather than attitude. If, as Egon Schwarz has said, Schnitzler "enters into judgement on the Viennese mentality"[51] in severe terms, he does at the same time offer a positive counter-image, a guiding light in a confused and complex world, one which, for Schnitzler himself and his audience, was shortly to become even more difficult. We are reminded most forcefully of Eschenbacher when we read Schnitzler's own definition, in a letter to Leo Fromm of 24 January 1915, of true patriotism:

> Für mich ist in Friedens- wie in Kriegszeiten nur der ein Patriot, der die Sache seines Vaterlandes fördert, indem er an seinem ihm angewiesenen Platz, nach dem Maß seiner Begabung redlich seine Pflicht erfüllt, ohne seine Nachbarn in ihrem gleichen Bemühen durch scheinpatriotische Wichtigtuerei zu behindern.[52]

While it is true that Schnitzler avoids any analysis of the psychology of this character, whereas Medardus seems to come closer to the more "modern" situation of the characters in the almost contemporaneous *Das weite Land*, in which there is "keine Sicherheit mehr auf Erden" and "Das Natürliche . . . ist das Chaos" (DW 2, 281), and at times even teeters on the brink of breakdown, we should remember that Eschenbacher is in effect a finished character, while Medardus is striving to become one, to be "ganz ich selbst" (DW 2, 212). It could be that the final position to which Schnitzler brings him, by an admittedly tortuous route, is not so very far removed from Eschenbacher's. This is not tragedy,[53] but neither is it comedy, or, as *Das weite Land* is designated, tragi-comedy. Modernity is tempered here by the (less exclusively "dramatic") spirit of the "History in dramatic form," an approach which Schnitzler himself highlighted in his subtitle. The play was too "sceptical," not monolithically "heroic" enough, to please the German critics when it was put on in Berlin in 1914, but Schnitzler, who had sensed that this might be the reaction even before the outbreak of war, is surely justified in remarking to Elisabeth Steinrück that what he continues to cherish as a "prächtiges Theaterstück" contains, if anything, *less* "Fragezeichen" than most of his plays.[54] Even the vacillating, "inconsistent"[55] Medardus is a hero with a potential historical resonance.

The Austrian situation, then as now, is characterised, as Schnitzler sees it, by mess and muddle, and a great deal of "Theater," which is duly ironised. The spontaneous "Demonstration" of patriotic feeling which erupts at a performance of some quite harmless play by the deservedly forgotten Heinrich Zschokke ("weiter Krieg führen wollen . . . im Theater!" [DW 2, 198]) brings a smile to the lips, but it has its positive side as well. It shows the survival of a genuine Austrian feeling, and the possibility of a continuation of the struggle against Napoleon in the future, when conditions are more favourable. *Der junge Medardus*, Schwarz tells us, was applauded even by Schnitzler's natural enemies, ". . . weil sie ihren österreichischen Schiller und ihren zeitgenössischen Grillparzer, weil sie partout ihre vaterländische Tragödie haben wollten."[56] This was certainly not what Schnitzler was offering them, but perhaps they were not entirely led astray by wishful thinking. This is not "Land of Hope and Glory," but neither has Schnitzler turned his back on his homeland. As late as 2 August 1918, with collapse staring Austria in the face, he was able to write to Georg Brandes celebrating the many "positive Möglichkeiten in diesem Land."

Formally, Schnitzler has also taken account of the special needs of historical drama. The huge cast, the panoramic variety of its scenes (it was originally planned as "eine phantastische Historie in etwa 20 Bildern")[57] and its sense of constant movement and activity remind us, almost, of Goethe's *Götz von Berlichingen;* indeed, Schnitzler's friend Schlenther was so reminded.[58] By comparison with his other plays on historical themes, Schnitzler has gone to great lengths to endow the period and setting with historical solidity. There is a wealth of contemporary reference: to events such as Aspern[59] and Wagram,[60] the uprising in the Tyrol,[61] and to detail of contemporary actuality (such as Collin,[62] the Deutschmeister,[63] or Schrämbel's atlas),[64] the city of Vienna itself, in the images of the "Bastei" (act III) and of Schönbrunn (act V, scene 2) thrusts itself onto the stage as a physical presence. Austrian-ness in this play is not just an "atmosphere" or a "manner"; it has a local, and historically temporal, name and habitation.

Bertolt Brecht might well have claimed that with the advent of Marxist "historisches Denken"[65] (with its Hegelian roots),[66] it was possible for the first time to speak of a true "German historical drama." On the other hand, it might be claimed that with Brechtian "Historisierung," which submits all people and processes to examination from the point of view of socio-political "development,"[67] we are back with the Baroque concept that nothing can be distinguished as peculiarly "historical," since everything is. Marxist "historicality" is achieved by stripping away much of the individuality of historical fact. Heinrich Mann's *Madame Legros* (1913), a play set at the outbreak of the French Revolution, is "historical," for Kaufmann, by virtue of an "Analogieschluß."[68] "Historicization" is the ultimate alienation-effect: it enables the critical spectator to see his or her relation to society (which always has primacy), "als historisch und verbesserbar,"[69] and by the same token, the playwright to compose, and the actors play, "Stücke aus unserer eigenen Zeit als historische Stücke."[70] The present "becomes history," as Brecht has it in the *Messingkauf;*[71] the almost inevitable corollary is that the past can be seen in terms of the present. Only in such circumstances could Brecht, in the "Modellbuch" of *Mutter Courage und ihre Kinder*, reject the presentation of Courage's commercial activity in Zurich as "natural" and "human," whereas she should have been seen as a *petit-bourgeois* capitalist, and add: "Das Proletariat als Klasse kann den Krieg abschaffen, indem es den Kapitalismus abschafft."[72]

This might seem to contradict the view, expressed, for example in the *Messingkauf*, in the characteristically simplistic critique of Schiller's

Wallenstein given by the Marxist "philosopher,"[73] that it is not the "eternally human" aspects of character and motivation that need to be stressed, but rather those which are "historical" in the sense that they are socially conditioned and subject to change, and that the case should be seen as an "historische[n] Fall, mit Ursachen aus der Epoche und Folgen in der Epoche," and its moral issues as specific to a particular system in a particular society.[74] The fact is, however, that within his lights as an "enlightened" historical observer from the eighteenth century, Schiller did just that, and that in order to "historicize" the action, the conceptual Marxist playwright would have to abstract it altogether from any kind of recognizable seventeenth-century context and subject it to analysis from a totally foreign perspective, one which interprets the Thirty Years' War as, in Brecht's words, "einer der ersten Riesenkriege, die der Kapitalismus über Europa gebracht hat."[75]

Wallenstein as "capitalist" might have made an interesting figure: alas, he does not even rate a mention in Brecht's own "seventeenth-century" play, which resolutely refuses to pay more than intermittent, and ironic, attention to the doings of the "ruling class." They have made the war, but it is the struggle of the common people to survive within that war that concerns Brecht. The latter can also be said to have their history; unfortunately, it is very difficult to give them an historical identity, and Brecht has made very little attempt to do so. In the final analysis, they are of interest to him, not as people of the seventeenth century, but in class-terms which are in fact difficult to apply to that period. The reason why Courage "does not learn" (and cannot be allowed to learn) from what happens to her, is that she is a child, not of her time, but rather of her "class," the petty bourgeoisie: a concept which can only be squeezed into a discussion of life in the 1640s by main force, and by the substitution of Goethe's "grey theory" for the colour of life. Thus, Georg Lukács can say that Goethe is "historically authentic" (in the retrospective light of Marxian historical materialism), in showing the "necessity" of Götz von Berlichingen's defeat.[76] The Age of Absolutism is, in Marxist terms, at most one of "transition" between feudalism and capitalism, and it is stretching the definition considerably to speak of a "bourgeoisie" in the relatively retarded economic climate of seventeenth-century Germany. Yet we are told that the "Schlechtigkeit" Courage shows (in the "Capitulation" scene) is "nicht die Schlechtigkeit ihrer Person, so sehr als die ihrer Klasse."[77]

Courage is often critical of the "Great Ones" and their assumptions, and there is no reason why, as a member of the lower orders in the seventeenth century, she should not have been. One can see such criticism in Grimmelshausen too. But what we do not find in her is any trace at all of the "Baroque" mentality, of the conditioning of the social order into which she was born, which is present in even the most radically rebellious of all Grimmelshausen's characters, namely the "Erzbetrügerin und Landstörtzerin" Courasche, who gave Brecht's heroine her name . . . and precious little else.[78]

Certainly, Brecht does place his epic "chronicle" of the lives of "little" people within a lightly sketched framework of documented historical events and names. He begins with Gustavus Adolphus's campaign in Poland, which he seems to conflate with the German "Glaubenskrieg," though strictly speaking, it was not part of it at all, rather a distraction from which Sweden had to be extricated by French policy. Brecht's theme is the phenomenon of war as a whole (and its relation to capitalism), and so the absence of such fine distinctions, as indeed of any reference to seventeenth-century politics (above all the Habsburg-Bourbon conflict), or of any real attempt to understand the importance of religion for the period,[79] is not entirely surprising. It does, however, alienate (in a *non*-Brechtian sense!) the action from the substantial (as opposed to theoretical) historical reality of its location. Historically documented occurrences, indeed, are presented, not on the stage, but on the banners suspended across it, and comment among the stage-figures reflects no great understanding of, or interest in, the motivations, intentions and strategies of those who are conducting the war. These latter are subsumed into an impersonal "they," whose motive is "Gewinn"[80] pure and simple. Brecht would argue, of course, that this simplistic "purity" is the result of a true [Marxist] historicization, in which the details of the superstructure (historical accuracy and specific historical atmosphere) are not allowed to confuse the "real" historical issue, namely "the historicity of the thought-content."[81] But he could hardly deny that this in turn has involved a de-historicization of the subject-*matter*. How much knowledge of the seventeenth century he pre-supposed in his ideal spectator is not clear, but it is apparent that he did not wish him to deploy any such knowledge in the interest of a sense of distinction, and of historical community, between present and past.

The "community" which Brecht shows between the seventeenth and the twentieth centuries is, in fact, not historical in any meaningful sense, but (in his own terminology), "ewig menschlich." Brecht's instinct is correct in not allowing Courage to "learn" from her experience: the correct conclusions are such that only a generation in which a proletariat exists can draw them. Certainly, the "common people" in the seventeenth century could make reflections of the "When Adam delved and Eve span" variety, but for Courage, the Cook, or anyone else to proceed from that to revolutionary insights would have been, not prophetic, but absurdly anachronistic. Indeed, Courage comes perilously close to such an anachronism when she speaks of the common people "tolerating" an Emperor and Pope,[82] with the implication that they (that is, the "arme Leut" of the seventeenth century) had any alternative but to do so.

The scene in which this remark occurs (No. 6, following the death of Tilly) focusses quite strongly on the relation between the common people and the figures — none of them are *characters* in this play — who, *pace* Brecht, are the only historical ones mentioned in the text, because they are the only ones, praiseworthy or not, to whom the record has given an historical reality, of whom we can think that they *have* existed, both in time and in material reality. In particular in Courage's speech (144) on generals and emperors, his aim is to achieve historicization by debunking "history," seen as a record of the past. They have a time-oriented view of history: they wish to have their names survive into "künftige Zeiten," and though Brecht ignores this (inconvenient) fact, that is precisely what has occurred. When the Chaplain says of Tilly's interment that it is "an historic moment" (156), he means just that: it will go down in history: history, that is, as chronicle in *our* sense of the word. Courage's reply, namely that the injury suffered by Kattrin is *her* "historic moment" (157), makes a valid point, but at the same time denies her own, and Kattrin's historicity. She knows that her existence, and Kattrin's, will *not* be recorded. The fact that something has happened that threatens to ruin her daughter's life is certainly no less important, and no less worthy of sympathy, than the death of a general, but it is important either in its own present, or as an "eternal" symbol: it is not history. It cannot be said to have any potential influence on the outcome of the Thirty Years' War, or any other events which could reach out across time to the reader or spectator of a later age. Courage is indeed a vehicle for Brechtian "historicization," by dint of the de-historicization of the individual historical actuality in favour of Marxist "history."

We can leave aside the possible debate as to whether it is entirely true that the "great" can achieve nothing without the common people. What matters from our point of view is the fact that it is they who took the decisions and directed the battles that decided the fate of the Empire out of which, by an admittedly very tortuous historical development, the modern state, with Prussia rather than Austria as its nucleus, had arisen. Only through them, if indeed at all, could twentieth-century German spectators of this play have made contact with their own past. Brecht, quite evidently, is not interested in evoking such a sense of historical community. This is not, of course, to imply that his use of the material, historical omissions and inaccuracies and all, is in any way illegitimate. He has his own clear and consistent point of view, and has written a play that can stand alongside Schiller's *Wallenstein,* but whereas the latter belongs to the history of historical drama, *Mutter Courage* does not. It is simply another confirmation that whereas history itself continues, in modern times, to fascinate, and to have its uses for the playwright as well as the historian, at some time around the end of nineteenth century, historical drama as we have conceived it, grew pale and spectre-thin. Whether it can ever recover its vigour is very much a moot point.

Notes

[1] Quoted by Klaus Ziegler in the essay "Das moderne Drama als Spiegel unserer Zeit" in *Der Deutschunterricht* 13 (1961): 12.

[2] J. L. Styan, for example, speaks of the "special effort of perception" required by a Chekhov play, of the "unending complexity" of the thematic threads and the "submerged character relationships" (*Modern Drama in Theory and Practice. I: Realism and Naturalism* [Cambridge: Cambridge UP, 1981; paperback edition, 1983], 88 and 89). Ibsen, on the other hand, retained elements of the "well-made play" (83).

[3] E.g. (as one for many others), Leroy R. Shaw, in *The Playwright and Historical Change* (Madison/Milwaukee: U of Wisconsin P 1970): "By century's end, it was obvious that this secure and 'real' world [of the nineteenth century] was changing": 21.

[4] E. Brock-Sulzer, *Friedrich Dürrenmatt. Stationen seines Weges,* 3rd edition (Zurich: Arche, 1970), 24, and Friedrich Dürrenmatt, *Die Wiedertäufer* (Zurich, 1967), 107.

[5] See the article "Expressionismus" in the *Reallexikon der deutschen literaturgeschichte,* 2nd edition, ed. W. Kohlschmidt and W. Mohr (Berlin: de Gruyter, 1958), 423.

[6] Hans Kaufmann, et al., *Geschichte der deutschen Literatur vom Ausgang des 19. Jahrhunderts bis 1917* (Berlin: Volk und Wissen, 1974), 513.

[7] Friedrich Sengle, *Das deutsche Geschichtsdrama* (Stuttgart: Metzler, 1952), 189.

[8] P. Sprengel, *Geschichte der deutschsprachigen Literatur 1870–1900. Von der Reichsgründung bis zur Jahrhundertwende* (Munich: Beck, 1998), 220 and 221, 67.

[9] Sengle 188.

[10] See M. Sinden, *Gerhart Hauptmann: The Prose Plays* (Toronto-London: U of Toronto P, 1957), 97.

[11] K. L. Tank, *Gerhart Hauptmann* (Hamburg: Rowohlt, 1959), 78.

[12] Cf. Geyer's speech in the Second Act: "Ich dank Euch, liebe bäurische Brüder! . . . Ich gehe von Euch, damit das Gottestreiben dieser Zeit zu einem seligen Ende geführt werde. Im Kyffhäuser ist es lebendig worden . . . etc.": Gerhart Hauptmann, *Gesammelte Werke* (Jubiläumsausgabe), vol. 2 (Berlin: S. Fischer, n.d.), 126.

[13] Cf. Karl S. Guthke, "Der 'König der Weimarer Republik,'" in K. S. G., *Erkundungen. Essays zur Literatur von Milton bis Traven* (New York-Frankfurt-Berne: Peter Lang, 1983), 313.

[14] There was even, sad to relate, an SS cavalry division that bore the title "Florian Geyer."

[15] F. Martini, *Geschichte im Drama — Drama in der Geschichte* (Stuttgart: Klett/Cotta, 1979), 106.

[16] Sengle 189.

[17] Among other examples of that period are Emil Ludwig's *Friedrich, Kronprinz von Preußen* and Hermann Burte's *Katte* (also 1914). As with the "Nibelungen" theme, one can trace that of "Preußentum" into the darker waters of the twentieth century, that is, in the thinking of a "conservative revolutionary" such as Ernst Jünger, as Loewy shows (*Literatur unterm Hakenkreuz* [Frankfurt/Main: Europäische Verlagsanstalt, 1967], 212 and 233). Jünger was, of course, no Nazi, but he did, perhaps, contribute to the heroic cult of Germanic "Stärke" which they exploited. Bracher, for example, believes that in *Der Arbeiter* (1932), Jünger "fixed the heroic accents for what was to come" (185). See also Ketelsen 258–85. On Nazi attempts to revise the image of history in their own spirit, which included "the glorification of Frederick the Great," see Bracher 328.

[18] To Elisabeth Steinrück. Quoted by Robert A. Kann in "Die historische Situation und die entscheidenden politischen Ereignisse zur Zeit und im Leben Arthur Schnitzlers" *Literatur und Kritik* 161–62 (1982): 20. For Redlich's remark, see Hugo Hantsch, *Geschichte Österreichs*, 2nd edition, vol. II (Graz-Vienna-Cologne: Styria Verlag, 1953), 520. "Die Flammenzeichen eines beinahe unausweichlichen Schicksals," writes Hantsch (539) "häuften sich."

[19] Brecht writes in the "Modellbuch" for *Mutter Courage:* "Das Stück ist 1938 geschrieben, als der Stückeschreiber einen großen Krieg voraussah": Brecht, *Schriften zum Theater*, vol. 6, ed. W. Hecht (Frankfurt: Suhrkamp, 1964), 148.

[20] Stadler 68–69. "We don't need to be kind to the Czechs and similar people," Lagarde is quoted as saying.

[21] Guiseppe Farese calls the novel a "Querschnitt des Lebens im Wien des fin de siècle." See G. F., "Untergang des Ich und Bewußtsein des Endes bei Arthur Schnitzler," *Literatur und Kritik* 161–62 (1982): 27.

[22] E.g. Bermann in *Der Weg ins Freie,* and the "hero" of *Professor Bernhardi:* "Mein lieber Flint, die Politik gedenk ich auch weiterhin dir ganz allein zu überlassen": Arthur Schnitzler, *Die dramatischen Werke,* 2 vols, vol. 2 (Frankfurt: Fischer, 1981), 457. Discussion of Schnitzler's plays is based on this edition, cited as DW.

[23] In his "Nachruf" in the *Neue Freie Presse,* 22 October 1931.

[24] As Rollin says: "Sein . . . spielen . . . kennen Sie den Unterschied so genau?" DW 1, 54. For Schnitzler and Pirandello, see Hans Hinterhauser, "Arthur Schnitzler und die Romania," *Literatur und Kritik* 161–62 (1982): 70–71.

[25] R. A. Kann, *A History of the Habsburg Empire* (Berkeley: U of California P, 1977), 223. It is striking how often Schnitzler refers to Aspern in his text.

[26] A. Schnitzler, *Tagebuch 1909–1912,* ed. Werner Welzig (Vienna: Verlag der österreichischen Akademie der Wissenschaften, 1981), 205 (25 December 1910).

[27] DW 2, 212: "ich werde für sie sterben."

[28] Cf. Eschenbacher's important speech (DW 2, 107: "Doch wohl um das Wort, Etzelt [that is in this case, 'revenge' as a conventional principle] — wie meistens, glauben Sie nicht . . . etc").

[29] ". . . dieses Krieges letzter und seltsamster Held": DW 2, 215.

[30] Letter to Eduard Korrodi, 2 April 1915.

[31] Joseph Redlich, *Austrian War Government* (New Haven: Yale UP, 1929), 67.

[32] Hantsch, *Die Geschichte Österreichs,* vol. 2, 530.

[33] Kann (1977), 412.

[34] Karl Kautsky, in his pamphlet "Wie der Weltkrieg entstand" (Berlin: Paul Cassirer, 1919), quotes von Bülow's reference to such promises, 27. Naumann, always on the look-out for signs of a "Central European consciousness," seizes on Bülow's "Nibelungentreue" as a "mitteleuropäische Weissagung" (56).

[35] Cf. Richard Miklin, "Heimatliebe und Patriotismus: Arthur Schnitzlers Einstellung zu Österreich-Ungarn im Ersten Weltkrieg," *Modern Austrian Literature* 19 (1986): 199.

[36] DW 2, 36, Eschenbacher: "Glaub' schon, daß es echt war. Ich hab' schon allerlei Echtes erlebt in Wien, und von der verschiedensten Art." The reference is to the patriotic emotion with which the people of Vienna sang Collin's song "Habsburgs Thron wird dauernd stehn." Frau Klähr, wary of her brother's [Schnitzlerian] scepticism, has insisted on its genuineness.

[37] Ernst Mach, in *Analyse der Empfindungen* (1903), questions the notions of "Self" and "personality" and seems to think rather in terms of a pattern of "impressions" and stimuli.

[38] DW 2, 155: "Und es gibt kein Schicksal, das ein Narr, wie ich es bin, nicht als ein wohlverdientes hinnehmen müßte."

[39] For Helene's view of the power of the will, see DW 2, 191.

[40] The Self as "ein Resultat aus Stimmungen"; cf. Klaus Günther, "Bemerkungen zu Arthur Schnitzler und Ernst Mach" in H. Scheible, ed., *Arthur Schnitzler in neuer Sicht* (Munich: Fink, 1981), 113.

⁴¹ DW 2, 162, Medardus: ". . . Das Gestern ist so fern wie der Tag, da die Welt erschaffen wurde, das Morgen so ferne wie der Tod, — so ruh ich in meinem Glück. Das kann nicht dauern, Etzelt!" Other "escapers" into happiness in time-less time include the ageing Casanova in *Casanovas Heimfahrt* (cf. my article: "Schnitzler and the Experience of Time: From Anatol to Casanova" in *Modern Austrian Literature* 19 [1986], 163–77), and Frau Berta Garlan, in the novella of that name.

⁴² There are hints of this in the title. The epithet "jung" could suggest Werther, and "Medardus" certainly recalls the schizophrenic hero of Hoffmann's *Die Elixiere des Teufels.*

⁴³ DW 2, 39: "Ich aber war in die Kirche hineinkommandiert . . . etc."

⁴⁴ DW 2, 58.

⁴⁵ Cf. Naumann, *Mitteleuropa* (Berlin: Georg Reimer, 1915), 101: "Mitteleuropa wird im Kern deutsch sein."

⁴⁶ Cf. particularly Naumann, 11–14: "Zwei verschiedene Temperaturen, verschiedener noch als Wien und Budapest!"

⁴⁷ Naumann, in approaching his peroration, indulges freely in "big words": he speaks (262) of a "weltgeschichtliches Wort" that must be spoken, a "Weltgeschichtstag" that must not be missed, a "große[r] Gesichtspunkt der Weltentwicklung" that will inspire the Austrian peoples.

⁴⁸ Hugo von Hofmannsthal, "Grillparzers politisches Vermächtnis" in *Gesammelte Werke in Einzelausgaben, Prosa III* (Frankfurt: Fischer, 1964), 257.

⁴⁹ DW 2, 117: "Wir stehn auf unserm Posten, Schwester."

⁵⁰ In particular in the contrast with the "patriotic" scoundrel Wachshuber in act III, scene 1.

⁵¹ Egon Schwarz, "Milieu oder Mythos? Wien in den Werken Arthur Schnitzlers," *Literatur und Kritik* 163–64 (1982): 32.

⁵² A. Schnitzler, *Briefe 1913–31,* 71.

⁵³ Cf. *Briefe,* 633–34.

⁵⁴ Letter of 22 December 1914.

⁵⁵ "ein ausnehmend inkonsequentes Subjekt"; cf. Schnitzler's letter to Hermann Bahr of 17 November 1910.

⁵⁶ Egon Schwarz 32.

⁵⁷ Cf. the letter of 16 March 1908 to Otto Brahm.

⁵⁸ *Tagebuch 1909–12,* 76. Schlenther also applied to the play an appellation which Wieland, in his day, had given to *Götz:* he called it "ein angenehmes Monstrum" (84).

⁵⁹ DW 2 157, 163, 178, 197.

⁶⁰ DW 2, 200.

⁶¹ DW 2, 36, 58.

⁶² DW 2, 35, 51, 62, 81.

⁶³ DW 2, 115, 163.

[64] DW 2, 145–47.

[65] Cf. *Der Messingkauf,* Brecht, *Schriften zum Theater,* vol. 5, ed. W. Hecht (Frankfurt: Suhrkamp, 1963), 179: "Die Auffassung des Menschen als einer Variablen des Milieus, der Milieus als einer Variablen des Menschen . . . entspringt einem neuen Denken, dem historischen Denken."

[66] Cf. Shlomo Avineri's study, *The Social and Political Thought of Karl Marx* (Cambridge: Cambridge UP, 1968). The aim, says the author, is to bring out Marx's "ambivalent indebtedness . . . to the Hegelian tradition" (7).

[67] Brecht, *Schriften zum Theater,* 5, 295: "Bei der Historisierung wird ein bestimmtes Gesellschaftssytstem vom Standpunkt eines anderen Gesellschaftssystems aus betrachtet. Die Entwicklung der Gesellschaft ergibt die Gesichtspunkte."

[68] *Vom Ausgang des 19. Jahrhunderts bis 1917,* 489.

[69] Brecht, *Kleines Organon für das Theater; Schriften zum Theater,* vol. 7 (1964), 65.

[70] *Schriften zum Theater,* 7, 29–30.

[71] Brecht, *Messingkauf,* 155: "Nicht länger flüchtet der Zuschauer aus der Jetztzeit in die Historie; die Jetztzeit wird zur Historie."

[72] *Schriften zum Theater,* vol. 6, 135–36. Courage is described as "kleinbürgerlich" earlier in the "Modellbuch" (125).

[73] The fundamental significance of Marx's doctrine is established by the philosopher (*Messingkauf,* 47): "Der Satz, daß das Bewußtsein der Menschen von ihrem gesellschaftlichen Sein abhängt . . . etc."

[74] *Messingkauf,* 48–49.

[75] "Modellbuch," 152.

[76] G. Lukács, *Goethe and His Age,* trans. R. Anchor (London: Merlin Press, 1968), 164. Keith Dickson makes a similar point in connection with Brecht's other important drama on an overtly historical theme, *Leben des Galilei:* Brecht has "X-rayed history" (*Towards Utopia. A Study of Brecht* [Oxford: Oxford UP, 1978], 89).

[77] "Modellbuch," 91.

[78] Certainly not her children! While Grimmelshausen's anti-heroine insists that she is not telling her "life-story" to save her soul, it would hardly have occurred to her to deny that she had one, as Brecht's Courage does (see Brecht, *Stücke* 7 [Frankfurt: Suhrkamp, 1957], 150: "Ich hab aber keine Seel").

[79] That religion played no part at all in Gustavus's intervention is hard to sustain, and that Ferdinand II was a devout Catholic is clear, if from nothing else, from the fact that he continued to insist on the Edict of Restitution when its withdrawal might have united the country under Habsburg leadership.

[80] Courage: "Aber wenn man genauer hinsieht, sinds [that is, 'die Großkopfigen'] nicht so blöd, sondern führen den Krieg für Gewinn"; *Stücke* 7, 103.

[81] H. Kaufmann, quoted by Dickson, 60.

[82] *Stücke* 7, 150: "Daß sie einen Kaiser und einen Papst dulden . . . etc."

Works Cited

Adel, K., ed. *Josef Friedrich von Hormayr und die vaterländische Romantik in Österreich.* Vienna: Bergland, 1974.

Asmuth, B. *Daniel Casper von Lohenstein.* Stuttgart: Metzler, 1971.

Avineri, S. *The Social and Political Thought of Karl Marx.* Cambridge: Cambridge UP, 1968.

Baumann, G. *Franz Grillparzer. Sein Werk und das österreichische Wesen.* Freiburg-Vienna: Herder, 1954.

Behrens, E. *Friedrich Schlegels Geschichtsphilosophie (1794–1808).* Tübingen: Niemeyer, 1984.

Benjamin, W. *Ursprung des deutschen Trauerspiels.* Revised by R. Tiedemann. Frankfurt/Main: Suhrkamp, 1963.

Beyer, M. *Ibsen. The Man and his Work.* Trans. Marie Wells. London: Souvenir Press, 1978.

Blunden, A. G. "Schiller's Egmont," *Seminar* xiv (1978).

Borchmeyer, D. Contributions to Žmegač (1979), I: 1 and 2.

Bracher, K. D. *The German Dictatorship. The Origins, Structure and Consequences of National Socialism* (1969). Trans. Jean Steinberg. Harmondsworth: Penguin U Books, 1973.

Brock-Sulzer, E. *Friedrich Dürrenmatt. Stationen seines Weges.* Zurich: Arche, 1970.

Cassirer, E. *The Philosophy of the Enlightenment.* Trans. F. C. A. Koelln and J. Pettegrove. Boston: Beacon Press, 1960.

Christiansen, O. *Gerechtigkeitsethos und rhetorische Kunst in Grillparzers "Ein Bruderzwist in Habsburg."* Uppsala: Almqvist & Wiksell, 1980.

Clédière, J. "Idéal cosmopolite, vertus allemands et l'image de la France dans la *Deutsche Chronik* de Schubart" in G. L. Fink (1985), 253–70.

Collingwood, R. G. *The Idea of History* (1946). Oxford: Oxford UP, 1961.

Coupe, W. A. "Hutten, Meyer and the Use of History" in *For Lionel Thomas* (see "Mc Innes"), 35–52.

Davis, R. H. C. *A History of Medieval Europe. From Constantine to St Louis* (1957). London: Longman, 1968.

Dickson, K. A. *Towards Utopia. A Study of Brecht.* Oxford: Oxford UP, 1978.

Eggers, W. *Wirklichkeit und Wahrheit im Trauerspiel von Andreas Gryphius.* Heidelberg: Winter, 1963.

Farese, G. "Untergang des Ich und Bewußtsein des Endes bei Arthur Schnitzler." *Literatur und Kritik* 161–62 (1982).

Field, W. G. *The Nineteenth Century. 1830–1890.* London-New York: E. Benn, 1975.

Fink, G. L. "Wieland und die französische Revolution" in *Christoph Martin Wieland* (ed. H. Schelle), Darmstadt: Wissenschaftliche Buchgesellschaft, 1981, 407–43.

———, ed. *Cosmopolitisme, patriotisme et xénophobie en Europe au siècle des lumières.* Strasbourg: Actes du colloque international 2–5 October 1985.

Fischer-Lamberg, H., ed. *Der junge Goethe*, vol. 2. Berlin: de Gruyter, 1963.

Flemming, W. *Andreas Gryphius. Eine Monographie.* Stuttgart: Kohlhammer, 1965.

Flitner, W. *Goethe im Spätwerk.* Hamburg: Claasen & Goverts, 1947.

Flygt, S. G. *Friedrich Hebbel's Conception of Movement in the Absolute and in History.* New York: AMS Press, 1966.

Fülleborn, U. *Das dramatische Geschehen im Werk Franz Grillparzers.* Munich: Fink, 1966.

Gagliardo, J. *Reich and Nation. The Holy Roman Empire as Idea and Reality.* Bloomington: Indiana UP, 1988.

Garland, M. *Hebbel's Prose Tragedies.* Cambridge: Cambridge UP, 1973.

Gerhard, M. *Schiller.* Berne: Francke, 1950.

Gerresheim, H-M. "Christian Dietrich Grabbe" in von Wiese (1969).

Görlich, E. J. *Grundzüge der Geschichte der Habsburgermonarchie und Österreichs*, Darmstadt: Wissenschaftliche Buchgesellschaft, 1970.

Gundolf, F. *Goethe*, 2nd edition. Berlin: Georg Bondi, 1925.

Günther, K. "Bemerkungen zu Arthur Schnitzler und Ernst Mach" in Scheible (1981).

Guthke, K. S. *Erkundungen. Essays zur Literatur von Milton bis Traven.* New York-Frankfurt-Berne: Peter Lang, 1983.

Habersetzer, K.-H. *Politische Typologie und dramatisches Exemplum.* Stuttgart: Metzler, 1985.

Hantsch, H. *Die Geschichte Österreichs*, 2nd edition. Graz-Vienna: Styria Verlag, 1953.

Heald, D. "Hebbel's Concept of Realism," *New German Studies* 1 (1973).

Heckmann, H. *Elemente des barocken Trauerspiels. Am Beispiel des "Papinian" von Andreas Gryphius.* Darmstadt: Gentner/ Munich: Hanser, 1959.

Heitner, R. R. *German Tragedy in the Age of Enlightenment*. Berkeley: U of California P, 1963.

Hettner, Hermann *Geschichte der deutschen Literatur im achtzehnten Jahrhundert*. Berlin: Aufbau, 1961.

Hinck, W. "Georg Büchner" in von Wiese (1969).

Jauslin, K. "Nackt in der Kälte des Raumes. Emblem und Emblematik in Grabbes historischer Maschine." *Grabbe-Jahrbuch* 9 (1990): 46–70.

Jespersen, U. "Detlev von Liliencron" in von Wiese (1969).

Joachimsen, P. *Vom deutschen Volk zum deutschen Staat* (1920). Ed. J. Leuschner. Göttingen: Vandenhoeck und Ruprecht, 1956.

Kampmann, C. *Reichsrebellion und kaiserliche Acht*, Münster, 1992.

Kann, R. A. "Die historische Situation und die entscheidenden politischen Ereignisse zur Zeit und im Leben Arthur Schnitzlers," *Literatur und Kritik* 161–62 (1982).

———. *A History of the Habsburg Empire 1526–1918*, 2nd edition. Berkeley: U of California P, 1977.

Kaufmann, H. *Geschichte der deutschen Literatur vom Ausgang des 19. Jahrhunderts bis 1917*. Berlin: Volk und Wissen, 1974.

Kayser, W. *Das sprachliche Kunstwerk*, 2nd edition, Berne: Francke, 1952.

Ketelsen, Uwe-K. *Literatur und drittes Reich*, 2nd, revised edition. Vierow bei Greifswald: S-H Verlag, 1994.

Kiszling, Rudolf. *Fürst Felix von Schwarzenberg. Der politische Lehrmeister Kaiser Franz Josephs*. Graz-Cologne: Hermann Böhlaus Nachf, 1952.

Kluckhohn, P. *Das Ideengut der deutschen Romantik*. Tübingen: Niemeyer, 1966.

Koch, F. *Heinrich von Kleist. Bewußtsein und Wirklichkeit*. Stuttgart: Metzler, 1958.

Kohn, H. *The Mind of Germany. The Education of a Nation* (1960). London: Macmillan, 1968.

Korff, H. A. *Geist der Goethezeit*, 2nd edition. Leipzig: Koehler und Amelung, 1958.

Kreuzer, H. "Friedrich Hebbel" in von Wiese (1969).

Krofta, K. *A Short History of Czechoslovakia*. London: Williams and Norgate, 1935.

Lamport, F. J. "Patzke's *Virginia*." *New German Studies* 8 (1980): 19–27.

Linder, J. *Schillers Dramen. Bauprinzipien und Wirkungsstrategie*. Bonn: Bouvier, 1989.

Loewy, E. *Literatur unterm Hakenkreuz.* Frankfurt/Main: Europäische Verlagsanstalt, 1967.

Lukács, G. *Der historische Roman.* Berlin: Aufbau, 1955.

———. *Goethe and His Age.* London: Merlin Press, 1968.

Marchand, J. W. "Wieland and the Middle Ages" in *Christoph Martin Wieland. Nordamerikanische Forschungsbeiträge zur 250. Wiederkehr seines Geburtstages 1983.* Ed. H. Schelle. Tübingen: Niemeyer, 1984.

Marcuse, H. *Reason and Revolution. Hegel and the Rise of Social Theory.* London: Routledge, 1941.

Martens, Wolfgang *Die Botschaft der Tugend. Die Aufklärung im Spiegel der deutschen Moralischen Wochenschriften* (1968). Studienausgabe, Stuttgart: Metzler, 1971.

Martini, F. *Geschichte im Drama — Drama in der Geschichte.* Stuttgart: Klett/Cotta, 1979.

Matt, P. von. *Der Grundriß von Grillparzers Bühnenkunst.* Zurich: Atlantis, 1965.

Mc Innes, E. "Moral, Politik und Geschichte in Goethes Götz von Berlichingen." *Zeitschrift für deutsche Philologie* 103, Sonderheft (1984).

———. "Scepticism, Ideology and History in Büchner's *Dantons Tod,*" in *For Lionel Thomas.* Ed. D. Attwood, A. Best and R. Last. Hull: U of Hull, 1980.

Meinecke, F. "Schillers Spaziergang" in *Deutsche Lyrik von Weckherlin bis Benn.* Ed. J. Schillemeit. Frankfurt/Main: Fischer, 1965.

Menhennet, A. "Grillparzer, Shakespeare and Historical Drama." *German Life and Letters* 44 (1991).

———. "Historical Ambivalence in Goethe and Scott." *New German Studies* 13 (1985).

———. "Historical and Dramatic Truth in Lessing." *Lessing Yearbook* xix (1987): 67–83.

———. "History or Drama? The Curious Case of Grillparzer's 'Treuer Diener.'" *Quinquereme* 11 (1988): 129–45.

———. "Schnitzler and the Experience of Time: From Anatol to Casanova." *Modern Austrian Literature* 19 (1986): 163–77.

———. "Vom 'friedewünschenden Teutschland' zum 'bedrängten Deutschland.' Die Schicksale der 'deutschen' Tradition in der deutschen Literatur von dem Barock bis zur Aufklärung" in *Tradition, Norm, Innovation. Soziales und literarisches Traditionsverhalten in der Frühzeit der deutschen Aufklärung.* Ed. W. Barner. Munich: Oldenbourg, 1989.

Michelsen, P. "Goethes 'Götz': Geschichte dramatisiert?" in *Goethe-Jahrbuch* 110 (1993).

Miklin, R. "Heimatliebe und Patriotismus: Arthur Schnitzlers Einstellung zu Österreich-Ungarn im ersten Weltkrieg." *Modern Austrian Literature* 19 (1986): 197–212.

Möller, H. "Nicolai als Historiker," in *Friedrich Nicolai 1733–1811.* Ed. B. Fabian. Berlin: Nicolaische Buchhandlung, 1983.

Moser, H. "Ludwig Uhland," in von Wiese (1969).

Müller, G. *Deutsche Dichtung von der Renaissance bis zum Ausgang des Barock* (1927). Darmstadt: H. Gentner, 1957.

Mullan, B. *Grillparzer's Aesthetic Theory. A Study with Special Reference to His Conception of the Drama as "Eine Gegenwart."* Stuttgart: Heitz, 1979.

Murat, J. "Klopstock, citoyen français et patriote allemand," in Fink (1985).

Nadler, J. *Grillparzer.* Vienna: Bergland, 1952.

Newald, R. *Die deutsche Literatur vom Späthumanismus zur Empfindsamkeit,* 4th ed. Munich: Beck, 1953.

Nipperdey, T. *Deutsche Geschichte 1800–1866.* Munich: Beck, 1983.

Palacký, F. "Eine Stimme über Österreich" in *Österreichs Staatsidee* (1866). Vienna 1974.

Paulin, R. *Ludwig Tieck. A Literary Biography.* Oxford: Oxford UP, 1985.

Periam, A. *Hebbel's Nibelungen.* New York: Macmillan, 1906.

Popper, K. R. *The Poverty of Historicism* (1957). London: Routledge, 1961.

Purdie, E. *Friedrich Hebbel* (1932). Oxford: Oxford UP, 1969.

Ranke, L. von. *Geschichte Wallensteins* in *Historische Meisterwerke.* Ed. H. Michael. Vienna-Hamburg-Zurich n.d. Vol. 13–14.

Ratz, A. E. "Ausgangspunkte und Dialektik von C. M. Wielands gesellschaftlichen Ansichten" in Schelle (1981).

Reddick, J. *Georg Büchner. The Shattered Whole.* Oxford: Oxford UP, 1994.

Redlich, J. *Austrian War Government.* New Haven: Yale UP, 1929.

Reisiger, H. *Johann Gottfried Herder.* Hildesheim: Olms, 1970.

Reiss, H. S. "Goethe, Moser und die Aufklärung. Das Heilige Römische Reich in Goethes Götz von Berlichingen" in H. R., *Formgestaltung und Politik. Goethe-Studien.* Würzburg: Königshausen und Neumann, 1993.

Rietra, M. *Jungösterreich. Dokumente und Materialien zur liberalen österreichischen Opposition 1835–1848.* Amsterdam: Rodopi, 1980.

Sagarra, E. *Tradition and Revolution. German Literature and Society 1830–1890.* London: Weidenfeld and Nicolson, 1971.

Sahmland, I. *Christoph Martin Wieland und die deutsche Nation.* Tübingen: Niemeyer, 1990.

Sautermeister, G. *Idyllik und Dramatik im Werk Friedrich Schillers.* Stuttgart: Kohlhammer, 1971.

Scheible, H., ed. *Arthur Schnitzler in neuer Sicht.* Munich: Fink, 1981.

Schelle, H., ed. *Christoph Martin Wieland.* Darmstadt: Wissenschaftliche Buchgesellshaft (Wege der Forschung 181, 1981).

Schings, H-J. *Die Brüder des Marquis Posa. Schiller und der Geheimbund der Illuminaten.* Tübingen: Niemeyer, 1996.

———. *Die patristische und stoische Tradition bei Andreas Gryphius.* Cologne-Graz: Böhlau, 1966.

Schöne, A. *Emblematik und Drama im Zeitalter des Barock.* Munich: Beck, 1964.

Schuhmann, D. W. "Goethe and F. C. von Moser. A Contribution to the Study of Götz von Berlichingen." *Journal of English and Germanic Philology* 111 (1954).

Schulz, G. M. *Die Überwindung der Barbarei. Johann Elias Schlegels Trauerspiele.* Tübingen: Niemeyer, 1980.

Schwarz, E. "Milieu oder Mythos? Wien in den Werken Arthur Schnitzlers." *Literatur und Kritik* 163–64 (1982).

Sengle, F. *Das deutsche Geschichtsdrama.* Stuttgart: Metzler, 1952.

———. "Klassik im deutschen Drama." *Der Deutschunterricht* 5 (1987).

Sharpe, L. *Friedrich Schiller. Drama, Thought and Politics.* 2nd edition. Cambridge: Cambridge UP, 1994.

———. "Schiller and Goethe's Egmont." *Modern Language Review* 77 (1982).

Shaw, L. R. *The Playwright and Historical Change.* Madison/Milwaukee: U of Wisconsin P, 1970.

Sinden, M. *Gerhart Hauptmann. The Prose Plays.* Toronto-London: U of Toronto P, 1957.

Smallmann, B. *The Background of Passion Music. J. S. Bach and his Predecessors.* London: SCM Press, 1957.

Soergel, A. *Dichtung und Dichter der Zeit* (1911). 19th edition. Leipzig: R. Voigtländer, 1928.

Spellerberg, G. *Verhängnis und Geschichte. Untersuchungen zu den Trauerspielen und dem "Arminius"-Roman Daniel Caspers von Lohenstein.* Bad Homburg: Gehlen, 1970.

Sprengel, B. *Geschichte der deutschsprachigen Literatur 1870–1900. Von der Reichsgründung bis zur Jahrhundertwende.* Munich: Beck, 1998.

Srbik, Heinrich Ritter von. *Deutsche Einheit. Idee und Wirklichkeit vom Heiligen Reich bis Königgrätz.* Munich, 1935. Reprint: Darmstadt: Wissenschaftliche Buchgesellschaft, 1963.

Stace, W. T. *The Philosophy of Hegel.* London: Macmillan, 1924.

Stadler, Karl R. *Austria.* London: E. Benn, 1971.

Staiger, E. *Grundbegriffe der Poetik.* Zurich: Atlantis, 1946.

Steiger, M. "Grillparzers 'Alfred der Große' und die Zeitgeschichte." *Euphorion* 17 (1910).

Steinhagen, H. "Schillers Wallenstein und die französische Revolution." *Zeitschrift für deutsche Philologie* 109 (Sonderheft Schiller), 1990.

———. *Wirklichkeit und Handeln im barocken Trauerspiel.* Tübingen: Niemeyer, 1977.

Stern, F. *The Politics of Cultural Despair. A Study of the Rise of the Germanic Ideology.* New York: Doubleday Anchor, 1965.

Stern, J. P. *Idylls and Realities. Studies in Nineteenth-Century German Literature.* London: Methuen, 1971.

Storz. G. *Der Dichter Friedrich Schiller.* Stuttgart: Klett, 1959.

Styan, J. L. *Modern Drama in Theory and Practice. 1: Realism and Naturalism* (1981). Paperback edition: Cambridge: Cambridge UP, 1983.

Szarota, E. M. *Lohensteins "Arminius" als Zeitroman. Sichtweisen des Spätbarock.* Berne-Munich: Francke, 1970.

Tank, K. L. *Gerhart Hauptmann.* Hamburg: Rowohlt, 1959.

Taylor, A. J. P. *Bismarck. The Man and the Statesman* (1955). London: Arrow Books, 1961.

———. *The Course of German History.* U Tutorial P edition: London: Methuen, 1961.

Taylor, R. *History and the Paradoxes of Metaphysics in "Dantons Tod."* New York-Berne: Peter Lang, 1990.

Treitschke, H. von. *History of Germany in the Nineteenth Century.* Trans. E. and C. Paul. London: Jarrold, 1915.

Valjavec, F. *Die Entstehung der politischen Strömungen in Deutschland.* Kronenburg/Düsseldorf: Athenäum, 1978.

Wangermann, E. *The Austrian Achievement 1700–1800.* London: Thames and Hudson, 1973.

Wedgwood, C. V. *The Thirty Years War* (1938). Harmondsworth: Pelican Books, 1958.

Wehrli, M. *Das barocke Geschichtsbild in Lohensteins Arminius.* Frauenfeld-Leipzig: Huber, 1938.

Wells, G. A. "The Enigma of Hebbel's *Nibelungen.*" *New German Studies* 13 (1985).

von Wiese, B. *Die deutsche Tragödie von Lessing bis Hebbel* (1948). Munich: Deutscher Taschenbuch Verlag, 1983.

———, ed. *Deutsche Dichter des neunzehnten Jahrhunderts. Ihr Leben und Werk.* Berlin: E. Schmidt, 1969.

Wittkowski, W. "Octavio Piccolomini. Zur Schaffensweise des 'Wallenstein' — Dichters" in *Schiller. Zur Theorie und Praxis der Dramen.* Ed. K. L. Berghahn/R. Grimm. Darmstadt: Wissenschaftliche Buchgesellschaft, 1972. 428–44.

Wolf, P. *Die Dramen Johann Elias Schlegels.* Zurich: Atlantis, 1964.

Yates, W. E. *Grillparzer. A Critical Introduction.* Cambridge: Cambridge UP, 1972.

Ziegler, K. "Das moderne Drama als Spiegel unserer Zeit." *Der Deutschunterricht* 13 (1961).

Žmegač, V., ed. *Geschichte der deutschen Literatur vom 18. Jahrhundert bis zur Gegenwart.* Vol. 1, parts 1 and 2. Königstein Ts: Athenäum, 1979.

Index